Military Economics

Also by Ron Smith

Consumer Demand for Cars in the USA

The Political Economy of British Capitalism, with Sam Aaronovitch, Jean Gardiner and Roger Moore

Energy Demand in Asian Developing Economies, with M. Hashem Pesaran and Taka Akiyama

The Economics of Militarism, with Dan Smith

L'effort economique de defense: France et Royaume-Uni, editor with Jacques Fontanel

The Peace Dividend, editor with N.P. Gleditsch, O. Bjerkholt, A. Cappelen and J.P. Dunne

Arms Trade Security and Conflict, editor with Paul Levine

Military Economics

The Interaction of Power and Money

Ron Smith

Professor of Applied Economics, Birkbeck, University of London

palgrave
macmillan

First published 2009
Published in paperback 2011 by
PALGRAVE MACMILLAN

Palgrave Macmillan in the UK is an imprint of Macmillan Publishers Limited, registered in England, company number 785998, of Houndmills, Basingstoke, Hampshire RG21 6XS.

Palgrave Macmillan in the US is a division of St Martin's Press LLC, 175 Fifth Avenue, New York, NY 10010.

Palgrave Macmillan is the global academic imprint of the above companies and has companies and representatives throughout the world.

Palgrave® and Macmillan® are registered trademarks in the United States, the United Kingdom, Europe and other countries.

ISBN 978–0–230–22853–5 hardback
ISBN 978–0–230–33717–6 paperback

This book is printed on paper suitable for recycling and made from fully managed and sustained forest sources. Logging, pulping and manufacturing processes are expected to conform to the environmental regulations of the country of origin.

A catalogue record for this book is available from the British Library.

A catalog record for this book is available from the Library of Congress.

10   9   8   7   6   5   4   3   2   1
20   19   18   17   16   15   14   13   12   11

Printed and bound in Great Britain by
CPI Antony Rowe, Chippenham and Eastbourne

Contents

List of Figures and Tables

Figures

Tables

Preface

War and the preparation for war have shaped much economic development, since trade, specialisation and the growth of markets require some mechanism to control violence and provide order. Economic issues are central to military planning which involves balancing resources, capabilities and commitments. Thus the interaction of military and economy, power and money, is central to the modern world. Economists have studied issues of war and peace since, at least, Adam Smith's *Wealth of Nations*; but modern defence economics or peace economics, like most other economics, is usually written in a mathematical and statistical language that makes it incomprehensible to many of those who would be interested. The economic dimensions of conflict matter to those in the military, the peace movement or in non-governmental organisations concerned with conflict, like Amnesty International or Oxfam. This book draws on the technical defence economics literature to provide an accessible introduction to the elements of military economics: security, military expenditures, the acquisition of troops and weapons, the arms industry, the arms trade, military operations and the economic consequences of defence spending. In the process, the book explores the many links between the military and the economy; provides a guide to non-technical literature; explains the economic concepts used; and illustrates these concepts with a range of military examples, contemporary and historical. Among the many links between the military and the economy is the fact that fighting and finance are often both driven by the same basic motives, fear and greed.

1
Introduction

Money matters to the military; it is needed to finance fighting, and desire to acquire it is often the motive for fighting. Fighting matters for the economy, since military power and conflict have shaped economic development. Both fighting and finance are often driven by the same basic human motives: fear and greed. This book examines the interaction of economics and conflict. There is a large economic literature devoted to conflict and to finance and resource allocation by the military, which is known either as defence (or defense) economics or as peace economics. The journal of the subject is called *Defence and Peace Economics*. Economists are the specialists in studying money, though not usually in making it, and they have contributed much to military analysis. For instance, Thomas Schelling gained a Nobel Prize in Economics for his game-theory analysis of strategy, particularly nuclear strategy. Since defence economics is often about attack and peace economics is often about war, I have used the title military economics: the economics of the use of organised force.

Military money also matters because a large amount is spent on the military, about $1300 billion in 2007, and military equipment is expensive, US B2 bombers cost about $2 billion each. This money plays a major role in issues of war and peace which have repercussions on economic development. In 2008, major conflicts were continuing in Iraq and Afghanistan and there were about 20 other wars in progress, mainly intra-state civil wars, many involving substantial loss of life. One cannot understand the economies of many countries, particularly poor countries, without understanding the role of war. The genocide in Rwanda in 1994, where about 800,000 were killed, was the beginning of over a decade of conflict in the Great-Lakes Congo region in which perhaps millions died, large numbers from disease and malnutrition. As well as

Rwanda and Zaire/Democratic Republic of Congo the war involved combatants from Angola, Burundi, the Central African Republic, Chad, Libya, Namibia, Sudan, Uganda and Zimbabwe plus foreign mercenaries. Despite a ceasefire in 2003, elections in 2006 and 17,000 UN peace-keepers stationed in the area, the conflict in the Democratic Republic of Congo restarted in late 2008. The area is a source of crucial minerals, so conflicts there have global economic implications.

Defence and peace economics, like much of the rest of economics, uses a mathematical and statistical language that makes it incomprehensible to many who might be interested, but do not have a quantitative training. This includes many students on courses in war or peace studies, many in the military, and many of those working with non-governmental organisations (NGOs), campaigning on military issues. This book draws on the mathematical literature, but presents the economic aspects of defence in a non-technical way without equations or regressions. It tries to provide a self-contained account which explains the economic concepts used and introduces related literature. Just as different military services – army, navy and air force – have their own cultures, so do different academic disciplines. These cultural differences extend to how they reference and refer to the literature. Relative to work in history or international relations, economists tend to economise on references, thus there will not be quite as many citations to sources of alleged facts, ideas or opinions as is usual in other subjects. Economists also use a different referencing system. Where literature is referred to in the text, it will mainly be to material that is accessible to a non-mathematical audience and presented in the author-date format, as in Schelling (2006), with a page or chapter number where necessary. Full details of the book or article can be found in the reference section at the end. Because I have tried to cite literature that is accessible to non-specialists, I have not given credit to the authors of most of the mathematical and statistical literature that I have used. I apologise to them for this. The final chapter contains some more general discussion of the various approaches in the literature. Both economists and the military use abbreviations heavily and a list of abbreviations can also be found at the end.

The book uses a very simple framework to try and organise a range of questions about the interaction between the spheres of economy and strategy. It looks at a process by which money, the defence budget, is used to acquire forces, troops and weapons; these forces are used to provide military capability, the potential to prevail in combat; and this military capability contributes to security or insecurity, peace or conflict.

This structure is very similar to one used in relating ends to means in military operations. A military plan is based on: the desired ends, the political aims of the campaign (security); the military objectives to support those aims (capability); the means to attain those objectives (forces); and the resources to provide those means (budgets). Analysing these four elements occupies the bulk of the book and these elements operate at an individual, national and global level. The rest of this chapter provides some background to how they will be analysed.

Economics

The birth of economics as a discipline is usually dated to the publication in 1776 of *The Wealth of Nations*, by the Scottish moral philosopher Adam Smith. Besides providing a general framework for economics, Smith addressed a range of military questions and he will be referred to a number of times. Since then economists have examined the economic dimensions of many aspects of war and military preparations. Financing war and managing the war economy have been recurrent issues throughout history. The economic analysis they generated includes David Ricardo's involvement in the Bullion Controversy provoked by the suspension of the Gold Standard during the Napoleonic Wars and John Maynard Keynes's advice on how to pay for World War II. The economics of war remains an issue of current concern. Within much of the poor world, particularly Africa, civil wars are a major cause of economic dislocation and the international financial institutions are struggling to come to terms with this linkage. It has proved difficult to manage post-conflict stabilisation and reconstruction and to provide incentives for combatants to return to civilian life.

Economics can contribute to understanding the causes of conflict, particularly when there may be economic elements in those causes. Such economic elements include the liberal view that free trade and economic integration promotes peace; the mercantilist-Leninist view that war is the continuation of national economic competition by other means; and the materialist view that wars, including civil war in poor countries, are explained by the drive to control natural resources like oil, water or diamonds. Economic analysis has also been applied to military effectiveness. This runs from Smith's discussion of the relative advantages of standing armies and militias to 20th-century applications of economic and mathematical models, to optimise military procedures. The more general application of quantitative methods to military problems is often called operational analysis.

The application of game theory to nuclear targeting is a classic example of the use of economic models in strategic analysis. In 1964 Stanley Kubrick made a dark comedy about nuclear war: *Dr Strangelove or: How I Learned to Stop Worrying and Love the Bomb*. Dr Strangelove may seem a mad and implausible character, but he was sufficiently recognisable that there is considerable dispute about which members of the nuclear–academic community contributed to the composite. Candidates include the mathematician-economist John von Neumann, who developed game theory; Edward Teller, who developed the Hydrogen bomb; Herman Kahn, who wrote the text book on Thermonuclear War; and Wernher von Braun, who developed the US rocket programme and had been a Nazi, like Strangelove.

This book approaches the military from the perspective of an economist, thus there is an emphasis on the incentives people face and how these incentives can shape choices. Fear and greed will be the motivators we focus on. However, people have other motives and there are other perspectives on the military that are not discussed or only mentioned in passing. These include environmental, feminist, legal, philosophical, psychological and sociological perspectives. The fact that they are not discussed does not mean that they are unimportant. War and the military have many dimensions and this book focuses on the economic dimension. For instance, gender issues are central to the military because the role of women in the armed forces, particularly in combat, is a matter of dispute in many western countries; these western armed forces, including women, may serve in countries like Iraq or Afghanistan where the role of women is quite different; and in most wars women are prominent among the victims, not least because rape is endemic in war. Similar points could be made about legal and environmental dimensions. However, despite the importance of these other dimensions, this book will emphasise the economic perspective. The economic influences are important but not deterministic. An analogy is the influence of the wind on a yacht. The wind does not determine the path of a yacht, the skill of the skipper matters. But the wind is a constraint. Without wind the yacht cannot move, and you cannot understand the course of the yacht without knowing the wind. As Karl Marx put it: men make their own history, but not under circumstances of their own choosing. Economic circumstances are not the only ones that shape history, but they do matter.

There is one respect in which the economic perspective may appear strange: economists usually assume that people are rational. While this rationality assumption has been questioned in many areas, in the military area in particular, it can seem to fail to capture the reality of war with its waste, passions and emotions. Carl von Clausewitz, in his 19th-century classic *On War*, saw war as uniting the trinity of passion, chance and reason. We will return to passion later in this chapter and to chance in Chapter 2, but reason does play a role. Rationality is not a straightforward concept and there are many types of rationality. It may be instrumental and apply to the decision itself (was it in the person's best interests, an action consistent with their objectives and beliefs) or procedural, the process by which the decision was made. In terms of process, economists sometimes assume that decisions makers can effortlessly calculate the optimum solutions to complicated probabilistic problems and face no obstacles to implementing the solution. If this was the case most wars would not happen. Uncertainty is fundamental to military matters and can rarely be represented by probabilities. Information is suspect, tainted by secrecy, deception and the fog of war. Acceptable let alone optimal solutions are rare and implementation is problematic, constrained by hierarchy, bureaucracy, standard operating procedures, inter-service rivalry and logistical difficulties.

The traditional image of economic man, the self-interested calculator, is an approximation that has been qualified by recent experimental work in behavioural economics. This work suggests that emotions matter and that people are less selfish, more altruistic and more co-operative than traditional economic theory predicts. Optimists are pleased that people are nicer than economists supposed; pessimists worry that such selfless, altruistic individuals, who are happy to co-operate within groups, can be easily mobilised to slaughter other groups. Motivating the selfish, individualistic, economic man for war could be more difficult. Although sometimes neglected by economists, psychological biases play an important role in war. For instance, leaders tend to be over-optimistic about their military capabilities and, like rogue traders in banks, take big gambles to try and recover from losses.

Military problems are hard in ways that are not captured by certain economic models, hence the prevalence of apparent irrationality. Clausewitz emphasised the fog of war: 'everything in war is simple, but the simplest thing is very difficult.' In particular, control is difficult. Tolstoy, writing about the Battle of Borodino, said: 'It was not Napoleon who directed the course of the battle, for none of his orders was carried out and during the battle he did not know what was going on.' Optimisation is a good place to start, and it is where we will usually start, it is a bad place to finish. One must go on from simple optimisation to the realities of military decision making, with its uncertainties, organisational constraints and often perverse incentives. There are a range of other sorts of economic models that allow for these factors and can help one understand the systemic reasons for certain types of failure: rules, structures and standard operating procedures that are functional from one perspective, but profoundly dysfunctional from another.

In the application of economics to military issues it will become apparent that military problems have a lot of similarities to economic problems. Not only are fear and greed central to both fighting and finance, but so is competition. Military competition is closer to real economic competition, with agents striving for relative advantage, rather than the abstract perfect competition of elementary economics text books. There are other analogies. In 2002 the renowned investor, Warren Buffett, possibly the world's richest man, compared derivatives to financial weapons of mass destruction. Though unlike neutrons bombs, which kill people and leave the property untouched, derivatives can destroy property and leave the people alive, if without jobs. The analogy of derivatives and weapons is pursued in Satyajit Das's (2006) *Traders, Guns and Money*. Das examines the racy realities of finance and those from a military background should be warned that financial traders make an infantryman sound like a well-spoken, sensitive, moralist.

Economics was traditionally regarded as the study of the allocation of scarce resources between competing ends: the problem of allocative efficiency given resource constraints. More recently, there has been a shift to the study of the rules by which resources are allocated: the problem of incentive efficiency and the constraints that people face in allocating resources. The focus then shifts to the nature of social institutions (rules, beliefs and behaviour patterns) as mechanisms for communicating information between people and co-ordinating their actions. The Nobel Prize lecture by Roger B. Myerson (2008) explains this approach to economics. The general problem of aligning incentives to achieve co-ordination is known in economics as a principal–agent or contracting problem. One partner to the trade, the principal has some goal. To reach that goal, the principal must employ an agent with specialist knowledge and skills, which the principal does not have; there is asymmetric information. The problem is that the agent has different objectives from the principal, so the principal cannot easily get the agent to do what the principal wants. The principal then has to try to design a contract or institution that aligns their conflicting interests. This might be done by providing some incentives to the agent that encourage them to implement the principal's objectives, such as threatening to shoot any soldier who refuses to advance into battle.

The principal–agent problem is pervasive; it arises when owners of a firm hire managers and when people hire professionals like doctors, lawyers or builders. The builder who comes to work on your house may say that they are acting in your interest, but they also have their own agenda and goals. To align these interests you have to try and agree terms, design a contract, so that the builders have incentives to turn up and do the work on time, in the way that you want it done, to an acceptable quality standard. The incentive problems are bad enough when you hire builders; they are much worse when you hire heavily armed killers. Brauer and van Tuyll (2008) discuss the problems of designing contracts between the Renaissance Italian Cities and the Mercenaries they employed to fight for them. These private military contractors were known as Condottieri, from the Italian for contract. The difficulties included the fact that the Condottieri often had more incentive to take over and loot the City that had hired them, rather than to fight that City's enemies. Similar issues apply to governments that fear military coups or hire modern private military companies.

A major element of the principal–agent problem is asymmetric information: the two sides of the contract know different things. This information difference, which arises with regular armies, has two aspects that are given names taken from insurance. The first is adverse selection, where there are hidden characteristics of the agent, such as whether the general you hire is brave or not. The second is moral hazard, where there are hidden actions by the agent, such as whether the general tries very hard or not. The problem gets more difficult when the principal cannot monitor the actions of the agent, just observe the outcome. In the early years of the US Civil War, President Lincoln (the principal) could only observe the lack of progress by General McClellan (the agent) in fighting the war. But Lincoln did not know how much of this lack of progress was a consequence of General McClellan's psychological aversion to fighting (an adverse selection problem, Lincoln had hired the wrong sort of General); how much was a consequence of a lack of effort by McClellan (a moral hazard problem) and how much was really a consequence of the strength of the Confederate enemy.

Such principal–agent problems recur throughout the book. For instance, most ministries of defence see their main enemy not as the country they might fight, but the finance ministry that controls their budgets and the audit office that evaluates their expenditures and publicises their mistakes (in the US the Government Accountability Office, GAO, in the UK the National Audit Office, NAO). This hostility may be well founded; finance ministers can be the most effective disarmers.

The disputes between defence and finance ministries about balancing resources and commitments play a major role in many military decisions.

The military

While this book may often appear critical of military procedures, like Norman E. Dixon's (1976) classic *On the Psychology of Military Incompetence*, it is not an attack on the armed forces. Although I may have met a unrepresentative sample, most members of the armed forces and defence civil servants that I have met are well intentioned, intelligent people who have good reasons for what they do, however unhappy the consequences. Often the military personnel are the most articulate critics of the unhappy consequences, though they are usually ex-military by the time it gets into print. Lewis Page (2006) is a recent UK critique of waste and blundering in the armed forces by an ex-officer. There are many similar books.

Unlike Dixon's book which emphasises psychological factors, I emphasise organisational incentives, though the explanations are not mutually exclusive. His focus was on failures in combat under great pressure with little time for deliberation; but there can also be failures in defence ministries, with less pressing time constraints. Organisational structures that are functional, providing the right incentives, in certain respects are dysfunctional, giving the wrong incentives, in other respects. These are often peacetime mistakes. War is rightly usually presented as a period of great uncertainty, but in some respects the uncertainty is reduced. In war you know who you are fighting, where and how, which you do not in peacetime. All organisations face the same issue: how to ensure that individuals that comprise it are encouraged to act in ways that support the organisation's objectives. This problem is not unique to the military; every commercial firm faces it. But in commercial firms the objectives are generally clearer and the contribution of an individual's behaviour to those objectives can be determined much more quickly than in the military. If the sales staff alienates the customers, this is reflected in sales and profits, which prompts some response by management. How quickly this response occurs depends on competition. In a very competitive market the response tends to happen quickly or the firm goes out of business. If the firm has a near monopoly and customers have few alternatives, the response can be very slow. Likewise the speed of military response tends to be determined by the nature of the competition, being much faster in war.

In military activities, the objectives are vaguer (particularly in peace-time, when there is no direct pressure from the competition) and the effect of individual actions on those objectives much harder to determine. These two themes recur: the lack of clarity about objectives and the difficulty of evaluating how actions contribute to objectives. Even in war these can be issues. While the overall objective, defeating the enemy, is clear, the best way to do it is less clear. It may be better achieved by unconventional and indirect means, such as deception, than by more conventional direct assault. Partly because of these difficulties, the military is also prone to a pattern of goal displacement, switching objectives in response to difficulties. The intangible objective, having troops that can prevail in combat, is replaced by more tangible objectives, such as having troops that look smart, are disciplined and perform well on parade. Goal displacement is not peculiar to the military; academics are equally prone to it: replace a messy, difficult, important problem by a simpler formal one to which there is an answer.

Values

We saw above that Clausewitz thought war united passion, chance and reason. Passion covers not only the strong feelings aroused by particular conflicts but the strong feelings about conflict itself. War and peace involve fundamental values about how conflicts of interest should be resolved, on which people differ. Some believe that all violence is wrong thus organising violence, as the military does, is inherently immoral. Some value peace equally sincerely, but believe that the best way to preserve peace is to prepare for war. Some believe that 'might makes right' and the powerful are entitled to what they can take. Each of these views tend to regard war as instrumental, a means to an end; but some regard it as an end in itself: an exciting and enjoyable activity in which one can realise oneself and attain honour and glory. While the enjoyment often fades with the experience of war, such views were once very widespread. Max Hastings (2005) quotes Winston Churchill on the exhilaration he felt fighting in the Boer War. Such enthusiasm for war would now be regarded as politically incorrect; but once admiration of the warrior spirit and prowess in war was pervasive. War was thought a proper source of education and amusement for the younger members of the upper classes. Joanna Bourke (1999, chapter 1) uses letters and diaries to illuminate perceptions of the pleasures of war.

Despite their need for military skills, modern developed societies are understandably ambivalent about the warrior spirit. In 2008 the issue of reintroducing awards for military bravery generated contro-versy in Germany. Germany had abolished awards, like the Iron Cross, after World War II; but the combat experience of German troops in Afghanistan prompted reconsideration of the issue. Since soldiers risk their life for their country, societies have traditionally recognised this sacrifice by remembrance services and awards for valour like the Con-gressional Medal of Honor in the US and the Victoria Cross in the UK. It can be difficult to separate recognition of sacrifice, by those who served or died in war, from glorification of the war in which they served. This is most obvious in the political sensitivity of recognition of Germans and Japanese who died in World War II, but is also an issue in unpopular wars like Vietnam in the US and the current war in Iraq.

These conflicting values about war and preparation for conflict are important, but they will not be the focus of this book; economists have no special expertise in judgements on values. The book tries to describe what happens from an economic perspective, in the hope that readers will find it useful, whatever their values. Some readers may find this economic approach rather amoral, because it takes the objectives and preferences of the actors as given, rather than something to be judged. In the past I have presented this material to many military groups and to many anti-military groups in the peace movement. Both groups seem to have found it helpful to understand the economic issues and they have even invited me back on occasion. Knowing your enemy is as important to anti-militarists as it is to the military. Many people would be surprised at the similarity of what is taught on War Studies and Peace Studies courses. The values of those attending the courses may differ, but the issues they study are largely the same.

Language cannot be value free. While I have tried to avoid value-laden words, it is impossible to do so completely. The problem is made more difficult by the fact that particular words have different connotations to different people. I tend to see fear and greed as quite useful emotions; fear stops people hurting themselves and greed motivates them to great achievements. Others may see fear and greed as bad things to be disap-proved of. I tend to refer to groups using force to oppose governments as insurgents (rather than terrorists or freedom fighters) without imply-ing whether their opposition is legitimate or illegitimate, but even the term insurgents has connotations. Many economic terms have implicit connotations. While efficient markets, Pareto optimality and the natural rate of unemployment have specific technical meanings, there may be a temptation to think that things which are efficient, optimal or natural must be good. This need not be the case; markets for illegal drugs and weapons can be very efficient. The main empirical implication of the efficient market hypothesis is that future changes in prices are unpredictable; but had it been called the unpredictable prices hypothesis, it may have had less impact.

Facts

People differ not only on values, but also on the evidence: what the facts are and how they are to be interpreted. For instance, there currently appears to be a pattern by which poor countries are more prone to civil war. This fact depends on particular measures of poverty and civil war, which could be disputed, issues we return to. Even if we agree on this association or correlation in the data, we may disagree on interpretation. War may cause poverty, poverty may make war more likely, or some third factor, such as the quality of the country's political institutions, may determine both war and poverty. Even if we think that poverty causes war, it may be because governments in poor countries cannot afford to maintain security or because some people find insurgency attractive, given the low income provided by peaceful alternatives. To resolve such issues of interpretation, natural sciences can often use experiments, which control the variation in factors. Social sciences have to rely on observed variations, not controlled variations. For instance, one might observe a poor country rapidly becoming rich and consider whether this changed the probability of the country being involved in a war. But the reason for a poor country becoming rich, such as the discovery of oil, will have other effects; including on the likelihood of war. We would also need to observe a number of such cases to be sure that the association was not just chance in that particular case.

There is the further problem that very few events have a single cause, so mono-causal explanations tend to be inadequate. In Oscar Wilde's phrase, the truth is rarely pure and never simple. Outcomes tend to be the result of the interactions of a large number of factors with luck and chance playing an important role. People make fun of the way economists qualify their theory with the Latin phrase *ceteris paribus*, other things being equal. The qualification is important, because there are always so many different factors operating. But the multiplicity of factors makes for more complicated explanations and disputes about the events themselves (what happened) and the interpretation of the events (why they happened). I will try to indicate the uncertainties and where the facts or interpretation are controversial; but when in doubt assume that they are controversial and that there will be disagreement about both the facts and interpretation. I am afraid that this may result in the reader having sympathy with the US President Harry Truman who is reputed to have asked for a one-armed economist who could not say 'on the one hand...on the other hand...'.

In many cases, the facts are numbers: how many were killed in a war or how much was spent on defence. There are three issues about the numbers. Firstly, the numbers are often very big. The Stockholm International Peace Research Institute (SIPRI), a standard source, estimates that world military expenditure in 2007 was about $1339 billion and had increased by about 45 per cent in the previous decade, from a low in the mid 1990s. Almost half of this total was spent by the US. A billion is one followed by nine zeros; $1000 billion, sometimes called a trillion, is one followed by 12 zeros. To get a feel for big numbers, like world military expenditure, it sometimes helps to relate them to something else. For instance, world population is just over 6 billion, so military expenditure is about $200 a year for every person in the world. For the large number of people who subsist on less than a dollar a day that is a big number; for the world as a whole it is not a large number, about 2.5 per cent of world output.

Secondly, the numbers are often very inaccurate. We will spend quite a lot of time discussing how they are measured. For instance, there are many different definitions of what constitutes military expenditure or what constitutes a war. Because of the large uncertainties attached to most of the numbers in this book, they should be regarded as rough orders of magnitudes rather than precise figures. While it is useful to know how the details of how the numbers are constructed, there is rarely a right answer, just a range of probabilities. For instance, on one measure (using market exchange rates) China's annual military expenditure in 2006 was about $50 billion. On another measure (using purchasing power parity (PPP) exchange rates) it was estimated to be about $190 billion in 2006 and $140 billion in 2007. The fall between 2006 and 2007 was not a result of a reduction in Chinese military expenditure, but a result of the World Bank getting better estimates of Chinese prices and changing their estimate of the PPP exchange rate. These measures are discussed in more detail in Chapter 4. As another example of the uncertainty attached to the numbers, in early 2008 the estimates of the number of Iraqis who had died in the 5 years since the invasion in 2003 ranged from 60,000 to 600,000. The figures differ in which deaths are included (just directly conflict related deaths or also indirect deaths from the disruption and disease caused by the conflict) and in the sources of information on which the estimates are based (such as press reports of casualties, morgue and hospital records, bodies in mass graves, or household surveys). While most of the numbers are just rough order of magnitudes, the remainder are not even that good and should be regarded as someone's best guess. Despite the uncertainties, working with the numbers gives you a feel for the order of magnitudes, possible relationships and the degree of uncertainty, the estimated margin of error around the number.

At times the reader may feel that I am being a little cavalier with the numbers. That is because I think it better to be roughly right rather than precisely wrong. One can be wrong in a number of ways with numbers. One is treating them as being less uncertain than they actually are and becoming anchored to them. Another is switching the focus from the relevant uncertain magnitudes to irrelevant but more precisely measured magnitudes. This tendency is common and generates many stories. One is about the drunk who searched for his lost coins by the lamp post, because the light was better there than where he dropped them. Another is about the balloonist, blown off course and lost, coming down and asking a person on the ground, where he was. The person on the ground replied 'in a balloon'. To which the balloonist said the man on the ground must be an accountant: providing information that was perfectly accurate but perfectly useless. The accountant's response was that the man in the balloon must be a general: completely screws things up and then drops from the sky to blame the people on the ground.

There is a third, more subtle, issue with the numbers. Many variables, such as the height or weight of individuals, show a pattern of a strong central tendency with some dispersion around it. There are short people and tall people but they represent relatively small deviations around typical values. We do not see people who are ten times average height. With variables like height or weight, adding or subtracting the observation for an individual from the group does not change the total, or the average for the group, by very much. As the sample of observations gets larger the estimate of the average gets more precise. This is called the law of large numbers in statistics. Variables with this sort of pattern also often follow a bell-shaped curve, called the Gaussian or normal distribution. This results from, what statisticians call, the central limit theorem. Economic and military variables tend not to follow a normal distribution; they have highly skewed and unequal distributions: we observe people with 100 times average income. As a result totals and averages can be very sensitive to the set of observations used. Since the US accounts for almost half of world military expenditure, including or excluding the

US makes a big difference. Many economic and military variables have skewed distributions like this; and the processes that generate them may not satisfy the assumptions required for central limit theorems or laws of large numbers to work.

One, though not the only, source of the very unequal, skewed, distribution of outcomes observed in economic and military numbers is that they reflect multiplicative rather than additive processes. Suppose that there are three elements that contribute to success in combat: the quantity of forces, their quality and logistics. Side A scores 4, 4, 1 and Side B scores 3, 3, 3. When the elements are added the two sides are equal; both sum to 9. But when multiplied, they are very unequal. For side A the product is 16, for side B it is 27. Although A is better than B on two of the three elements it is only about half as effective overall. If side A had scored 0 for logistics it would be even more obvious, the product would be 0. Although side A is better in quality and quantity of forces than side B, A is let down by logistics. Because A cannot get enough fuel and ammunition to its troops, they suffer severely despite their quality and quantity. This interactive effect is recognised by the military who often talk of 'force multipliers'. What often counts in military and commercial competition is the weakest link in the chain, get one element wrong and it can mean disaster, however good the other elements. This is a major factor in strategic skill. The ability to combine arms (archers, cavalry and infantry, or artillery, aircraft and tanks) in a way that maximises the effectiveness of their interaction is a rare skill in generals.

Theories

There are deep theoretical disputes in economics, international relations and strategic studies. Within economics the dominant theory is labelled neo-classical or marginalist economics, but there are also Keynesian, Marxist and many other approaches. The theories differ about the nature of rationality and social interactions and their perceptions of the relative efficiency of states and markets. Within international relations, there are also theoretical divisions, such as between realists and idealists. Realists tend to see war as an inevitable outcome of the interaction of sovereign states, each with their own interests, operating in an anarchic international system. Idealists, also called liberals, tend to see an inherent harmony of interests among people and war as an aberration which could be avoided by appropriate political institutions within and between states. Throughout this book, I use liberal in the classical sense of those who believe in free markets, free trade and free elections. In the US the term liberal is often given a socialist tinge, and a classical liberal would probably be regarded as a neo-conservative who is soft on the use of force.

Many books in economics and international relations are organised around these theories; this book is not. Instead it adopts a relatively eclectic approach to the questions that arise in the interaction of the spheres of power and money. Theory is used; it is impossible to avoid using some theory, whether implicit or explicit, to organise the information. However, there is no grand unified theory to provide an integrated explanation. One consequence of the lack of a unified theory is the danger of inconsistency and one example of such inconsistency is the treatment of the state. It will prove useful at some times, to treat the state as a rational actor making decisions for the country as a whole; and at other times, to treat it as an arena of conflict between various interests. The state is the term used for the whole apparatus that runs a country, including politicians in government, bureaucracy, military, legislature and judiciary.

Part of the reason for not using more explicit theoretical structures is that the theories in economics and international relations do not really overlap: the theoretical divisions in economics do not match those in international relations. There are some overlaps; rational actor models are widely employed both in economics and in other subjects and there are Marxist theories both of economics and of international relations. But even here the match is not close. Rational actor models in different disciplines involve different conceptions of rationality and Marxists in different disciplines tend to read different parts of Marx. There are also differences in how social interactions are perceived. There is some evidence that people have a tendency to co-operate within groups and compete between groups. This raises the question of how the groups (families, firms, football teams, *Fedayeen* cells) are defined and the forms that competition takes. One theory of international relations, the constructivist, emphasises the cultural determination of group identity and the role of modes of discourse, how people talk about things, in determining when this competition takes the form of conflict. This provides a useful insight. Economics and international relations have non-overlapping modes of discourse and different assumptions about the relevant groups and forms of conflict. For instance, in international relations, *securitisation* refers to the classification of certain phenomena, such as illegal drugs or resource shortages, as security issues; existential threats requiring emergency and possibly military responses (e.g., Collins 2007). In economics *securitisation* is the process where certain debts, such as mortgages, are bundled into assets which are traded as securities on financial exchanges. Such asset-backed securities played a starring role in the credit crunch, the global financial crisis that started in August 2007.

In such cases of multiple meaning, I have tried to signal which meaning is involved. Oil is securitised in both senses. It is seen as a major security issue which may cause conflict and it is the basis for a range of derivatives which are traded on markets as securities. Derivatives are contracts, such as futures and options, whose value derives from the price of some underlying asset such as oil. The term derivative also has multiple meanings. The *Financial Times* reported that in 2002, when the US Congress was debating whether to close the 'Enron Loophole' – that is, to require that over-the-counter energy markets be brought under the full oversight of the US futures regulator – Republican Trent Lott rose to his feet in the Senate chamber, brandishing a dictionary; the senator looked up a definition of 'a derivative', a term referring to the complex futures contracts used in the energy markets to hedge the risks associated with holding physical supplies of commodities such as oil and natural gas. The dictionary told him that it was 'the limit of the ratio of the change in a function to the corresponding change in its independent variable as the latter change approaches zero'. Mr Lott turned to his colleagues with a warning: 'We don't know what we are doing here. I have serious doubts how many senators really understand [this] and it sounds pretty complicated to me.'

Adopting an explicitly theoretical structure would also involve digressions into the controversial, but peripheral, issue of what really constitutes the essence of the various types of theory: Marxist, realist, idealist, neo-classical or constructivist. Another justification of the eclectic approach is that the subject is inherently eclectic. Lawrence Freedman, discussing War Studies in a paper entitled *Mindless Eclecticism or Creative Synthesis?* (chapter 10 of Clarke, 1993), concludes that strategy is unavoidably eclectic. Although it is not ideal to use different theories for different applications, it is not uncommon. While I would not wish to claim any similarities between economics and physics, physicists use a different theory for the very large, general relativity, than they do for the very small, quantum mechanics.

Outline

The interaction between strategy and economy, power and money, is discussed in Chapter 2. This examines a set of relations in which military budgets are used to buy forces, which provide military capability that may be used to provide security. Such relations are often called input–output processes: there is an input, budgets, and an output, forces, which itself is an input into the processes determining military capability and security. The final output, security, is discussed in Chapter 3. While economists have written about war since, at least, Smith in 1776, defence economics emerged as a distinct speciality in the 1960s. Charles H. Anderton (2003) provides an introduction to this history. The 1960s defence economists were largely working in the US Department of Defense (DoD), or at a think-tank, RAND, that advised DoD. Their original questions were about the defence management aspects of budgets, forces and military capability. While one might not agree with their answers, they provided a good set of questions and I will use them to organise my discussion of military economics. However, I will do it in a much wider historical and geographical context than the narrow issues of contemporary military management in industrial countries. Although current military technology and organisation differs from that of the past, many of the fundamental issues are timeless. Thus the historical perspective is illuminating. Because the issues are timeless, works like Sun Tzu's *On the Art of War*, written in China about 450 BC, and Thucydides' *History of the Peloponnesian War*, written in Greece about 400 BC, are still taught in military academies and widely cited.

The first of the questions raised by the defence economists of the 1960s is about the optimal size of the defence budget: 'how much is enough?'; this is the subject of Chapter 4. Their second question was about force acquisition: 'how to get the biggest bang for a buck?' Force acquisition is examined in two stages. Chapter 5 looks at the demand side of force acquisition, how to recruit the troops and procure the weapons required. Chapter 6 looks at the supply side: the arms industry and the arms trade, the so-called merchants of death who provide the weapons. Their third question concerned how to organise these forces to produce the maximum military capability, how to win in combat; this is the subject of Chapter 7. The final question posed by the 1960s defence economists was about the opportunity costs of defence, what you have to give up: 'guns or butter?' or as the Bible has it 'swords or plowshares?' This choice is the subject of Chapter 8.

The questions posed in each chapter are rhetorical, there are rarely clear answers beyond 'it depends'. Neither the study of strategy nor the study of economics provides clear answers; they are primarily ways of thinking about issues. Thus rather than providing overall conclusions, the final chapter examines the methods used to understand military economics and the literature on these issues. But we begin with issues that relate to the wider interactions between economy and strategy and the production of security.

2
Power and Money

This chapter reviews the overlap between the economic and strategic spheres, introduces some economic concepts and illustrates how they can be used to illuminate military issues. Military and economic calculations involve inherent uncertainty so it discusses how to analyse uncertainty. Finally, it considers some examples of economic–security interactions.

Defence and peace economics studies a set of questions that arise in the intersection between the sphere of power and strategy (the art of a general, the specialist in violence) and the sphere of money and the economy (the processes of production, distribution and exchange and incentives that shape the allocation of scarce resources between competing ends in those activities). These questions concern how the forces of production interact with the forces of destruction. These forces are often seen as operating in separate spheres with their own rules and logic; but this is not the case, they interact. Economic development and the operation of markets require some mechanism to control violence, provide order and secure property rights. Most economic theory is part of peace economics: it takes for granted the ability of people to safely specialise, trade and hold property. In practice, the conventional economic forces of supply and demand are often shaped by violence and power. Military groups were probably the first formal social organisations and wars have played a major role in economic development. Success in war is influenced by economic factors, such as the wealth of nations and their ability to finance military activities.

Adam Smith in Book V chapter I of *The Wealth of Nations*, on the expense of defence, matched the development of different types of military preparations and employment of force to the different modes of economic development: hunting, pastoral, agricultural and manufacturing. He saw the propensity to war increasing then decreasing with development. It was not until the development of manufacturing, and guns, that agricultural states could feel safe from their nomadic neighbours, like Scythians, Tartars and Mongols, who regularly overran them. Europe would be very different had the Mongols, who reached Vienna and the Adriatic in 1242, not turned back. The Mongols established the largest land empire in history. They conquered China and northern India, defeated Christian armies in Poland and Hungary in 1241 and destroyed Baghdad in 1258, ending the Caliphate, the central authority of Islam. Europe was spared because the Mongol general Sabotai took his army home on the death of Ogadai, son of Genghis Khan, and the Mongols never bothered to return. Timothy May (2007) describes the Mongol way of war.

Money is a very concrete category, power is not; it has many dimensions. One dimension is the ability to get others to do what you want. This requires understanding why people do things, the many things that might motivate them to action. People are motivated by: coercion, they are forced to do it; material gain, they are bribed to do it; beliefs, they think it is the right thing to do; enjoyment, they get pleasure from doing it; reputation, they gain approbation from others for doing it; solidarity, they support their group in doing it. Our emphasis will be on coercion and material gain, fear and greed, but the other motivations are often more important. The soft power that comes from the ability to persuade can be more effective than the hard power that comes from the ability to coerce. It is not coercion or material gain that usually drive religions and charities, or the open source movement that produces products like Linux and Wikipedia. Similarly the motivations that make military risk death are often wider than coercion and material gain, though both can play a role.

Generally power and money are fungible: one can be transformed into the other. The rate at which they can be transformed is not a constant, but will change over time with the cost of force. In some circumstances, people or nations acquire power in order to extract money from others. In other circumstances people make money in order to acquire power. Often acquiring power and money go together. The 'Robber Barons' who made their fortunes creating late-19th-century American industry took the associated violence for granted. As Richard B. Mellon said, 'You couldn't run a coal mine without machine guns' (Von Hoffman, 1992, p. 24). Paul Kennedy (1988) describes the rise and fall of the great powers in terms of how their growing wealth gave them power and their attempts to maintain that power undermined their wealth.

Cyclical theories of power are very old. Ibn Khaldun, the 14th-century North African Islamic scholar, described how hardy warriors became softened as they took advantage of the riches of the civilisations that they had conquered, leaving themselves vulnerable to the next wave of hardy warriors.

This intersection or overlap between power and money is a contested terrain fought over by different disciplines. This overlap occurs at the individual, the national and the global levels. At the global or systemic level, the international system of states and markets, there is constant dynamism as new economic and strategic competitors enter this overlap. Life in this overlap between economics and strategy is complicated by the 'separate tracking' of issues in the two spheres. Different people are involved in international economic negotiations and international security negotiations. Those who go to the World Trade Organisation (WTO), which regulates trade in civilian goods, do not go to the organisations that regulate the trade in military goods. While there is just one organisation, the WTO, to regulate trade in civilian goods, there are four to regulate trade in weapons: the Wassenaar Arrangement for trade in conventional weapons; the Australia Group for chemical and biological weapons; the Nuclear Suppliers Group for nuclear technology; and the Missile Technology Control Regime for longer range missiles. Both the WTO and the European Union (EU) explicitly exclude weapons from their rules on trade. There would be interesting implications of applying WTO and EU rules to weapons, but there seems no political will to do so.

Similarly, except at head of government level, the people who go to the United Nations (UN) and North Atlantic Treaty Organisation (NATO) are not the same as the people who go to meetings of the World Bank and International Monetary Fund (IMF). This separate tracking can be functional in that it insulates the spheres: countries can be in dispute in one sphere and cooperating in another. But there is a danger that it can be dysfunctional: actions in one sphere having unintended consequences in the other. This separate tracking can also cause hostility between the Ministry of Defence, the lead department in the strategic sphere, and the Ministry of Finance, the lead department in the economic sphere. The hostility can run deep. During the Cold War, in the event of a nuclear attack, the 210 top people in the UK were to be spirited away by the military to a hideout under Box Hill. The military, who compiled the list of those to be saved, did not include anybody from the Treasury (Hennessy, 2002).

A recent description on life in this overlap between economy and strategy is provided in *Global Financial Warriors* (Taylor, 2007).

John B. Taylor is an eminent US monetary economist, best known for the 'Taylor Rule' which specifies how central banks should set interest rates. He was US Treasury Under Secretary for International Affairs from 2001 to 2005. After 9/11, he was responsible for cutting off terrorist money, organising the financial aspects of the invasions of Afghanistan and Iraq and attempting to reform the World Bank and IMF. Beyond the *Financial Times* and *Wall Street Journal* his book got less attention than it deserves. This may be partly because the issues are technical and partly because, unlike most such memoirs, he does not have a bad word to say about anybody, even George W. Bush. Early in the book (p. xxiii), he says:

> Financial Issues have always been a third pillar of foreign policy, along with political and military issues. Over two thousand years ago Thucydides wrote how 'The Athenians,' needing money for a siege, 'sent out twelve ships to collect money from their allies, with Lysicles and four others in command.' In the modern age of globalization the role of finance in foreign policy is even more important, and it is growing rapidly.

Taylor gives a nice example of how communications between economic and security specialists can fail. This arose during a National Security Council presentation he made to President Bush in the Situation Room in May 2003, shortly after the invasion of Iraq. The presentation was on Iraqi finance and a central issue was the movements of the Iraqi currency, the dinar. Exchange rates are usually quoted in units per dollar, the number of dinars required to buy a dollar. When a currency strengthens, fewer dinars are required to buy a dollar, so the rate goes down. Taylor comments (p. 228):

> One of my briefing charts showed how the value of the dinar had declined sharply at the start of the war, but then recovered rapidly and had since stabilized. As is typical in charts of currencies, an *upward* movement in the number of dinars per dollar is a *depreciation*, which causes no end of confusion to people who do not study the currency markets every day (which included, of course, everyone in the Sit Room that day except me).

He got the charts changed for future presentations.

The interaction of economics and security means that decisions taken in one sphere can have unintended consequences in the other.

Economics is largely the study of unintended consequences. Sometimes the unintended consequences are positive. We get most of what we need, not because of the concern of others with our welfare, but as an unintended consequence of the pursuit of their self interest: to make money out of us. This process is often described as an 'invisible hand' which directs the self interest of one to the benefit of others. The idea is usually attributed to Adam Smith, though he did not actually use the term in this context. Some companies explicitly say their goal is 'to do well by doing good', but even when they do not intend to do good they only do well, and make money, by meeting the needs of their customers; if not other stakeholders.

Sometimes the unintended consequences are negative; the economic consequences of political self interest in the 1919 Treaty of Versailles, after World War I, were disastrous. The victors' pursuit of their short-term self interest, over the reparations paid by Germany and its allies and the allocation of inter-allied debt, contributed to the German inflation of the 1920s, the depression of the 1930s and the causes of World War II. This disastrous outcome was predicted by the English economist John Maynard Keynes, in his 1919 book *The Economic Consequences of the Peace*. Keynes (pronounced Canes), who was known as Maynard, not John, was involved in the management of economic–security interactions throughout his life. He worked in the Treasury during World War I, rising to being responsible for the external finance, despite feeling 'that I work for a government I despise for ends I think criminal' (Skidelsky, 1983, p. 295). He was Treasury Representative at the peace negotiations before resigning in disgust to write his book. He was heavily involved in war planning during World War II; wrote *How to Pay for the War*; helped develop the national accounting information that allowed better war planning; and tried to negotiate loans from the US. He played a major role in the Bretton Woods Conference of 1944 which created the post-war international economic order. Throughout this he was very conscious of the interaction of economic and security policy.

The activities of Keynes are well documented because, unlike most economists, he was interesting enough to justify a three-volume biography (Skidelsky, 1983, 1992, 2000). He influenced policy on issues of war and peace; revolutionised economics, by shifting the emphasis from microeconomics to macroeconomics; and was heavily involved in the arts, setting up the UK Arts Council. During World War I, he organised the purchase of many impressionist paintings, both for the nation and himself, when the contents of Degas's studio came up for sale in Paris. Prices at the auction were depressed by the sound of German guns in the distance. He was a member of the Bloomsbury group which included novelists like Virginia Woolf and painters like Duncan Grant, advising them on their finances. He also shocked them by abandoning his established homosexual ways in his early forties and happily marrying a Russian ballerina, Lydia Lopokova, of whom they disapproved. During World War I, he was torn between his conscientious objection to the war and his work, which his friends Bertrand Russell and Lytton Strachey described as the 'job of demonstrating how to kill Germans as cheaply as possible' (Skidelsky, 1983, p. 324).

Producing security

At each level (individual, national and global) within this interaction of economics and strategy one can imagine an input–output process of linked elements, what in business schools would be called the value chain (Porter, 1985). The first link in the chain is the defence budget or military expenditures. Governments decide how much to allocate to their military budget, in the light of the economic and strategic environment: the threats they perceive and what they can afford. This budget buys forces: troops, weapons and the organisations to support them. Estimates of the size of forces can be found listed in the International Institute for Strategic Studies (IISS), publication *The Military Balance*, which gives the number of personnel, tanks, aircraft and the like. The forces provide capabilities – the ability to achieve military objectives – which influence the probability of winning in certain types of conflict. The military capabilities can then be used for attack, defence, deterrence or peacekeeping, which are intended to contribute to perceived security, confidence in the safety of society and its interests. This process is most obvious at the national level, but also operates at the individual and global levels and each of these four elements (budgets, forces, capability and security) is linked to the economic and strategic environments.

There are similarities between the commercial and military value chains. Commercial entrepreneurs must raise a budget to finance the purchase of labour and capital. They then use this labour and capital, with the available technology, to produce a product that will thrive against competing products in the marketplace. The military entrepreneur must also raise a budget to finance the acquisition of troops and weapons. They then use these armed forces, with the available technology, to produce military capability that will thrive against competing militaries in the strategic sphere. Many military organisations, like many large firms, are bureaucracies following standard procedures.

But at times, just as some innovative economic entrepreneur, like Bill Gates of Microsoft, can develop strategies that transform the value chain and sweep through the market, some innovative military entrepreneur, like Napoleon, can develop strategies that transform the military value chain and sweep through their enemies. Of course, there is the danger that the innovative entrepreneur gets locked into strategies that were initially successful, not realising that the competitors, like Google or Wellington, had developed responses to these strategies.

Although useful analytically, each of these elements are difficult to define and measure. Measuring budgets raises difficult accounting issues and it can take a military expert to assess what forces are really available to a state. But budgets and forces are conceptually easier categories than capability or security, which can mean very different things to different people. There is massive variability and uncertainty in the links between each of these four elements, with the strength of each link subject to economic and strategic influences. The linkages operate within interacting societies. The interactions may be negative, increasing one countries security reduces that of the other; or positive, increasing trade benefits both.

Consider an example of the link between budgets and forces. In the mid-1970s the Central Intelligence Agency (CIA) doubled its estimates of the share of output that the USSR devoted to the military, from about 8 per cent to about 15 per cent. This was not because the CIA thought that they had underestimated the forces that the Soviets could field. Their estimates of the forces remained the same; they had counted them using what were then called national technical means of verification: satellites and spy planes. What changed was their estimate of the efficiency of the Soviet defence industry. They obtained information that suggested that those forces cost twice their previous estimate. Although the revision was widely interpreted as indicating that the Soviets were more threatening, in fact it indicated that they were less threatening, only half as efficient. At the time, many thought the CIA was exaggerating the Soviet military burden. Subsequent to the collapse of the Soviet Union, it was discovered that the share of their output that the Soviets were spending on the military was probably well over 20 per cent, much more than the CIA estimated. This high share of defence did considerable damage to the Soviet economy.

How much capability the forces provide depends on the military skills and intangibles that shape force deployment: leadership, training, strategy, tactics, logistics, morale and maintenance of the equipment. How military capabilities translate into security is a matter of grand strategy.

In particular, there may be more effective means of maintaining security than military means. In 1946 France had been invaded by Germany three times in the previous three quarters of a century. France could have constructed another Maginot Line to protect itself, as it did between the World Wars. Instead France tried to create such economic interdependence that war would be impossible. This was initially done through the Iron and Steel Community and subsequently through the Common Market and the EU. However, to be on the safe side, during the Cold War, France did keep some of its nuclear missiles targeted on Germany.

In principle, this input–output structure provides a way of determining the defence budget by thinking forward, deciding where you want to be, and reasoning back, deciding how to get there. In principle national powers should look at the threats to their security and what they can afford; calculate the military capabilities required to deter or defend against those threats; establish the forces necessary to provide those capabilities; and match the cost of those forces to the available budget. This is the basis for what is called the Program, Planning and Budgeting System (PPBS), developed in the US in the 1960s and widely used. The Program is designed to provide the capability to match the threat; the plans specify the forces required to do this; and the budget provides estimates of the cost of those forces. Budgeting is discussed in more detail in Chapter 4.

In practice, although the formal process reflects this command and control structure, actual defence budgeting is rarely done in this way. This sort of calculation is done on a small scale when deciding to acquire particular types of system. Then investment appraisal is combined with operational analysis of the effectiveness of alternative force structures to determine the costs and benefits of alternative solutions. In the UK this process is called combined operational effectiveness and investment appraisal (COEIA); David Kirkpatrick (1996) describes the process. But this sort of process cannot be applied to the whole budget. This is partly because the calculations are too difficult and partly because decisions are not made in this way. The calculations are difficult because of the uncertainties in all the links in the chain from budgets to security and the fallibility of any forecasting process. For instance, it can be difficult to judge the extent to which the threat can be countered by the use of military capability. In *The Utility of Force*, General Sir Rupert Smith (2005) examines the use of military force to achieve one's purpose. The book attracted a lot of attention and his scepticism about the current effectiveness of military power led to it being labelled by some as 'the futility of force'. Some threats can be deterred by military preparations, others cannot. He also points out an important difference in the use of our two central motivators, fear and greed, through the use of threats or bribes. Threats are expensive when they fail, bribes are expensive when they succeed (p. 384).

In addition to the difficulty of these calculations, actual defence budgeting cannot be done in this way because there is no single national decision maker, no unitary rational actor, to attempt these calculations. Any society is a mixture of different groups with various identities and possibly antagonistic interests. They compete within an arena established by a set of standard operating procedures that establish the rules of the game. These rules or institutions may be constitutional checks and balances and the rule of law, if it exists, but they may also reflect the procedures of the military and civil bureaucracy. In bureaucracies it is often said that where you stand on an issue depends on where you sit: the organisation you belong to. These standard operating procedures are not immutable but it may take much effort, even for an autocrat, to change them. The state is not a monolithic institution and the identities of the groups competing for control may be defined by their class or relation to means of production; their religion; their ethnicity; or their beliefs about particular issues such as the environment. There may be an elite, or ruling, class, which shares common interests, but its members are not homogeneous and their personal interests or values may conflict with their class interests. To implement the policies that promote their interests the ruling class have to operate through institutions and even the most autocratic dictators can have difficulty implementing their wishes.

Decisions are the product of various groups – political, military, industrial and bureaucratic – with their own interests and often conflicting objectives operating in a fluid system of institutions. These institutions and groups provide the transmission mechanism by which perceptions of threats and affordability are turned into decisions. This transmission mechanism reflects industrial and political interests, pork-barrel politics as elected representatives try to get military facilities in their constituencies, inter-service rivalry and various bureaucratic forces. The exact form of this institutional transmission mechanism is society specific. Who matters in different countries can be quite different. For instance, unlike most legislatures, the US Congress has great power over the details of the military budget: determining whether a particular piece of equipment is produced or not or whether a particular military base is closed or not.

In most countries there is inter-service rivalry between the army, navy and air force. This rivalry is partly for roles and resources. For instance in the 1950s, the US army, navy and air force, each fought to have their own nuclear weapons. Another example is a long dispute between the Italian air force and navy. A Mussolini law of 1926 gave the air force exclusive aviation rights, even though Italian military aviation had been pioneered by naval Lieutenant Mario Calderara. Despite defeats in World War II attributable to absence of aircraft carrier capability, the air force monopoly of fixed winged aircraft was maintained. In the 1950s naval pilots who flew two US-supplied Curtiss SC-2 Helldiver planes onto Italian soil were arrested and the planes mothballed. It was declared that 'everything that flies is Air Force property.' There was some co-operation between the services, such as in anti-submarine warfare, but over 30 years the two services devoted huge resources to lobbying on this issue. The navy acquired an aircraft carrier, despite being unable to put fixed-wing aircraft on it. Eventually in 1989 the navy was allowed aircraft, subject to a convoluted compromise retaining air force prerogatives. Monopolies, like the air force monopoly over aircraft, create excess profits, which need not be measured in money. Economists call these excess profits rents; and it is worth individuals or organisations, like the armed services, to invest in obtaining those rents. This 'rent-seeking' behaviour can absorb a lot of resources to no productive effect.

Thinking about the optimum solutions may be revealing in certain circumstances, particularly in revealing mistakes; but the limitations of optimisation and the importance of institutions must also be recognised. We will alternate between the two approaches, depending on which seems most useful for the purpose at hand.

At some points we will treat the state as an optimising rational actor and at others as an arena of conflict constrained by standard operating procedures.

Militarism

Military and society are closely linked. Society provides the resources for the military and the military have to respond to social trends, for instance in attitudes to gays, women and discipline. Conversely society may also be influenced by the military. The term militarism is usually used to describe the adoption of military values and symbols by the wider society. The military influence might involve an emphasis on an external or internal threat, justifying military expenditures and large arms industry; bellicose foreign policies and repressive internal security measures; the widespread use of uniforms and military ceremonial and procedures; or government by the military. The range of these examples indicates that militarism is not a single phenomenon, but describes various ways the military can influence society. At one extreme the whole society may be dedicated to the production of soldiers, like classical Sparta; at the other extreme the soldiers may merely provide ceremonial for public holidays.

The military values of patriotism, discipline, self-sacrifice and respect for tradition can be made part of an ideology which is used for other purposes. The values can be used to promote social solidarity and cohesion, encouraging people to unite against a common enemy. Such unity may be designed to over-ride conflicts of class, gender or ethnicity and mobilise the nation to serve some higher objective. In the face of domestic discontent or industrial unrest governments may be tempted to indulge in foreign adventures to divert attention from domestic disputes. Liberals traditionally ascribed militarism to the aristocracy, socialists ascribed it to the capitalists; but it can permeate whole societies, particularly when linked to deep nationalist feelings. Michael Howard (1981) says:

> At the dawn of the twentieth century Europe was a very bellicose, very militarist society, and the inflated spirit of patriotism and xenophobia which fuelled an alarmingly intensive arms race could not be laid at the old aristocracy. It was no less virulent among those 'industrious classes' which Saint-Simon and his successors had expected to propagate the spirit of peace.

Militarism may be dysfunctional, particularly when military styles are ineffective for more general economic and social purposes. The fact that different styles may be effective for different purposes is illustrated by the often unhappy relations between scientists and military during World War II, for instance in the Manhattan Project, constructing the atomic bomb. Soviet society was highly militarised at great cost to its economy. Military involvement in government may not only be damaging to the economy, but may make the military ineffective in combat as their goals are switched from military objectives to domestic politics. Military governments have a poor record of winning wars. Even in maintaining internal order, the military style may not be effective and most societies draw a strong distinction between military and police activities, with quite different modes of operation. Similarly, most military counter-insurgency strategies recognise that the military contribution is a small, though necessary, part of the package of measures required.

Economic concepts

Just as the military approach to running the economy may be ineffective, the economic approach to running the military may be ineffective. Edward N. Luttwak (1985) attacks the materialist bias in much military planning, which comes from the economic approach. In his chapter 'Why we need more fraud, waste and mismanagement in the Pentagon' (p. 139), he says

> But when it comes to material power, the relationship between material inputs and desired outputs is not proportional; it is in fact very loose, because the making of military strength is dominated by the nonmaterial, quite intangible human factors, from the quality of national military strategy to the fighting morale of individual servicemen.

He also says (p. 133): 'The trouble is that the outputs that count in war are very particular and very different from the outputs that count in peacetime and when civilian notions of efficiency are applied, the difference is routinely overlooked.' Despite the fact that Luttwak's criticism of the mechanical application of material targets is correct, the economic approach can still be useful, if applied carefully, with due respect for the intangibles. This section reviews some economic concepts, which can be useful in a military context.

Marginal analysis

Economics emphasises marginal analysis: the effects of small changes, a little more or a little less. Adam Smith noted that water was essential to life but very cheap, while diamonds are inessential but expensive. What determines their relative prices is not their relative value, but the relative cost of obtaining the last unit. The marginal cost of obtaining another glass of water is normally rather small, that of obtaining another diamond rather large. Some may argue that defence is so important, like water, that we should spend whatever is required. But what matters is the margin. When the defence budget is optimised, the marginal security benefit (the extra security got by a little more military spending) is equal to its marginal opportunity cost (benefits lost by that military spending not going to alternative uses, such as lower taxes or more government spending on health or education). Opportunity costs, resources used for one purpose are not available for other purposes, and equalising marginal costs and marginal benefits are central to economics. Marginal costs are additional costs, so the marginal cost of the Iraq War after the invasion of 2003 is different from the total cost. Much of the troops and equipment used in the war would have existed anyway, even without Iraq. Thus the marginal cost is the extra expenditure that would not have been incurred had the war not been fought.

Whether one measures marginal or total costs is one of the reasons that there have been disputes about the costs of the Iraq War. Donald Rumsfeld, then US defense secretary, initially estimated the cost as $50–60 billion; Bilmes and Stiglitz (2008) estimated it as $3000 billion. In the UK at the time of the invasion the Blair government 'prudently' allowed for £1 billion to cover the costs, but by 2008 the UK had already spent about £9 billion. Differences in estimates also arise because of the time period over which the costs are measured (over a year, over the period since the invasion) and what is included in the costs. In addition to the direct costs in Iraq, one may or may not include such things as: replacement military equipment; extra interest on the national debt; the risk premium added to the oil price; the future costs of medical care for those wounded; and imputed values of human lives for those killed.

Marginal analysis cannot be used where the idea of a little more or a little less is not applicable, because there are sharp breaks. Economists refer to such breaks as indivisibilities or discontinuities. For instance, it rarely makes sense to speak of being a little more dead, or a little less dead; you are either dead or not. However, averaging can make marginal analysis useful even here. Considering a large number of people, one can analyse the small changes in the probability of death that result from particular expenditures to estimate their marginal benefits.

There is a useful piece of marginal analysis, originally due to Ricardo in the early 19th century. Imagine a city, set in a fertile basin surrounded by mountains. The land close to the city is the most productive and fertility falls as you move further out. The price of food will be equal to the cost of production on the least fertile fields farmed, the marginal land. The cost of production will include the food and subsistence for those who work the land and any necessary investment such as the seed for the crops. If the price of food was higher it would be worth extending the area farmed, workers could move to unused land. If the price was lower, the marginal farms would not cover their costs and go out of business.

This equality of the price of food and the cost of production on the marginal land is called an equilibrium condition. In economics, equilibrium is a situation where nobody has any incentive to change their behaviour. An example is lines at supermarket checkouts; in equilibrium

they are all about the same length. If they were not, people would move
to the shorter lines, until lines were once more the same length. In equilibrium, people are indifferent about which line they join, since they
are all about the same length. The equilibrium need not be efficient.
A single line with people going to the next available checkout may be
quicker, but there is no mechanism for people to move to that alternative arrangement without some form of organisation. Notice that the
equilibrium does not determine the length of the lines, it just says that
they are equal. Nor does it make sense to ask which of the lines determines their length, they just equalise. Similarly it does not make sense
to ask whether price determines cost of production on the marginal
land or vice versa, they just equalise by people moving. The time it
takes to move to equilibrium, the speed of adjustment, varies. People
move between supermarket lines quickly, they move between farms
more slowly.

If the price of food is equal to the cost of production on the marginal
land, price will be higher than the cost of production on the more fertile
land. The owners of the more fertile land can extract the difference, the
surplus over the cost of production, as rent. Since the right to extract the
surplus is valuable, people will invest resources in trying to acquire this
right, by force if necessary; though this aspect of the model rarely makes
the economics text books. The rights may be acquired in various ways,
including driving the peasants off their common land, or by imposing
restrictions on the ability of the workers to move. While profitable for
individuals, this rent-seeking behaviour may be unproductive for society
as a whole. It is costly, absorbing resources, but does not add to the
total amount produced, just redistributes it. While often unproductive,
such conflicts over the ownership of land and control of other rents are
common and often violent.

Rents

Economists have extended the term rents from just land to any surplus
of price over the cost of production. The term rent-seeking is used for
attempts to control this surplus. Rents can be the product of state actions
which restrict supply. By imposing tariffs that stop foreign competition,
the state can raise the profitability of domestic industry. It then pays
domestic firms to invest in advertising, lobbying or bribing politicians
to get tariffs imposed. Even within a democracy, this may be effective,
since the few firms who each benefit a lot are better able to organise than the large number of consumers who each lose a little. Tariffs
are not always harmful; protection may allow the domestic industry to

attain the critical size for efficient production that allows it to compete effectively on the world market. Such protection was crucial in the early stages of industrialisation of the US, Germany and Japan. Economists know this as the 'infant industry' argument and while recognising its force, many are sceptical about the ability of the state to distinguish real infant industries from rent-seeking geriatrics.

The argument that rent-seeking conflicts over ownership are unproductive rests on the assumption that the form of ownership, the allocation of property rights, does not influence the total amount produced. The Coase (1960) Theorem shows that if there are no transactions costs, then unrestricted trade in property rights and resources can achieve an efficient allocation, regardless of the initial allocation of property rights. Whether the workers or the landlords owned the land, one would get the same outcome in terms of food produced and hours worked. It is a striking theoretical result, but it depends on a very strong assumption, no transaction costs that restrict free exchange; so its empirical relevance is questionable. Often economic transactions are governed more by the assumptions of Machiavelli, 'a prince never lacks legitimate reasons to break his promises' than the assumptions of Coase, where trade can be trusted. In practice, changes of ownership, such as after wars or land reforms, do have major effects on productivity. The enclosures in Britain drove the peasants off the common lands, but the enclosed land produced more. Cramer (2007, p. 281) argues that economic development is often an unintended consequence of violent conflict. War can influence the amount of wealth available for investment, change social and political organisation, and provoke technological and institutional innovation. It is important to emphasise that these are unintended consequences. The fact that development may follow a war is not a reason to conclude that the desire for development was a cause of war. Marx called this process, by which a ruling class can generate development by investing the surplus expropriated from peasants or workers, primitive accumulation.

Substitution

The economic approach emphasises opportunity costs, what you give up by taking an action, and the need to compare expected marginal costs and benefits of an action. It also emphasises substitution; if the costs of one alternative rises decision makers will tend to substitute another alternative. When increased airport security raised the cost of hijacking aircraft, terrorists substituted other tactics, including bombing. The Irish Republican Army (IRA) was quite efficient at substituting targets in the light of incentives, moving from military targets in Northern Ireland to targets on the mainland. The first mainland targets were civilian, such as pub bombings; then political, they killed Airey Neave, a leading Conservative MP, and got close to killing two prime-ministers, Mrs Thatcher in the Brighton hotel bombing and Mr Major when they mortared Downing Street, the Prime Minister's residence. Finally, they switched to high value financial targets like the Baltic Exchange and Canary Wharf. Nuclear and conventional weapons can be substitutes: the rising costs of conventional defence provide incentives to switch to cheaper nuclear substitutes. Brauer and van Tuyll (2008) discuss such substitution in the case of French nuclear forces. As income grows you may be able to afford more of both the substitute goods, more conventional and more nuclear weapons. Two goods are substitutes if raising the price of one causes you to increase your demand for the other. Two goods are complements if raising the price of one causes you to reduce your demand for the other. Guns and ammunition are complements: reduced demand for guns reduces demand for ammunition.

A particularly important form of substitution is between the present and the future. The extent to which you are willing to substitute short-term gains now for longer-term benefits in the future is central to much military and security analysis. This is described in terms of a discount rate. If you will give up $100 now for $110 in the future, this is a 10 per cent discount rate, the $110 in the future is discounted to a present value of only $100 now. The extent to which you discount the future partly depends on how uncertain it is. If you prefer a bird in the hand to two in the bush, you discount the two because of the uncertainty of catching them. We return to uncertainty.

Returns to inputs

Often each extra unit gives a smaller return. When you are thirsty, the satisfaction from the first glass of water is very large, but the satisfaction from subsequent glasses declines; there are decreasing or diminishing returns. Suppose you are selecting targets for a nuclear attack, and are targeting the enemy's society, called a counter-value strike. You select the most valuable target first, such as their leadership, then sequentially less valuable targets for each subsequent missile. Thus there are decreasing returns to nuclear missiles in counter-value targeting. Given the vast numbers of nuclear warheads in the US arsenal, it was difficult to find enough meaningful targets for them in the Single Integrated Operation Plan (SIOP) that controlled nuclear deployment. Decreasing returns are not universal and there can be increasing returns, each extra unit generates a greater reward. The coexistence of both positive and negative returns to increasing inputs is reflected in English proverbs. With increasing returns, 'extra hands make light work'; with decreasing returns, 'too many cooks spoil the broth'. To return to nuclear war, suppose you aim not at the enemy's society, as in a counter-value strike, but at its nuclear missiles in a counter-force strike. The objectives are different. A counter-value strike tries to maximise mega-deaths in the enemy country, a counter-force strike tries to minimise mega-deaths in your own country. The first missiles you launch provide little benefit. You destroy a few enemy missiles, but there are still more than enough left for a retaliatory strike that will completely annihilate your society. As you fire more missiles, the benefit increases, because there are fewer enemy missiles left to inflict retaliatory damage on you. Once you have reached the point where you can destroy all the enemy missiles, decreasing returns set in again; there is nothing left for your missiles to destroy.

There are two related economic concepts which sometimes get confused: returns to scale (more output or more missiles fired) and returns to one of the inputs (more labour, holding output constant; or better accuracy, holding the number of missiles fired constant). The effectiveness of each missile depends on a number of inputs such as its payload (the number of warheads and the destructiveness of each) and accuracy (usually measured by circular error probable (CEP)). Returns to inputs and returns to scale can be different. There may be decreasing returns to scale, each extra missile fired does less damage; but increasing returns to an input, each improvement in accuracy causes more damage. Esoteric calculations of this sort were common during the Cold War.

Earlier it was noted that economic power and political power were fungible, one could be transformed into another, but that the marginal rate of transformation, how much extra power you get for an extra bit of spending, was not constant. This exchange rate between power and money will depend on all the links in our chain: what military forces money can buy; the capability those forces provide; and the effectiveness of military capability in achieving your goals. There are also likely to be diminishing returns; initially some political power can be bought quite cheaply, but the more power you obtain the more it threatens others and the more expensive it gets to buy off resistance. The UK in the 19th century and the US in the 20th century used their considerable economic power to gain political leverage which allowed them to organise the international system, but the more powerful they became the more resistance they provoked. In the 21st century, China and other countries which acquired large international currency reserves, through running balance of payments surpluses, could use these reserves through Sovereign Wealth Funds to support political goals. For instance, China used its money to persuade other countries not to recognise Taiwan. Such use faces trade-offs: how much profit on foreign investments are you willing to sacrifice to meet your political objectives?

Brauer and van Tuyll (2008) argue that these economic concepts can illuminate many episodes of military history. They illustrate this with the role of opportunity costs in the choice between castles and standing armies in mediaeval Europe; the role of contracting issues in the private sector provision by the mercenary Condottieri in the renaissance; the role of marginal cost-benefit analysis in the decision by generals to offer battle in the 18th century; the role of asymmetric information during the American Civil War; the role of diminishing returns in strategic bombing during World War II; and the role of capital–labour substitution in the development of a French nuclear capability during the Cold War.

Public goods

Military preparations are usually, but not always, the preserve of governments. In most countries, individuals do not provide for their own defence against their country being invaded. They do protect themselves against local threats, by fitting locks and hiring private security firms, but not national threats. Defence is usually publicly provided, but in economics, the term public good has a more specific meaning. A public good is one where nobody can be excluded from consuming it and there is non-rivalry in consumption: if one person consumes a public good the ability of others to consume the good is not reduced. Since private producers of a public good cannot exclude people from consuming it, they cannot charge for it, so have no incentive to provide it. If the government provides it, welfare is maximised if the sum of the marginal benefits (often called marginal rates of substitution between public and private goods) over all consumers equals the marginal cost of production (often called marginal rate of transformation). There is a practical difficulty in applying this condition, since it requires determining each consumer's marginal benefits. Even if the consumers knew what these benefits were, they may have no incentive to report them truthfully, since governments could tax them on those benefits. Sometimes surveys of stated preferences are used to determine benefits. For instance, people are asked how much they would be willing to pay, for instance in extra airport taxes, for protection of aircraft against shoulder-launched surface-to-air missiles. Such protection is not a pure public good; those who refuse to pay can be excluded.

Defence is usually given as the example of a public good, but this is not clear. One might distinguish between defence, protection when attacked, and deterrence, discouraging attack through strength. Pure deterrence may well be a public good, since the expenditure deters enemies from attacking, everyone benefits and nobody can be excluded from that benefit. Protection from attack may not be a public good. The Spitfires that were defending airfields during the Battle of Britain were not defending London, so there was rivalry in consumption. There is also the problem that many of the benefits of the defence budget may be private benefits that accrue to those that determine it. The military spending may be motivated as much by the benefit that the elite gets from protecting themselves from attack by the people as by protecting the people from attack by outsiders. In calculating marginal benefits, strategic responses must be taken into account. If the defence spending provokes an antagonist to match that spending, the extra spending may not provide any extra security; the marginal benefit of the military expenditure is zero.

When there are reasonably free markets, the marginal benefits and costs of goods and services can be usually be approximated by their prices. This is not necessarily the case when there are public goods or restrictions on the prices, either from monopolies or from government regulations. Markets may also fail to allocate efficiently when individual choices, and thus market prices, do not reflect all benefits and costs. In such cases there are said to be externalities: benefits or costs that are imposed on others. When someone is vaccinated there is a positive externality. Not only are they less likely to get the disease, a private benefit, but they are also less likely to infect others with the disease, a public benefit. When cost-minimising firms cause pollution, they impose a negative externality on others. Externalities, like public goods, are cases where markets fail to allocate efficiently. Cases of market failure may justify government intervention, such as subsidised vaccination or regulations on pollution. However, the danger of government failure may be as great as the danger of market failure; the outcome after government intervention may be worse than no intervention at all. In some cases government regulations are introduced to benefit particular groups; there are then incentives for rent-seeking groups to pressure or bribe governments to introduce regulations that benefit them.

Calculating the benefits of military preparations involves identifying the possible threats, their likelihood and how military preparations would reduce them. Some might argue that the most likely security threats, such as global warming, pandemics and terrorism, are not amenable to a military solution. This would suggest a defence budget of zero, like Costa Rica or Iceland. Others might argue that while there are no obvious military threats, one never knows what may happen, so it is sensible to maintain a military as an insurance policy. Then it is a question of what is a sensible insurance premium: how much is enough? This question, which is considered in Chapter 4, involves a judgement fraught with uncertainty.

Uncertainty

Given that society has decided to maintain a military as an insurance policy, the military have to decide what risks to prepare for. This requires identifying the threats that have the highest probability or impact in terms of their potential consequences. It is impossible to prepare against all risks, since preparations are expensive; so priorities are essential. But to establish priorities requires predicting risks and this is fraught with difficulties in both the economic and strategic spheres. Furthermore, if the preparations are effective and deter the threat, then the preparations seem unnecessary since no threat materialised. The threats that materialise tend to be the unexpected ones, against which no preparations were made.

As Carl von Clausewitz emphasised, chance plays a central role in war and the outcomes of conflict are unpredictable. If one side was completely confident that it was going to be massively defeated it probably would not fight. An exception is where the group wants to establish a reputation for fighting to the death against impossible odds, which might be useful in future conflicts, to the group if not the individuals who die. In practice one can never be completely confident about the outcome: what appears inevitable after the event, may look very uncertain before it. Given the centrality of chance in military affairs, we need to analyse uncertainty.

The large role of chance in war tempts us to ask unanswerable 'what if?' questions. To illustrate the role of such uncertainties, consider the small, well documented, war between the UK and Argentina over the Falkland/Malvinas islands in 1982. The islands, 300 miles off the Argentine coast were held by Britain, though their ownership had always been disputed. Argentina invaded the islands on 2 April 1982 and established a large garrison. The British despatched a task force to the South Atlantic, which landed at San Carlos on 21 May, recaptured the islands and accepted the surrender of the Argentine forces on 14 June. From one perspective it can be presented as the inevitable victory by the professional armed forces of a major Western power, in a small colonial war against third world troops, led by a vainglorious and incompetent military Junta, trying to establish domestic political legitimacy by foreign adventures. From another perspective, it was a dangerous gamble by a bellicose British Prime Minister, Mrs Thatcher, which, against all the odds, paid off and where failure would have had major international repercussions.

Argentina is unusual in going from a developed economy in the 19th century to a developing one in the 20th century. In 1913 Argentina had a per capita income of $3797, close to that of Britain, $4921, when Britain was at the height of its power. In 1973, after a long period of relative decline Britain had a per-capita income of $12025, Argentine only $7962 (Maddison, 2007). Argentina had potentially effective armed forces that were well equipped, had operational experience in internal counter-insurgency and were trained for a possible war with Chile. The Argentine air force destroyed six British ships and damaged ten others. One of the ships destroyed was the Atlantic Conveyor carrying the Chinook helicopters on which the British plan of advance depended. The Parachute Regiment and the Marines were able to advance on foot. While it seemed anachronistic in an age of mechanised high-technology warfare to insist that Paras and Marines spent much of their training carrying heavy loads over boggy mountains in Wales, this paid off in the Falklands. Other units, like the Guards, who could not walk had to be shipped by sea suffering heavy losses from the Argentine air force at Bluff Cove.

To illustrate the role of chance, consider some things that, had they been a little different, might have changed the outcome. Had Argentina delayed the invasion by 9 months, as had originally been intended, Britain probably could not have sent a task force. Most of the ships and landing craft used in the task force would have been scrapped or withdrawn from service under the 1981 John Nott Defence Review. The delay would have also allowed Argentina to take delivery of more French Exocet missiles, which did such damage to British ships. The Reagan administration was split between supporting UK or Argentina, though eventually it backed Britain. Had it not, the UK would have lacked essential satellite intelligence and the AIM9L Sidewinder air-to-air missiles. These were rapidly purchased from the US and fitted to Harrier jets. Without Sidewinders, the Harriers could not have destroyed so many Argentine aircraft. Argentina sent poorly trained conscripts to the Falklands, keeping its elite units on the borders with Chile, fearing that Chile would exploit the situation to attack. The elite troops would have made the British task more difficult. Had Argentina extended the airport at Port Stanley to take fast jets, the Argentine air force would not have had to fly 300 miles before engaging the British, giving them more flexibility and forcing the task force to change their deployment. British losses of shipping would have been much heavier had Argentina mined the approaches to San Carlos Water, where the British landed, or correctly fused their bombs dropped. Many of the bombs that hit British ships did not explode or went straight through the ship. Had the Argentine Navy not retreated into port after the sinking of the cruiser, The General Belgrano, or used their submarines more aggressively, they could have restricted the task force. Had the Argentine garrison held out for a few weeks longer, for instance by counter-attacking and disrupting the British advance rather than staying behind defensive lines around Port Stanley, the British ships, which were already suffering from the prolonged campaign, could not have stayed on station any longer and would have been withdrawn.

The British also made mistakes. The attack on Goose Green and Darwin was a diversion from the main thrust on Stanley, to establish an early win for morale and political purposes. Contrary to the British expectations, the settlements were heavily defended and the battle went on for almost 3 days, delaying the main advance. The casualties included the commanding officer of the Para battalion. Had the war gone badly for the British and there been a danger of their losing the whole task force, it is not clear how they would have responded. Many of the ships in the task force had been on exercises before being diverted to the South Atlantic and some were still carrying nuclear weapons which could not be offloaded before they went south. All these issues are contentious and there are good reasons for some of the Argentine decisions. Had they postponed the invasion, the Junta may have been swept from power much earlier, instead of being deposed after the defeat. Chile might have invaded, had the elite troops been moved to the Falklands. Basing fighters at Port Stanley was not just a matter of extending the runway but providing the considerable infrastructure required to equip and maintain fast jets. The logistics of the conflict played a central role on both sides. These examples are primarily intended to emphasise the uncertainties of war, the impossibility of forecasting, the imponderables involved in any calculation and how things might have turned out differently.

Going back to the more general issues of uncertainty, humanity seems to have evolved with a set of decision-making rules, often called heuristics, which while effective in evolutionary terms, leave blind-spots about dealing with uncertainty and probabilities. Generally there tends to be some reluctance to believe in the importance of chance, instead people think that there must be some pattern or reason behind the outcomes. In areas where chance reigns supreme, such as sports, war or dangerous occupations, people tend to become superstitious, attributing importance to magical actions, or lucky pieces of clothing. This is despite the fact that it is said to be very unlucky to be superstitious.

When thinking about chance, it can be useful to distinguish three different types of uncertainty. With mild uncertainty, which economists often call risk, one can not only identify the possible outcomes or future states of the world, when tossed a coin may come up heads or tails, but also attach probabilities to them, heads has a probability of a half. This is typical of most gambling situations, such as horse races or casinos. With more fundamental uncertainty, which economists sometimes call Knightian uncertainty after Frank Knight, an American economist, one can identify the future possible outcomes, but not assign probabilities to them. When a coin is tossed, the possibilities are still either heads or tails, but you suspect that the coin is biased, so cannot attach a probability to heads. With a more extreme, but rather common, form of uncertainty one is not able to list all the possibilities let alone assign probabilities to them. Economists sometimes refer to this as unawareness and Nassim Nicholas Taleb (2007) calls it wild uncertainty. Military matters often involve such extreme uncertainties, what US Defense Secretary Donald Rumsfeld called 'unknown unknowns', things you don't even know you don't know about.

Probability is a late branch of mathematics. There does not seem to be any conception of probabilities as things that might be calculated before about 1650. During the 19th century probability was widely employed in science, but a proper axiomatic foundation for probability theory was only established in the early 1930s by the Russian mathematician Kolmogorov. Even now there is no agreement on what probabilities are. There are two broad interpretations, which go back to the origins of probability in the 17th century. On one view probabilities reflect relative frequencies, on the other they reflect degrees of belief.

The relative frequency approach measures probabilities as proportions. These are calculated from the number of occurrences of an event, such as the proportion of tossed coins that come up heads. So the probability of being killed when flying is calculated by counting the number of people killed in air crashes and dividing that by the distance travelled by air passengers. For the US this is about 0.1 deaths per billion passenger kilometres travelled. One can do the same thing for travel by road and one gets about 2.6 deaths per billion passenger kilometres, 26 times higher. After 9/11 many Americans chose to drive rather than fly and in the subsequent year road deaths rose by about 1600. This was reported in *New Scientist*, 30 August 2008 and prompted correspondence about the interpretation of this choice. This may have been because 9/11 changed their estimates of the probabilities; people expected more attacks on aircraft. However, people do seem to fear flying more than driving, despite the probabilities suggesting flying is much safer. This may be because of salience, air crashes get more publicity than car crashes; because of circumstances, people feel they have more control when driving; or because of preferences, people would rather die on their own, as is usual in a car crash, rather than with lots of other people, as is usual in a plane crash. What matters in choices, such as between flying and driving, are expected values, which depend both on the probabilities of the various outcomes and the consequences of those outcomes.

For many uncertain events, such as nuclear war, there are too few historical observations to estimate the probabilities by relative frequencies. The estimates are then based on some degree of belief informed by potentially relevant causal factors. The *Bulletin of Atomic Scientists* has a clock on the front cover showing the number of minutes to midnight, midnight being nuclear war. This is based on an assessment of the danger by experts. To illustrate how such probabilities might be used, consider a simplified version of the Cold War question of nuclear disarmament. It was generally thought that there were three possible outcomes or future states of the world: cold, red or dead. Cold was the maintenance of the Cold War pattern of armed confrontation; red was Soviet dominance and dead was nuclear annihilation. A fourth outcome, that the Soviet Union would peacefully disappear, was rarely included as a possible future state of the world. One then tried to compare the probability of each outcome, with and without nuclear weapons. For instance, if the West did not have nuclear weapons the probability of being red might be thought higher and the probability of being dead lower. But calculating the probabilities does not provide an answer; one also has to value the three outcomes: the perceived cost or value attached to being cold, red or dead. It is not clear what units you would use to express those relative values, but the quality adjusted life years (QALYs), used in medical cost-benefit calculations, might be a possibility. The expected value of nuclear weapons to the West is then the sum over the values attached to each outcome (cold, red or dead) multiplied by the probability of that outcome, given that the West has nuclear weapons. This can then be compared to the expected value without nuclear weapons. There is clearly scope for differences of opinion about the inputs to this calculation.

There are markets for certain sorts of uncertainties, which establish a price for risk. This price might be an insurance premium which provides cover against certain events, such as your house burning down; it might be a futures or forward market, which allows you to buy or sell a commodity for delivery in the future at a fixed price, irrespective of what happens; it might be a spread, the difference between the percentage return you can earn on a risky asset and on a safe asset; or it might be the odds on a horse winning a race quoted by a bookmaker. These prices provide information on risks. If you wanted to know whether the risk of piracy off the Horn of Africa had changed, you could consult Somali specialists and naval officers or you could look at ship insurance rates. Markets do not always get prices right and it is widely believed that markets systematically under-priced risk, prior to the credit crunch of August 2007. Markets are also supposed to pass risk to those best able to absorb it: risk specialists such as investment bankers, insurance companies and bookmakers. The risk specialists can absorb risk because they diversify; because they are specialists in calculating probabilities; and because they may also be able to influence the risk: early fire insurance companies helped establish fire brigades. The diversification benefits arise because insurance companies can pool over many risks, relying on the fact that not every house will burn down at the same time. The benefits of pooling depend on the risks being independent. If the risks are correlated, lots of disasters happening together as is common in crises, this undermines the benefits of diversification.

While in theory risk should be passed to those best able to absorb it, there is a danger that the risk will be packaged by financial engineers to pass it to those who are least able to understand it. In the case of the credit crunch it appears that those who least understood the risks were not the usual victims, uniformed consumers, but the large investment banks and insurance companies. All five of the large US investment banks had disappeared by September 2008. Bear Stearns, Lehman Brothers and Merrill Lynch failed and were taken over; Morgan Stanley and Goldman Sachs retreated to the safety of being regulated retail banks. The largest US insurance company, AIG, also had to be bailed out.

Even with mild uncertainty, when probabilities can be attached to events, people seem bad at judging risks and calculating the probabilities. Gerd Gigerenzer (2002) gives a range of examples, mainly drawn from health and medicine, of how people, including physicians, routinely make mistakes about judging risks and probabilities. He suggests various ways to avoid such mistakes. With wild uncertainty it is still more difficult; not only can you not calculate probabilities you cannot even imagine the events that might occur. Taleb (2004, 2007) argues for the importance of the highly improbable, calling such events Black Swans, the title of his 2007 book. Before Europeans went to Australia, every swan they had seen was white; they could not imagine black swans. Taleb was fortunate in the timing of his book. *Black Swans* was published in April 2007 just before the credit crunch of summer 2007. This nicely illustrated the type of improbable events he had in mind, including the first run on an English bank since the Overend-Gurney crisis of 1866.

Consider a simple example, where the probabilities often seem to surprise people. This example is usually given in terms of screening for a disease, but consider screening for spies. Suppose you run an intelligence agency and discover, through your own spies in the opposition agency, that you have been infiltrated and that the opposition estimate that they have recruited 1 per cent of your employees as agents. Suppose that there were procedures, such as some sort of future lie detector, to screen your employees and these were 99 per cent accurate: only 1 per cent of foreign agents escape detection and only 1 per cent of loyal employees are falsely accused. You undertake the screening process and identify the suspects. What proportion of the suspects are actually foreign agents? A common guess is 99 per cent, but in fact only half of the suspects are likely to be agents. To see why that is the case, follow one of Gigerenzer's suggestions and work with numbers rather than percentages. Suppose the agency has 100,000 employees, the opposition has recruited 1 per cent of them: 1000 employees are agents. Of those 1000 agents screening will identify 99 per cent of them correctly, 990 suspects. However, of the 99,000 loyal employees, screening will also wrongly identify 1 per cent of them as suspects, another 990 people; the same as the number of actual agents identified. So of the 1980 identified suspects, only half, 990, are real spies.

Whether such screening is worthwhile depends on the benefits of identifying agents (the programme identifies all but 10 of them) relative to the costs to morale, and to the individuals concerned, of wrongly identifying loyal employees as agents. In reality, life is more complicated. You are unlikely to know the actual proportion of agents or the accuracy of the screening and real screening methods are far less effective than 99 per cent. This is even better than the rates claimed, but not widely accepted, for possible future methods like functional magnetic resonance imaging (fMRI) brain scans. In addition, making an intelligence agency paranoid about its employees is an effective way of incapacitating it. So the information obtained from the opposition about their recruitment may have been fed to you to cause disruption. Had there been no foreign agents, the information about infiltration was false, your screening would have wrongly identified 1000 suspects (1 per cent of 100,000) and you would have thought that you had identified all the imaginary spies.

While reality is more complicated, the example is merely to illustrate that, even in simple cases, guesses about probabilities can be wrong. Economists sometimes argue that people will not make systematic errors of this type; because if they did, industries would grow up to make money from these errors and that the victims would learn from this, thus eliminating systematic errors. Part of the argument seems right. Large industries, such as gambling and advertising, have grown up to make money exploiting people's systematic mistakes. But the conclusion that such mistakes will be eliminated seems optimistic.

A common problem is to distinguish random fluctuations from systematic trends or patterns in a set of observations. Taking terms from communications technology the random part is often called the noise, the systematic part the signal. As the signal to noise ratio in the observations rises (less interference on the telephone), it is easier to distinguish the signal or message. Deception often relies on increasing the noise, so that the enemy finds it difficult to determine the signal. Before D-Day in World War II, considerable effort was put into creating information (noise) that suggested to the Germans that attacks would be made on Norway and the Pas de Calais. This was to swamp the signal, any indications that the attack would be in Normandy. The noise here included dummy units, with plywood tanks, located close to the launch point for an invasion of the Pas de Calais. Information supplied through double agents and extensive radio traffic reinforced the impression that these were active units.

Even with purely random noise it can be difficult to separate the signal from the noise. Random fluctuations tend to cancel out over time allowing one to determine the underlying message by averaging. In training, there tends to be an average trend improvement in performance, with fluctuations around that average: people do a bit better or worse but with a tendency to return to the average trend. A range of studies indicate that rewarding good performance leads to a faster trend improvement than punishing bad performance. However, experienced military trainers dismiss such theories as liberal sentimentality. They know that if they shout at recruits when they do badly, they do better next time; while when they praise them for doing well, they do worse next time. This is exactly the pattern one would expect with random fluctuations around a trend. A particularly good performance is likely to be luck, with a return to the average at the next attempt, similarly with the bad performance. Praise or blame does not stop that return to average but may have different effects on the trend improvement.

It is sometimes useful to distinguish what are called exogenous risks, determined outside of the system, from endogenous risks, which result from the operation of the system itself. Risks like the storms that caused D-Day to be postponed during World War II are exogenous; one can prepare for them, to provide protection against their consequences, but one cannot influence them. Risks like the storms that arise from man-made, climate change are endogenous; one can not only prepare against them but also influence the probability of them happening. In war many risks are endogenous, arising from actions by you that the enemy can exploit. Recognising uncertainty is crucial; certainties that do not correspond to reality, the things you think you know but are not so, can be very dangerous.

Big unexpected shocks, crises that come like storms out of a blue sky, are characteristic of both economics and the military. In economics they appear most often as financial crises, like the credit crunch starting in August 2007. Such economic crises can also have major political and strategic consequences. The book by Charles P. Kindleberger (2000) *Manias, Panics, and Crashes* provides a history of such crises and their economic effects. In their paper, 'This Time Is Different', Reinhart and Rogoff (2008) provide a panoramic view of eight centuries of financial crises. 'This Time Is Different' is what is usually said in the boom preceding financial crises. In international relations, crises like World War I, the Cuban Missile crisis and the collapse of the Soviet Union can also appear out of a blue sky.

Economic–security interactions

For some of the time, the spheres of money and power operate separately in their own manner; but at other times, particularly in times of crisis, they interact strongly. Military crises or wars may disrupt trade, production and financial flows. Economic crises may undermine the legitimacy of governments, as in Germany between the Wars. Since World War II, the UK has had a series of major defence reviews: Sandys in 1957, Healey in 1966, Labour in mid-1970s, Nott in 1982, Options for Change in 1991 and the Strategic Defence Review of 1997. It was not strategic reconsideration that drove these reviews; they were each driven by economic crises that meant that the UK could no longer afford its old defence policy.

Development of the currently rich countries is rooted in war. Their states were often forged in internal war like the British and American civil wars and the French Revolution or in the many international wars. Development was kick-started by protectionist tariffs; industrialisation was linked to deforestation, pollution and exploitation of natural resources; there was expropriation of large parts of the population: peasant enclosures in the UK, elimination of native Americans in the US. The unpleasant characteristics of the development of the rich countries are often forgotten. Poor countries have a case in accusing the rich countries of adopting a 'do what we say rather than what we did' when the rich condemn their civil wars, protection, environmental degradation, massacres and expropriation. But such unpleasant policies are not always effective routes to development, as many failed states illustrate.

On the British industrial revolution, Clark, O'Rourke and Taylor (2008) comment that 'The magnitude, scale and transforming power of the Industrial Revolution lay in its unification of technological advance with the military power that generated easy British access to the markets of Europe, the Americas, the Near East and the Far East.' They argue that success in trade in the mercantilist world of the 18th century was not just a product of comparative advantage, but of comparative advantage married to the musket and the cannon, globalisation with gunboats. Much of the state's legal and fiscal capacity, the ability to enforce contracts and raise taxes, have their origins in war; where the state is seen as representing a common interest, fighting an external enemy.

These are macroeconomic issues, the economic performance of whole economies, but microeconomics, the interaction of supply and demand in markets for particular goods, can also illuminate security issues. The illicit trade in drugs and firearms is an important security issue and prices can be a sensitive indicator of the success of supply side measures by governments to eradicate the trade. The failure of the war on drugs in most countries is clearly signalled by the falling prices of illegal drugs. Although rarely emphasised by champions of free markets, the vitality and flexibility of trade in illegal products is evidence of the power of markets. Economists tend to be biased against making products illegal, partly because all the profits from meeting illegal demand go to criminals, whose use of those profits tends to have adverse social effects.

A particularly interesting price for economic–security interactions is the price of money to governments: how much it costs them to borrow. This is measured by the yield lenders get paid on government bonds. Governments usually have to borrow during wars and war financing is discussed in more detail in Chapter 8. If government expenditure is greater than government revenue, the government runs a deficit which it must finance. One source of finance is the sale of government bonds. In return for the loan, the government promises to pay the bondholder an amount each year (the coupon) by way of interest. These bonds are then traded on financial markets and the yield or rate of interest (the amount the government pays each year divided by the price of the bond) reflects how much it costs the government to borrow. Wars tend to generate large deficits both because of the higher military expenditure and because they disrupt trade, reducing tax revenues. Large deficits increase the cost of borrowing, because the government must offer a higher yield to attract more savers willing to buy the bonds. Should the government lose the war, it is unlikely to be able to pay interest or repay what it borrowed; so the interest rate or yield has to be higher to compensate lenders for incurring this default risk. Financial markets are forward looking, so even the threat of war, with the danger of future deficits or default, will push up yields.

Niall Ferguson (2006) examines bond yields for the great powers (UK, France, Germany, Russia and Austria) between 1845 and 1914. Political risks and the threat of war are not the only things determining bond yields, fears of inflation and returns on alternative investments also matter; but he finds that, between 1845 and 1880, war or the threat of war pushed up the yields on the government bonds of the great powers. He looks for the big jumps in weekly data on yields and comments (p. 81): 'Once again it is remarkable that the biggest short-run jumps in yields occurred on dates that mean more to the political historian than the economic historian.'

The evidence indicates that Victorian financial markets were a sensitive indicator of political tensions. The puzzle is that in the run-up to World War I, an event traditionally seen as heralded by repeated international crises, bond yields hardly moved. He says (p. 85):

Indeed, until the assassination of the Archduke Franz Ferdinand on 28 June 1914, events in the Balkans coincided with falls in both Russian and Austrian bond yields. These events may have been important to diplomats. They have certainly been important to historians. They do not seem to have been very important to investors.

Keynes also did not believe that there would be a war and made investments which bet against a war. Ferguson concludes (p. 102):

> Yet even to the financially sophisticated, as far as can be judged by the financial press, the First World War came as a surprise. Like an earthquake on a densely populated fault line, its victims had long known that it was a possibility, and how dire its consequences would be; but its timing remained impossible to predict, and therefore beyond the realm of normal risk assessment.

The argument that World War I came as a bolt from the blue remains controversial. The military, on both sides, had been preparing detailed mobilisation plans for such a war and their rigid mobilisation timetables contributed to making war inevitable. However, the military always plan for possible wars, even when they do not expect them to happen; ideally the planning should deter war. During the Cold War, the US and Soviets had detailed plans for nuclear war, but it did not happen. Whatever the controversies, Ferguson's basic point remains valid. Detailed examination of financial markets can be illuminating about strategic assessments, providing an opinion poll of how people (or at least rich bond holders) perceived the future.

The integration of economy and strategy is central to post conflict reconstruction. During the World War II there had been intense discussions among the allies, and a major conference at Bretton Woods, to construct a blueprint for a new post-war order that would avoid the economic dislocation of the inter-war years. In the event there was a US security guarantee for Europe leading to NATO; a new set of international institutions (UN, World Bank, IMF and General Agreement on Tariffs and Trade (GATT)); the Bretton Woods monetary and exchange rate system; and US economic aid through the Marshall Plan. These all contributed to reconstruction and the creation of a new capitalist economic and security order particularly, but not only, in Western Europe and Japan. All the elements of this post-war settlement were controversial. There had been an alternative Morgenthau plan, which would have tried to de-industrialise Germany and turn it into a pastoral agrarian economy that could no longer threaten the world. This was rejected. It was not only Keynes, who was deeply involved in these negotiations, who was well aware of the damage that the vindictive peace after World War I had done to international stability.

With the end of the Cold War, more opportunities for intervention in civil wars arose and considerable effort was put into conflict resolution and reconstruction. But post-conflict situations are fragile and civil wars often resume. To reduce the risk of conflict resuming, one needs both to provide security and to boost the economy. Higher income and higher growth reduce the risk of conflict restarting. These may be contradictory. Interventions that boost economic development may increase the risk of conflict and vice versa. For instance, an autocratic government may reduce the risk of civil war restarting; but an autocratic government that terrifies people into peace is unlikely to promote economic development. Higher military expenditure after the conflict seems to increase the risk of the conflict resuming, since it signals an intention that the government is likely to renege on any peace agreement reducing its credibility (Collier, Hoeffler and Soderbom 2008).

In reconstructing societies after civil wars, or invasions like Afghanistan and Iraq, there are usually three transitions involved: from war to peace, to a different political structure and to a new form of economic operation. To make these transitions requires demilitarisation, political transformation and economic incentives that stabilise the situation and stop conflict breaking out again. Along with demobilisation, disarmament and economic reconstruction, post-war adjustment may require transformation in the role of the armed forces: security sector reform. Outside intervention may help these transitions and we return to peacekeeping in Chapter 7. Managing these transitions can be difficult: much of the population may have access to weapons, the issues that caused the conflict may not have been resolved and some of the participants in the conflict may have only reluctantly agreed to a ceasefire.

A classic example of reconstruction is in the Confederate States after the US Civil War. Some would argue that this was not completed until a century later when the federal government again sent troops into the south to enforce desegregation. Reconstruction could have been even more difficult. This example and a range of other historical 'what ifs?' are given in Cowley (1999). In April 1865, at the end of the war, the Confederate General Robert E. Lee was surrounded by Grant at Appomattox Virginia. Lee's subordinate, General Porter Alexander, suggested that the army scatter with their weapons and continue a guerrilla war. Lee rejected this and surrendered his whole army, making the classic wild west a little less wild. Of course, many ex-soldiers, like Jesse James of Missouri, became outlaws using their military skills to rob trains and banks, but there was not organised guerrilla war. The tendency for people to carry pistols and rifles, a feature of all classic westerns, was largely a post-civil war phenomenon in the US. A major source of alternative employment for demobilised troops was the construction of the railroad across the US. Stephen E. Ambrose (2000) notes that the men who built the Union Pacific Railway were mainly young ex-soldiers from both the Union and Confederate armies. The construction of the railroads also relied on experience in finance, organisation and logistics acquired during the war. Working on the railroad, or moving to frontier farms in the West, provided a relatively attractive alternative to organised violence.

The issue of dealing with the widespread ownership of guns after a civil war also involves some economic calculations. Let us assume that, unlike the US case, the post-war government thinks that widespread possession of guns is a bad thing. To reduce the stock of guns, it has to make the value of surrendering them greater than the value of retaining them. The value of retaining them will be influenced by people's expectations about how useful the gun may be in the future, what economists call an option value. The value of surrendering the gun will be determined by the price of guns. The government can make the price negative: possession of guns is made illegal and anyone caught with one is punished. To the person holding the gun, this price is the probability of being detected with the gun times the punishment on being detected. So unless the government can make the probability of detection high, this policy may not be effective. Offsetting a low probability of detection with a very harsh punishment may not work if the very harsh punishment is not credible: people think it unlikely that the government would actually implement such a harsh punishment. The government can make the price zero, essentially ignoring the issue. It can offer a positive price, people who hand in guns get paid for them and the guns are destroyed. This can take a large number of guns out of circulation and have social benefits which are much greater than the cost of the guns to the government. But the price offered must not be too high. In particular it has to be less than the cost of acquiring new guns, for instance from the illegal international market. Otherwise there is an incentive to buy extra guns to hand in and collect the money. This is a profitable activity which provides a source of finance and does not reduce the stock of guns. There is also a quality issue. People have an incentive to sell the bad, old or unreliable guns to the government and retain the good ones. It may be that the option value of retaining the gun is greater than the cost of acquiring new guns; so there is no market-clearing positive price that the government can offer. Calculating these values and costs is not easy.

Similar issues arise with policy towards the cultivation of illegal drugs such as coca, the base for cocaine, and poppies, the base for heroin. Alternative policies include: trying to eradicate the crops, for instance by spraying, which may drive the farmers to support the insurgents; trying to provide alternative crops which provide an equivalent income; buying the drug crops to stop them getting onto the illegal market, which may encourage the farmers to plant more; or reducing demand to lower price and the incentive to plant the crops.

The pace and nature of change in the spheres of economics and strategy is quite different. In economics change tends to be fast and continuous, in contrast to political change which tends to be slower and more discrete. Economic change is marked by volatility and financial crises. Financial crises and macroeconomic shocks are common. Over the past 150 years the probability of a macroeconomic disaster, a fall in GDP of over 10 per cent, is around 3.5 per cent a year, with an average size of 22 per cent and an average duration of about 3.5 years. Many of these are associated with wars or global recessions, such as the 29 per cent fall in US GDP between 1929 and 1933. The volatility of economic variables, like the price of oil, has political consequences, particularly on large oil exporters or importers. The price of oil can influence perceptions of the success of economic management and the political competence of a government. In 1998, when Russia under Boris Yeltsin defaulted on its debts and allowed the rouble to devalue, the price of oil was about $12 a barrel. A decade later in summer 2008 when Prime Minister Putin and President Medvedev began their double act, the price of oil almost touched $150 a barrel. Since 20 per cent of Russia's production and 60 per cent of its exports are accounted for by oil and gas, the price of oil has a large effect on Russian revenues. It is estimated that Russia requires the price of oil to be above $70 a barrel to balance its budget; well above the oil price of late 2008.

Crises and commodity price fluctuations can have immediate short-term political effects, but the political effects of long-term economic trends can be much slower. One may recognise unsustainable economic trends, but it can be almost impossible to predict their political consequences. Such was the case with the Soviet Union, where the adverse trends were evident from the late 1970s in falling life expectancy and worsening economic performance. But the political adjustments were not predictable. Similarly the first decade of the 21st century was marked by what economists called 'global imbalances', unsustainable financial flows. The primary feature was the pattern by which the US lived beyond its economic means, running a large balance of payments deficit financed by foreigners, primarily China, at very low interest rates. The US was fortunate; the interest rates it paid on its borrowings was much less than the return it got on its assets abroad. The US moved very rapidly from being the world's largest net creditor, its assets overseas being much larger than its liabilities, the amount it owed to foreigners, to being the world's largest debtor. Countries cannot continually increase their debts without prospect of repayment and what cannot go on forever, will not go on forever. But the economic and political adjustments that will restore balance are largely unpredictable.

As Ferguson's quote above indicated, the strategic sphere is more like plate tectonics: tensions build up, often as a consequence of economic pressures, but nothing happens; the system is locked in stasis. Then there is an earthquake, a rapid and extreme adjustment which upsets the system. Often these geopolitical earthquakes are associated with major wars, but not always; the collapse of the Soviet Union did not cause a major war, though it left various conflicts. Like real earthquakes, geopolitical earthquakes are hard to forecast.

3
Security: Are We Safe?

In *The Wealth of Nations*, Adam Smith argued that the origin of the division of labour, the growth of the market and thus the wealth of nations, was man's natural propensity to 'truck, barter and exchange'. But one might ask: why truck, barter and exchange when you can rob, pillage and loot? Of course, Smith considered this. In the *Theory of Moral Sentiments*, he argued that sympathy inhibited our baser instincts. In *The Wealth of Nations*, he argued that it was the duty of the sovereign to protect the nation from external violence; to protect the members of it from the injustice and oppression of each other; and to maintain public works and institutions. He also pointed out that the first duty of the sovereign, the protection of society, can only be performed by military force. Following Smith, I used to teach that it was the function of the state to maintain security by stopping people robbing, pillaging and looting. I qualified this after a student pointed out that in her country it was the state that did most of the robbing, pillaging and looting; not all states fulfil the first duty of the sovereign. This raises the issue of what constitutes security and how it may be provided and where we draw the line between the state robbing and taxing.

This chapter examines security at the level of the individual, the nation state and the global system and then considers three security issues: wars, oil and arms races. The division between individuals, states and system can only be rough. Individuals live in states and states exist in an international system and there is dispute about whether it is the nature of the individuals that shapes a society or the nature of the society that shapes the individual. Although rough, the division is useful. Security has various meanings, discussed extensively in Collins (2007). Individuals are secure if they are free from fear and can have enough confidence in their safety to be able to meet their basic needs, pursue a reasonable life and invest in their future. This view of security as the absence of fear largely matches the UN Development Programme definition of Human Security. Threats to security can come from many sources: from natural environmental forces, such as disease, earthquakes and floods; from economic forces, such as financial crises and mass unemployment; and from strategic forces, such as war or terrorism.

All of these threats may be difficult to forecast or prepare against, but economic and strategic threats differ from natural disasters because they are the product of interactions between people; though war or economic disaster can appear, to the individuals that suffer them, just as blind and impersonal as the weather. These interactions between people are often modelled using game theory; Dixit and Nalebuff (2008) is an accessible introduction. We suppose that these games have pay-offs, like the winnings in poker, but measured in terms of security. Depending on the context, the mechanism of the game, strategic games may be zero-sum (increasing one person's security reduces the other person's security by the same amount); negative sum (the actions of both reduce both of their security as in some arms races); or positive sum (the actions of both increase both of their security as in confidence-building measures). The tragedy is that what are potentially positive sum games are made into negative sum games by the structure of incentives. The 'prisoners' dilemma' game is the most famous example. In this game, the incentive to take advantage of the other leads both players to cheat or defect from an agreement, when they would both have been better off if they had cooperated. Trust and cooperation reduce the transactions cost in trade and increase economic efficiency, massively in many cases; but trust has to be created and maintained.

Individual security is reasonably straightforward but national security is a more problematic concept. It requires definition of the nation and how the security of its citizens gets aggregated to that of the nation. There may be national policies that make some individuals more secure and others less secure. In fact national security is rarely defined in terms of some aggregate of the security of its individuals. Often it is the interests of some elite or ruling class that defines national security and these are not always well aligned with the interests of their citizens. For instance, the security of the citizens might be greater if that particular nation state ceased to exist; but elites may not accept that as an acceptable outcome. Czechoslovakia is a rare exception, where a nation state peacefully split into two. The split of the Soviet Union into its constituent republics was not so peaceful. Some areas, such as Chechnya, did not want to be in Russia and areas in other republics, such as South Ossetia in Georgia, did want to be in Russia. National security may be narrowly defined in terms of the defence of the realm from attack, though how this defence may be implemented may not be clear for amorphous threats like terrorism. However, it is often broadened from the safety of the nation from attack to the safety of national interests, which in a globalised world are inevitably global. The global interests of a nation include its foreign investment, sources of essential inputs such as natural resources like oil, protection of trade routes, nationals abroad and export markets. Thus national security interests can easily be extended beyond protection of the nation from attack.

At the global level, there is the issue of how international public goods, like security, are provided. International or global security might be regarded as the security of most people in the world, though national leaders might see it as the security of most nations in the world, which is how the UN Security Council usually sees it. During the Cold War the major threat to the security of a large proportion of the world's population was the danger of a nuclear war. Now the major threats are probably environmental including global warming and pandemic diseases, against which military responses are ineffective. We now consider individual, national and global security in more detail.

Individual security

Imagine a world without a state to enforce laws. People consume what they produce themselves or gain by exchanging their products for the products of others; but they can also consume what they steal from others. They then have a choice about how much time and other resources they allocate to fighting (either to steal from others or to stop others stealing from them) as against how much they allocate to production. There are returns to specialisation and the division of labour, so it will pay some to invest in becoming specialists in violence, acquiring weapons and skill in using them. Thus there may evolve a dedicated warrior or bandit class. In practice, there is substitution between different roles. Despite the efforts of Scandinavian museums, the stereotype of the Vikings is of bearded warriors, with battleaxes and horned helmets, leaping from their long-ships to rob pillage and loot. This stereotype is misleading, since there is no evidence that they had horns on their helmets. However, the dispute about whether the Vikings were really pirates, traders or farmers seems irrelevant. From an economic perspective they were an adaptable people, with some effective technologies, who switched between occupations depending on the relative returns to each role, which would differ over time and place.

Having made the decision to invest in fighting skills, the warrior or bandit faces further economic problems. If he is, what Mancur Olson (1993) called, a roving bandit, he steals everything and rides on. But if he is a stationary bandit, who hopes to come back and steal again, it is not sensible to do this. If the bandit steals everything, all the peasant's grain, then the peasants will have neither seed to plant nor food to survive on; so the peasants will not be able to produce food for the following year. Thus there will be nothing for the bandit to steal the following year. Genghis Khan planned to depopulate northern China and turn it over to horses, until persuaded by an adviser that live Chinese paid more taxes than dead Chinese. Thus, if the bandit is stationary and expects to come back the following year, it is sensible to steal (impose a tax rate) less than 100 per cent, to encourage diligence and investment by his victims. The incentive to moderate this theft tax arises because the tax reduces his victim's ability and incentives to produce and thus the bandit's tax base. A stationary bandit has an incentive to encourage productivity because that increases what he can steal. This also provides incentives for the roving bandit to become a stationary bandit; by staying put he can deter other bandits, increase productivity and maximise the amount he can steal. By the point the bandit has got to this stage, he discourages people from calling him a bandit. Although it is not his intention, the stationary bandit may bring benefits to the people he steals from. To the victims, organised crime is often preferable to disorganised crime; without a Mr Big you are open to raiding by everyone else.

The strength of the incentive to moderate theft depends on the probability of coming back, how long the bandit will be around to steal from the population. This is reflected in the bandit's discount rate: how much he discounts future consequences. If the future is very uncertain (his gang may depose him as leader, the peasants may fight back, rival gangs may displace him), then his discount rate will be high; it is better to live for today and steal everything. Unfortunately, governments in some parts of the world have a high discount rate; they fear being deposed; so like the roving bandit they steal as much as they can now. There are economies of scale in bandit gangs, bigger is usually better, and this raises further economic problems. The leader has to worry about feeding his gang, ensuring that the attraction of being a bandit is as good as their alternative occupations, and establishing a more formal organisation that maintains his position. A fairly non-technical source on the economics of conflict is Hirshleifer (2001).

These economic calculations are implicit in many books and films. In the western *The Magnificent Seven*, based on a Japanese movie, *The Seven Samurai*, a bandit returns to rob a village again. The bandit never takes everything always leaving the villagers enough to live on, and subsequently worries that he had been too nice in the past (used too low a discount rate). He worries about feeding his men over winter (making required investments). To defend themselves against him, the villagers go off to the border and have to calculate the relative cost of buying guns or men with guns (capital–labour substitution). The villagers know that hiring gunmen will change their relationship with the bandit (implicit contracts and irreversible investments). Subsequently one of the seven opposing the bandit agonises about the relative attractions of being a gunman or farmer (opportunity costs of career choices).

One can think of security as being maintained by some level of enforcement of rights to life, liberty and property. The question 'where does such enforcement come from?' arises at all three levels: individual, national and global. If two parties interact, meet for trade or mutual celebrations, what stops one or both of them cheating, by stealing or using force? The enforcement may be third party: fear of the law or the social group who will punish cheating. It may be second party: fear of retaliation by the person cheated. It may be first party: morality or consideration of long-term self interest in reciprocity. Stealing from your trading partner now cuts you off from what he may bring you in the future: killing the goose that lays the golden eggs. It is often said that there is no international law because there is no supranational enforcement mechanism. But even at a national level enforcement may not be third party, from an external agency; other mechanisms may be equally effective. This is the basis of the Geneva Conventions and other aspects of international law. It is in the interests of the parties to follow them from concern about correct behaviour or about reciprocity: how the enemy will treat your troops held as prisoners of war will be influenced by how you treat their troops you hold prisoner. It was for this reason that many in the US military resisted the removal of restraints on the treatment of captives by President Bush during the Global War on Terror. Of course, many combatants do not abide by the Geneva Conventions, but that does not make them useless, since many do abide by them.

Some rules do not require enforcement. All one needs is that the rule, norm or convention is known; then it will generally be followed. Driving on the right is almost completely self-enforcing in countries that follow that rule. It is not generally in one's interest to drive straight into the oncoming traffic on the other side of the road. This is what is called a Nash equilibrium, after John Nash whose life was loosely interpreted in the film *A Beautiful Mind*. In a Nash equilibrium everyone plays their best strategy assuming that everyone else does the same. A Nash equilibrium may not be unique: driving on the left is also a Nash equilibrium if everybody does it. Just as in some countries everybody drives on the left and in others everybody drives on the right, in some countries nobody carries a gun and in others everybody carries a gun, or has a bodyguard who does. With multiple Nash equilibria, intermediate positions (heavy vehicles driving on the left, passenger cars on the right) are unstable, and the move from one equilibrium to another can be very rapid. Places like Beirut can move from an unarmed to an armed equilibrium, and back, very quickly.

If there is neither external enforcement nor internal norms, any rules must be maintained by the threat of retaliation: those that suffer a wrong will inflict punishment on those that committed it. In such circumstances a reputation for vengeance can be a useful deterrent to rule-breaking and it can become embodied in the norms of the society so that an individual's perception of honour or self-worth requires them to take revenge. Such norms, while functional in some circumstances, by acting as a deterrent, can generate highly dysfunctional blood-feuds and honour killings. As Mahatma Gandhi is supposed to have said, 'An eye for an eye makes the whole world blind'. Naci H. Mocan (2008), who gives the quote, reviews the literature on vengeance and analyses evidence from a large UN international survey on people's desire for vengeance, as expressed in terms of an appropriate punishment for a specified crime. The question asks

> people have different ideas about the sentences which should be given to offenders. Take for instance the case of a 20 year old who is found guilty of burglary for the second time. This time he has stolen a colour TV. Which of the following sentences do you consider appropriate for such a case?

The prison term thought appropriate differs between countries: about 40 per cent of people in China, Romania and Botswana prefer a prison sentence of 4 years or more as compared to about 1 per cent in Belgium and Spain. Heavier punishments are preferred in countries that are poor, have low levels of education, lack a rule of law or have experienced recent armed conflict. But responses overlap: poor people in rich countries are as vengeful as rich people in poor countries. There are, of course, many difficulties in interpreting such statistical data which

Mocan discusses. A colour TV is, relatively, much more valuable in poor countries and in countries where the usual penalty for burglary is losing a limb, 4 years in prison may seem extremely lenient.

Often establishing enforcement requires a group of people to act together. Such collective action problems are central to much of the analysis of the interaction of economy and strategy, at the individual, national and systemic levels. For instance, in an alliance there is an incentive for the smaller countries to 'free ride', let the bigger countries take the burden of enforcement. Olson points out in the introduction to Todd Sandler (1992) that sometimes, when each individual considers only his or her interests, a collectively rational outcome emerges automatically. This is the basis of market mechanisms, the so-called invisible hand. Here the term, 'collectively rational', has a very special meaning. It means that nobody can be made better off without making somebody worse off. This is what economists call Pareto optimality, which does not reflect how income is distributed. It is Pareto optimal for one person to have 99 per cent of the resources and the other person only 1 per cent, if the only way to make the poor person better off is to take away from the rich person. However, even under this very limited criterion, sometimes, no matter how intelligently each individual pursues his or her interest, no socially rational outcome can emerge spontaneously. Individual rationality is not sufficient for group rationality; some coordination between individuals to take collective actions or construct institutions is required.

In small groups people are usually able to negotiate collective actions between themselves, it is the basis of human survival; but in large groups it can be difficult. One must then examine the incentives that help or hinder people or nations working together in their joint interests. The costs and benefits of cooperation will determine whether individuals are willing to trade together, fight together against some common threat or jointly enforce some rules. Cooperation involves trade-offs. There are costs, particularly loss of autonomy, but there are also benefits from interdependence. When it is said that the international community should do something, such as intervene in Darfur, it tends to be assumed that this collective action problem has been solved, which it rarely has. Olson (1982) is a wide-ranging discussion of the rise and decline of nations in the light of collective action problems. It should be noted that the benefits may not be material benefits. Many factors, such as shared beliefs or community solidarity, may provide individuals with the incentives to solve collective action problems and cooperate as a group.

One can look at the world as a pessimist and ask 'Why is there so much conflict?' This is a common liberal or idealist response, starting from the perspective that people are naturally peaceful and war an unfortunate aberration caused by the vested interests of militaristic groups. Alternatively, one can look at the world as an optimist and ask 'Why is there so much less conflict than we might expect?' This is a common conservative or realist response, starting from the perspective that people are naturally acquisitive and will take what they can get. Quite a lot of the interesting economics of conflict is now about the economics of lack of conflict: how, even without legal enforcement of property rights, peaceful cooperation can arise. It may do this, not because people are naturally peaceful, but because cooperation dominates conflict in terms of self-interest. Cooperation within a group has been central to human survival since pre-historic times, lone individuals could not survive. Cooperation between groups is more problematic but again evolved very early as the evidence for pre-historic long-distance trade shows, though the social meaning of trade then may be different from the social meaning of trade now. Paul Seabright (2004) discusses the evolution of trust, Avinash Dixit (2004) discusses how alternative institutions to support trade can arise in the absence of state enforcement; both from an economic perspective.

Recent behavioural and experimental economics suggest that people are less selfish and more cooperative and altruistic than traditional economic theory predicts. Optimists are delighted with this evidence that people are nicer than the hypothetical calculating 'economic man'. Pessimists worry that this selfless, altruistic cooperation within a group can be used to mobilise people to slaughter members of other groups. Economic man was too calculating to be a good soldier.

National security

The focus in most of this book will be the nation. But both in the economic sphere and in the strategic sphere there is a perception that the power of the nation state to act is reduced, that states are more constrained and less able to meet their national goals. This should not be exaggerated. There is a saying that economists study how people make optimal choices, while sociologists study how people have no choices to make. So it is with nation states. The fact that it is often optimal for nation states to surrender sovereignty does not mean that they have no choice about it; it merely means that the costs of not doing so are very large. Countries can try to be autarkic, like Albania did for many years, but the costs are very high.

Though it is over-simple, it can sometimes be useful to think of states falling into three types. First there are predatory states, dominated by acquisitive individuals or groups who see power as an opportunity for personal gain. They are part of the globalising system, though not well integrated into it, and are subject to occasional interventions by it. They have little in the way of impersonal national bureaucracies and impartial legal structures; they have difficulty in establishing either legitimacy or stability and are prone to succession crises, since power is personal and easily challenged. Their rulers have a high discount rate. The kingdoms of feudal Europe and the modern kleptocracies are of this sort. For the international system and for international capital the problem is seen as 'state failure', the inability of governments in such countries to meet the minimal functions of a state: monopolising violence and maintaining order. When international firms operate in these countries (primarily in extractive industries or to sell them arms, since there are few other profitable opportunities) they are likely to provide their own order through heavily armed private security forces. Paul Collier (2007) describes the economics of development and conflict in such states. Predation is not confined to failed states and a recent book, *The Predator State* (Galbraith, 2008), is not about Mobutu and Mugabwe but about the US.

The second type of state can be thought of as the typical modern states which arose in Europe from the 17th century, though centralised states existed much earlier in China and elsewhere. In Europe, they are often dated from the Peace of Westphalia, which ended the Thirty Years War, in 1648. Such states are based on a permanent state apparatus and a notion of loyalty to a nation, often based on an ethnic identity. They rest on a notion of sovereignty as the state being the ultimate power within an area and subject to no power above it. One of the main characteristics of modern states in Europe was their tendency to fight each other to establish their claims over territories and resources and their relative power. In Europe, the process of state formation was a brutal business, the product of centuries of internal and external wars. Whether new states in the rest of the world need a protracted series of wars to establish themselves as modern states has been extensively debated (Cramer, 2006).

As states become more highly integrated both economically and socially into the international system they may evolve into a third, less warlike, type. Such states are typically rich and perceive the cost of military conflict as being very high and dispute resolution by non-military means as more effective. The cost of military conflict is high because it disrupts economic interdependence, provokes international reaction and because it is expensive to project force at a distance. As an example of the power of non-violent international reaction, Britain and France, both naturally warlike, were persuaded to withdraw from Suez in 1956 by threats to their currencies from the US. This interest in peace is reinforced by norms, developed over long periods of time, which reinforce that interest. These norms are most developed in traditionally neutral countries, like Sweden and Switzerland. However, the links between neutrality and military expenditure may be complex. During the Cold War Sweden and Switzerland tended to spend a higher share of their output on the military than similar small European states who were members of NATO and could free-ride on the alliance. Multilateral organisations can act as an alternative to the use of force, either through insurance, arbitration, international pressure or conflict resolution. Many see one of the great successes of NATO as stopping two of its members, Greece and Turkey, going to war. There are various international institutions and they play a crucial coordinating role on various important technical issues, where common standards are essential. But on many issues their effectiveness depends on the willingness of the nation states to support their activities, the collective action problem.

While the US is constrained by systemic interests, these interests constrain it in ways that are quite different from the ways that smaller states are constrained. It has this special position because of its unique ability to project military power and its central role in the global economic system. In the early 21st century, this hegemonic role allowed it to borrow cheaply and extensively from the rest of the world, in particular China, to finance large government and trade deficits. While such deficits are not sustainable, there is, at time of writing, no agreement about how adjustment might come about.

Nations remain important; the vast bulk of economic production and activity takes place within nation states, but it is the times that it does not, such as offshore gambling over the Internet and uncontrolled international financial transactions that attract attention. Most nation states provide at least the minimal law and order and infrastructure that is required for economic activity to proceed. But again it is not the majority but the minority of failed states that attracts attention. Despite their importance, permeable economic and security borders make states nervous and they feel threatened by global movements, from outsourcing of jobs to the pressures of immigration, that seem outside of their control. It is unclear whether this nervousness is justified. Rather than there being a reduction in the power of nation states, it may be that states do have the power to act independently if they have the will; it is just that it is rarely in their interests to do so.

This discussion takes the definition of a nation as given, but the number of nations in the world and the size of each is determined by international politics and economics. Over history, nations come into being, expand, contract and sometimes disappear. There are economic forces that make bigger better for nations. There are fixed costs in being a nation, and spreading those fixed costs over more people is efficient. International representation is largely a fixed cost, having embassies in other countries, sending representatives to the UN and the WTO and the like, though these costs can be shared; the members of the EU have a common trade negotiator. There are also some increasing returns to scale, for instance, in trade negotiations: the EU carries more weight than any of its members would individually. There are also increasing returns to scale in defence: small states find it difficult to protect themselves against large predatory neighbours. Large nations find it easier to recruit world-class talents, whether athletes, central bankers or generals, since they can be chosen from a larger pool. Large nations have the resources to absorb shocks like banking crises, Iceland was not big enough to support its banks in 2008.

The political disadvantages of size come from heterogeneity, which may arise from ethnic, linguistic, religious or ideological differences within the nation. The larger the state, the more likely it is that some groups will feel that national policies do not reflect their interests. The EU spreads some fixed costs to the advantage of smaller nations, but also faces the political costs of heterogeneity and countries may feel that the EU trade negotiator does not represent their interests as well as a national negotiator would; for instance, France may feel that the EU trade negotiator does not care as much about French farmers as a French representative would. The heterogeneity may prompt disaffected groups to use violence to secede; from the UK in the case of Northern Ireland Republicans or from Spain in the case of Basque separatists. The disruptive influence of heterogeneity may be reduced either by repression or by encompassing institutions, such as those of Switzerland, which has four languages and religious differences. Post-colonial borders in Africa generated great heterogeneity since they rarely reflected political and economic realities, but given the potential for conflict, the convention that the borders were to be treated as sacrosanct was rapidly adopted. The optimum economic size may not match the optimum

political size. In economic terms Belgium is too small; for economic purposes it often combines with the Netherlands and Luxembourg to form
Benelux, an economic rather than a political entity. In political terms,
Belgium is too large; the smooth running of the country is impeded
by the disputes between the two major linguistic groups, Flemings and
Walloons. The advantages of size are reduced when there is a degree
of international order, so small countries do not need to fear invasion
by large neighbours, and there is fairly free trade, so small countries
do not have to rely on their own resources. This seems to be the current position and the number of countries in the world has steadily
increased.

There tends to be a presumption that any state, however bad, is better than anarchy, no state at all. Since most of the discussions of the
characteristics of anarchy have been rather speculative, there has been
considerable interest in the consequences for Somalia of state collapse,
which provides a rare modern example of a country without a state.
Peter T. Leeson (2007) and Powell, Ford and Nowrasteh (2008) consider this case. The predatory Somali state collapsed with the fall of Siad
Barre's dictatorship in 1991 and the country sank into civil war. The UN
and US interventions from 1993 to 1995 failed, but following their withdrawal from 1995 to 2005 there was a period of relative peace until the
attempt to restore a state, the Ethiopian invasion and renewal of Civil
War in 2006. This period of statelessness was one of Somali progress on
a wide range of development indicators. Economic performance during
this period seems good, not only relative to its own history but also
to the performance of comparable African countries with states. Various non-state mechanisms ensured the provision of law and means of
exchange. Although this is only one example and the interpretation is
controversial, people may be better off with no state at all than a bad
state. The difficulty is that no-state is an unstable position: the incentives for internal and external groups to try to re-impose a state are
very great.

Global security

At the systemic level, military economics concerns the overlap between
the global economic environment and global strategic environment.
The economic environment is the sphere of trade, globalisation, the
price of oil and the future of the dollar. The strategic environment is
the sphere of nuclear proliferation, interacting national interests, threats
and failed states. The main examples of analyses of the interaction of

economy and strategy at the systemic level are historical works, such as Paul Kennedy's *The Rise and Fall of the Great Powers* (1988) that examines the interaction of economic change and military conflict since 1500 and Jared Diamond's *Guns, Germs, and Steel* (1998) that examines the interaction between material forces, particularly those shaped by geography, and power over the last 13,000 years. Diamond takes a very long perspective on the question of why Europeans and their offshoots in the US and Australia are so rich. He points out that the people of Eurasia had more crops and animals that could be domesticated compared to the Americas or Africa. Flows of peoples and ideas were easier along the east–west axis of Eurasia than along the north–south axis of the Americas or Africa. From their domestic animals, the Eurasians got diseases, to which they became partially immune. These diseases then wiped out peoples in the Americas.

In *Power and Plenty*, Findlay and O'Rourke (2007) provide a history of international trade over the last millennium. Early in the book (p. xviii) they comment: 'a feature of the book that may strike some economists as surprising, but will seem commonplace to historians, is its sustained emphasis on conflict, violence and geopolitics.' The interaction between politics and trade, the mutual dependence of power and plenty, has shaped world history. From about 1250 to 1350 a major spur to trade was the Pax Mongolica that followed the victories of Genghis Khan and his successors. This opened up the Central Asian Trade routes between Europe and China that allowed Marco Polo to make his travels. It was the closing of this route that spurred Europeans to find another way to the East that avoided the problems and predations of the sea route though Middle Eastern ports. In the explosion of European trade in the 17th and 18th century, commercial expansion was inter-twined with war between Dutch, English and French over trade routes and colonies. During this mercantilist period one could not make war without trade, because one had to acquire strategic naval supplies from abroad, and one could not trade without war, because countries used force to establish monopolies over crucial products and stop others using their trade routes. While the economic advantages of such monopolies may seem obvious, in fact they were a very mixed blessing, the costs, including the military costs, often outweighed the benefits. Many of the profits of mercantilism were more apparent than real, as was increasingly realised. The French revolutionary wars largely ended this period of mercantilism. The 19th century saw trends towards less restrictions on trade, stable currencies under the gold standard and increased globalisation. Such trends were ended by World War I.

In analysing the interactions between global economic and strategic processes there are various systemic theories. Mercantilism/Leninism sees strategic conflict as a continuation of economic competition by other means. Liberalism/idealism sees close trading links as inhibiting military conflict; there is more to lose from loss of economic integration. Both have their adherents today. There is a large literature examining whether increased trade increases or reduces the probability of war between states. Trade and economic integration is highest within states, but it is civil wars that tend to be the most violent, perhaps because the stakes are higher.

Globalisation is a vague term that is used to encompass various elements. One element is the internationalisation of economic processes through the movement of goods via trade; capital via foreign investment; labour via migration; and technology via knowledge transfer. A second element is the transformation of firms from being multinational, operating in many countries, to being transnational, having no home country. A third element is the tendency of global markets and international organisations to reduce the power and autonomy of national governments. A fourth element is a process of cultural homogenisation as nations share brands, movies, sports and music. The novelty and extent of these elements remains controversial.

The perception of globalisation is not new. In *The Manifesto of the Communist Party* of 1848, Marx and Engels say, 'Modern industry has established the world market... This market has given an immense development to commerce, to navigation to communication.' That was over 150 years ago. They go on to say:

> The bourgeoisie, by the rapid development of all the instruments of production, by the immensely facilitated means of communication, draws all, even the most barbarian, nations into civilization. The cheap prices of its commodities are the heavy artillery with which it batters down all the Chinese walls, with which it forces the barbarians' intensely obstinate hatred of foreigners to capitulate.

This passage was quoted in an article on the implications for China of joining the WTO, which took China joining the WTO as an event of historic significance comparable in importance to its opening after the Opium Wars. That was a case where Britain promoted free trade, in among other goods opium, by battering down the Chinese Walls against trade with real artillery. The first Opium War between Britain and China was from 1839 to 1842, so Marx and Engels writing in 1848 were possibly being ironic about the artillery.

The telegraph reduced the time taken to transmit a message from New York to London from 2 weeks to 2 minutes. Steamships disrupted European agriculture and politics in the late 19th century as cheap North American grain arrived. These changes in communications technology had effects that were as large as, or larger than, modern innovations. The 19th-century flows of labour were massive compared to the immigration some worry about today. On some measures, the world has only recently reached the degree of globalisation attained in 1913. This also makes it clear that globalisation is not inevitable; it was ended by World War I and the inter-war depression. It might be ended again.

As the system globalises, it increasingly requires forms of organisation and the provision of international public goods. There are large benefits, for instance, in having a common system of exchange which allows trade to take place far away. Some organisation arises spontaneously, but much comes from dominant states or international institutions. Empires have always provided one form of organisation. The conquests of Alexander the Great, the Romans, Islam or the Mongols all provided a stimulus to trade. But organisation by a dominant state can be more informal. During the 19th century Britain had a large formal empire but it also had substantial influence on the rest of the world, an influence often labelled hegemony. Although British hegemony was driven by its own interests, the Pax Britannica did have some benefits for the world as a whole. These included establishing freedom of the seas; acting to restrict slavery; encouraging free trade; and acting as a banker to the world, providing convenient means of exchange. Though Britain was a victor in World War I, it emerged impoverished, unable to maintain its hegemonic role. After World War II, the US took on a hegemonic role within the capitalist system, providing similar functions. Many explanations of the economic and political disruption of the inter-war period attribute it to the lack of a power able and willing to provide leadership, a hegemonic organising role.

The alternative to organisation by a dominant power is organisation by international institutions. Some had their origins in the 19th century, like the International Committee of the Red Cross established in 1863 and agreements to regulate post and telegrams; but they blossomed after World War II. Kennedy (2006, p. xi) says,

In the course of the twentieth century, there occurred a development unique in the story of humankind. States, which had defined themselves from Thucydides to Bismarck by their claims to sovereign independence, gradually came together to create international organisations to promote peace, curb aggression, regulate diplomatic affairs, devise an international code of law, encourage social development and foster prosperity.

There are a vast number of such international organisations to provide the coordination that makes globalisation possible. They range from the overarching UN; through those with broad economic responsibilities like the IMF, WTO and World Bank; to narrow technical organisations, few have heard of, to negotiate the allocation of the electromagnetic spectrum and similar essential specialist details. Such international organisations tend to live on a fine line of effectiveness. They are subject to various restrictions which limit their effectiveness, but those restrictions enable them to maintain their membership. One of the most important of those restrictions is at the end of Chapter I of the UN Charter: 'Nothing contained in the present Charter shall authorise the United Nations to intervene in matters which are essentially within the domestic jurisdiction of any state.' Given such restrictions, the extent to which the international institutions will be able to inhibit major war is unclear. The EU, initially motivated by the desire to prevent another war between France and Germany, has become one of the most extensive international institutions and probably reduces the likelihood of war between its members.

A global system tends to be a system of alliances. Sandler and Hartley (1999) give a good non-technical discussion of alliance issues, particularly as they relate to NATO. When a country starts to increase in power, other countries have a choice between joining the bandwagon, becoming allies of the rising power, or balancing, forming alliances that will keep the rising power in check. British policy towards Europe was always one of balancing: joining or forming coalitions against any continental power that seemed likely to become dominant. This was nicely summarised by the fictional Sir Humphrey in the TV series *Yes Minister*.

Britain has had the same foreign policy objectives for at least the last five hundred years – to create a disunited Europe. In that cause we have fought with the Dutch against the Spanish, with the Germans against the French, with the French and Italians against the Germans, and with the French against the Italians and Germans.... In other words divide and rule. And the Foreign Office can see no reason to change when it has worked so well until now. It was necessary for us to break up the EEC, so we had to get inside. We had previously tried to break it up from the outside, but that didn't work. Now we are in, we are able to make a complete pig's breakfast out of it. We have now set the Germans against the French, the French against the Italians, the Italians against the Dutch, and the Foreign Office is terribly happy. It's just like old times.

Lynn and Jay (1981, p. 117)

As with nations, alliances provide both economies of scale and political diseconomies of heterogeneity. Economies of scale arise from military integration; since if nations pool their resources, they share fixed development costs and may be able to afford jointly large indivisible systems like aircraft carriers or military satellites that they could not afford individually. With longer production runs unit costs fall, as producers learn how to make the items more efficiently. A unified command avoids duplication, many small national forces trying to do the same thing on an inefficiently small scale. Having inter-operable weapons increases efficiency: shared training, shared supplies of ammunition and saving on logistics. While there are benefits of coordination, costs arise from divergence in perceptions of national interests, clashes between different military traditions and national political objections. Coordination costs are reduced if one nation dominates the alliance, as the Soviet Union did the Warsaw Pact. But this also reduces the benefits to the other members of the alliance, who may see membership as a cost rather than a benefit.

As an alliance expands, its borders expand. This increases its vulnerability. This is an issue in the extension of NATO to countries on the border of Russia, like Georgia and Ukraine. Alliances also involve commitments, such as collective security guarantees. Article V of the Washington Treaty which established NATO in 1949 requires all member states to come to the aid of any allied nation subject to an armed attack. There is some ambiguity in this requirement. The treaty says that if such an armed attack occurs, each of the members 'will assist the Party or Parties so attacked by taking forthwith, individually and in concert with other Parties, such action as it deems necessary, including the use of armed force'. Thus the decision to respond remains a matter for each individual state and 'such action as it deems necessary' may be no action at all. During the Cold War this commitment was given credibility by members stationing troops on the territory of vulnerable allies bordering the Warsaw Pact. When former Warsaw Pact countries joined NATO, there was no comparable forward basing of troops by other members.

War

Among the earliest humans, it seems likely that competition over reproduction and resources spilled over into violent conflict. This conflict probably took the form of opportunistic raids rather than pitched battles, but rates of violent death were high. Azar Gat (2006) discusses the pre-history of war in an evolutionary context. With the development of culture, the basic sources of conflict – reproduction and resources, sex and shopping – became elaborated with social elements such as status within groups and vengeance between groups. So by classical times, Thucydides thought that men fought for reasons of fear, honour and interest. Some see war as an inevitable consequence of the existence of separate sovereign states; others see it as an unfortunate accident that could be prevented by better national and international institutions. In either case, war requires the two groups to have both the desire and the ability to fight. The desire to fight often has economic dimensions, the ability to fight always does. In analysing wars there tend to be three questions: what causes them to start? what causes them to end and after how long? and what causes them to restart? The causes have got the most attention but the recurrence is also a major policy issue because of the prevalence of enduring antagonisms, both within and between countries, which cause repeated wars.

From an economic perspective wars are puzzling. Given the vast waste of life and resources involved, there ought to be a potential deal or agreement between the parties that would share the wasted resources between them to their mutual benefit, leaving them both, victor and vanquished, better off than they would have been after fighting the war. Nineteenth century economists, like John Stuart Mill and Jean-Baptiste Say, believed that the cost of war had made it obsolete. They were correct about the cost, but not the obsolescence. World War I cost the lives of perhaps 11 million people, though on most estimates this was less than the perhaps 25 million who died in the influenza epidemic that followed it. The war destroyed three empires, the Russian, German and Austro-Hungarian; completed the destruction of a fourth, the Ottoman; and impoverished a fifth, the British. One might imagine that the leaders of the combatants, had they anticipated its possible consequences, would have put more effort into prevention. Its proximate cause, the murder of an Archduke in the Balkans, was to the international system, if not the Duke, a minor matter. Its more fundamental causes, what it was really about, remain a matter of dispute. Among the many interacting causal influences, militarism and the fact that few anticipated such a long and brutal war were probably factors. The few European wars between 1815 and 1914 had been short, that in Crimea 1854–1856 the longest. Of course, judging what people then believed is difficult, though the data on bond yields discussed earlier do suggest that the war was unexpected, certainly by the financial community.

Agreements to prevent wars may not be possible because of the uncertainty about the outcome and the difficulties of enforcing a deal. While a deal could be based on the relative strengths of each side, there may be no way to determine relative strengths other than by fighting, because it is in the interest of each side to exaggerate their relative strength. In such circumstances, wars are just a costly way of communicating relative fitness. While an agreement may be beneficial, there are strong incentives to renege on the agreement once it has been made and great difficulties in pre-committing to future behaviour. Anglo-Saxon Kings bought off Viking attacks by the payment of the Danegeld, but that just encouraged the Vikings to return and ask for more Danegeld, rather than stay away. Wars recur because while both sides have incentives to make promises in advance, they have no incentive to keep them. Given that they cannot pre-commit to their future actions, both sides may fear that if they postpone conflict they will be in a weaker position later; thus it is better to strike now. Thucydides ascribed the cause of the Peloponnesian War to the growth of Athenian power and the fear that it inspired in Sparta. Economic explanations of war tend not to focus on specific motivations for fighting, but emphasise feasibility (can the two sides mobilise the resources to fight) and credibility (can the two sides have any confidence in alternatives to war such as peaceful agreements).

Despite the fact that most wars result from many interacting influences, there is always a temptation to ask what the war was really about. Even long after the war is over, there may be no agreement about the issue: whether the US Civil War was about the abolition of slavery or about state's rights, for instance. Students of history tend to think all wars have seven causes, one for each paragraph of a one-hour exam answer. The answers can fall back on stereotypes. During the Cold War, wars around the world were categorised as capitalists versus communists, though often the combatants were unsure of their ideology until they had determined which superpower was making the better offer.

The fashionable stereotype can change through time. The war between north and south Sudan has been variously characterised as capitalist–communist, Arab–African and Muslim–Christian. While it is common to use standard dimensions (reproduction, resources, class, religion, ethnicity, territory and ideology) they over-simplify and can be misleading. Not only do the causes of any particular war become more obscure with study, there are situations with similar antecedents where war was avoided. For instance, while demographic factors, such as the presence of a bulge of young men without employment, can be a force for war, some societies find other ways to occupy their excess of young men. The picture is complicated by the fact that many will take advantage of the disorganisation of war to settle their own private grievances, which may have nothing to do with the main conflict. Conversely even within countries that are scarred by war there are often pockets that escape violence for local reasons. During what were almost universally called the 'Troubles' in Northern Ireland, there were parts of the country that lived in complete peace. There are rarely sharp distinctions between war and peace; rather there is a continuum of violence with a complex pattern in who is killing who, how, why, where and when.

Many reasons have been given for the 2003 invasion of Iraq: weapons of mass destruction, countering global terrorism, stabilising the Gulf region, spreading liberal democracy, oil, profits, the need for US military bases and the relations between Bush the Father and Bush the Son; and its cause seems likely to remain a matter of dispute. Christopher Cramer (2006, p. 96) quotes Tolstoy in *War and Peace*: 'The deeper we delve in search of these causes the more of them do we discover; and each separate cause or whole series of causes appears to us equally valid in itself and equally unsound by its insignificance in comparison with the size of the event.'

Clearly a range of behavioural factors and cognitive biases contribute to the prevalence of war and these factors are important in finance as well as war. In both there is a tendency to look for evidence that confirms rather than questions one's beliefs; to overestimate one's own capabilities and underestimate those of the competition; to follow a strategy that has been successful; and to be unwilling to cut losses when that strategy runs into trouble. Both rogue traders in finance and wartime leaders can respond to large losses by taking bigger gambles in the hope of recovering their position.

In the liberal view, wars were the product of vested interests, such as aristocratic elites, who used their social dominance to shape popular perceptions to their own ends; and that increased trade, by increasing the contacts and dependence between states, would reduce the risk of war. The traditional socialist view was that wars were the product of capitalist interests, in particular their imperial interest to expand markets. The fact that the working classes in both Germany and Britain, as represented by the Second International, supported World War I was put down to false consciousness. While there are clearly interests that benefit from war, war can also become a source of meaning and identity for many.

While democracies are, on average, as warlike as other states, they do not seem to go to war with other democracies. This pattern is known as the democratic peace. The hypothesis of a democratic peace has been quite controversial, depending on the definition of democracy, of peace and of the historical periods considered. It may also reflect other factors, such as democracies tending to be richer and to trade more with each other, both of which may reduce the risk of war. Goldsmith and He (2008) also argue that democratic states were more likely to give their colonies independence without war; though this is a probabilistic relationship and there were democracies, like France, that fought decolonisation.

While it is natural to want to know how many wars there are at any particular moment and whether war is becoming more or less common, it is difficult to give a quantitative answer because there is no unambiguous definition of war. Definitions used in the literature usually involve a number of elements. War might be defined as a contested incompatibility that concerns government and/or territory where the use of armed force between two parties, at least one of which is the government of a state, results in a specified number of battle-related deaths. Relating the definition to the number of deaths is quite common. Lewis Fry Richardson, a Quaker meteorologist, was one of the founding fathers of the quantitative study of conflict. Richardson (1960a) provided statistics, not on wars but on 'deadly quarrels', where people were killed in the course of a dispute. Data on such deaths are highly skewed, a few large wars account for most of the deaths. Data on non-war violent deaths are also quite skewed. Homicide rates differ substantially between countries and are particularly high in Latin America. More people may die violently in countries that are at peace than in countries that are at war.

Using some threshold number for a certain type of death, such as 1000 battle deaths, is a common criterion for a conflict to count as a war. This excludes other militarised international disputes, like the Cod Wars between the UK and Iceland over fisheries, where despite their name not enough people died to be counted in lists of wars. Basing the criteria on battle deaths exclude the large number of deaths from general violence, massacres of civilians and the disease and malnutrition associated with war. Battle deaths can account for a small proportion of war deaths, often less than 10 per cent. Wars are usually distinguished from other deadly quarrels, such as homicides, by the involvement of a government. Where there is no government, as in Somalia, the conflict then does not count as a war. To distinguish wars from massacres or genocide it is also common to require that there be some resistance, so that the state doing the killing should also suffer some casualties. It is normal to distinguish wars between states, inter-state, from intra-state, civil, wars. A civil war which leads to the formation of a new state, such as between Ethiopia and Eritrea, then becomes an inter-state war. National liberation struggles which lead to the independence of colonies are sometimes labelled extra-state or extra-systemic wars, the system being the system of states. In some civil wars, the neighbours join in; these are labelled internationalised intra-state wars. Some ethnic insurgencies are against more than one country; the Kurds have fought Iraq, Iran and Turkey.

Dating wars raises further difficulties. World War II is usually dated by the British and French as starting in 1939, when they declared War on Germany, after the invasion of Poland. But for its first two years it was largely a European War, though the British Commonwealth and colonies were involved. It was only when Japan and the USA became involved in 1941 that it could be regarded as a World War, so it is sometimes dated 1941–1945. This shortens the war, some might want to lengthen it. One could treat the Spanish Civil War as a trial run, where fascist and communist powers tested their military technologies for the war they anticipated. Eric Hobsbawm (2007, p. 15) argues 'The period from 1914 to 1945 can be regarded as a single "Thirty Years War" interrupted only by a pause in the 1920s, between the final withdrawal of the Japanese from the Soviet Far East in 1922 and the beginning of the Japanese attack on Manchuria in 1931.' World War II also involved a large number of separate conflicts and a number of countries, including the Soviet Union and Italy, changed sides during the course of it, so specifying participants is difficult.

There are two major sources of data on wars: the Correlates of War (COW) project and the Upsala Conflict Data Program (UCDP). UCDP cover a shorter period than COW, since 1945, but give more detail. UCDP define a major armed conflict as a contested incompatibility concerning government or territory over which the use of armed force between the military forces of two parties, of which at least one is the government of a state, has resulted in at least 1000 battle-related deaths in a single calendar year. Once a conflict passes 1000 battle-related deaths in a particular year, it is maintained in the list until the contested incompatibility has been resolved or there are no recorded battle-related deaths. UCDP also count minor armed conflicts, more than 25 battle-related deaths, and provide lists of unclear cases. As UCDP note, often little precise information is publicly available on number of deaths. UCDP tend to be conservative in their estimates and for cases where they can be compared, World Health Organisation (WHO) estimates of deaths tend to be much larger. Identifying and dating wars raises formidable difficulties and Cramer (2007, chapter 2) gives a good account of them. These difficulties are real, but the attempt to compile a systematic list of wars in a database is useful, in that it does clarify the difficulties.

The bulk of the conflicts are intra-state, civil wars, in poor countries. Blattman and Miguel (2009) provide a survey of the economics of civil wars. Since 1945 there have been about four times as many civil wars as inter-state wars, causing about four times as many casualties. Inter-state wars are usually more intense, more deaths per year, but civil wars last longer. Civil wars usually have an international dimension; the intra-state parties gain support from abroad, either from foreign governments or from a diaspora: people from the country living abroad. These conflicts can last a long time, sometimes subsiding for a while before being rekindled. Colombia has a long history of intermittent violence, which is sometimes separated into distinct conflicts. While most conflicts are in poor countries, there are also long-standing violent conflicts in rich countries, which may or may not be counted as civil wars. These include the UK conflict with the IRA and various other paramilitary groups in Northern Ireland, which started in 1969 and may have finished in the early years of the 21st century, and the Spanish government conflict with the Basque separatist movement ETA, which also started in the 1960s and continues.

UCDP report figures on wars each year in a number of places; the figures below come from the 2007 SIPRI Yearbook. They are likely to be revised as new information becomes available. In three of the 17 major armed conflicts that were active in 2006, there were more than 1000 battle-related deaths: Iraq, Afghanistan and Sri Lanka. UCDP note that estimating the number of deaths in the August–July 2006 conflict between Hezbollah and Israel in Southern Lebanon was particularly difficult and it is unclear whether it should be treated as an aspect of the Israel–Palestine conflict or a separate conflict. Over the last 10 years there has been a downward trend in the number of major conflicts from a total of 26 in 1998 to 17 in 2006.

Locations of major armed conflicts, 1997–2006

Africa

Algeria, Angola, Burundi, the Democratic Republic of Congo (formerly Zaire), the Republic of the Congo, Eritrea-Ethiopia, Guinea-Bissau, Liberia, Ruanda, Somalia, Sudan and Uganda.

Asia

Afghanistan, Cambodia, India (Kashmir), India–Pakistan, Indonesia (East Timor), Myanmar (Karen State), Nepal, Philippines and Sri Lanka.

Middle East

Iran, Iraq, Israel (Palestinian Territories) Turkey (Kurdistan).

Americas

Colombia, Peru, US v Al-Qaeda.

Europe

Russia (Chechnya) and former Yugoslavia (Kosovo).

Some locations, such as Sudan and Uganda, had more than one conflict.

In the late 1990s a heated debate emerged about whether civil wars were better explained by 'greed or grievance', economic or political motives. Greed covers both the motive for conflict, to acquire resources, and the feasibility of conflict, how the combatants obtained the resources to fight. Like all good debates it was excessively polarised, obviously both matter; but it did prompt more examination of the economic dimension of civil wars. The book on the new economics of war edited by Arnson and Zartman (2005) is a recent survey which discusses the economic dimension and provides a number of case studies.

The source of the greed–grievance debate was unusual. The main sources were a technical piece of econometrics, Collier and Hoeffler (1998) in *Oxford Economic Papers* on economic causes of Civil Wars and an *Adelphi Paper* of the London-based International Institute for Strategic Studies (IISS) by David Keen on the economic function of violence in civil wars. Policy makers, including those at the World Bank, where Collier became head of research for a time, and NGOs picked up on the issues relatively quickly. This debate also contributed to the Kimberley

Process against blood diamonds and the extractive industries initiative, both of which aimed to stop these commodities financing war.

In the ensuing debate there was much emotion and many misinterpretations. Some wrongly interpreted the greed to refer solely to that of the insurgents, thereby having a conservative implication, but the greed of the incumbent state was as likely to be a cause. Greed and grievance may be two sides of the same coin: the greed of one prompting the grievance of the other. There were also disputes about method and the relative advantage of detailed case studies of particular conflicts as against statistical analysis of lots of countries. One of the results of the statistical analysis was that the degree of ethnic heterogeneity in a country did not seem to predict conflict. This was surprising since ethnic disputes (Serb–Croat or Hutu–Tutsi) seemed to play a role in a large number of conflicts. Subsequent work indicated that this result depended on how ethnic heterogeneity is measured. Although the usual measure of ethnic fragmentation does not predict conflict, a measure of ethnic polarity does seem to predict both civil wars and genocides. This is discussed by Montalvo and Reynal-Querol (2008) in a rather technical article. The example illustrates the care that must be taken in quantifying qualitative concepts.

Quantitative analysis over a large number of conflicts can often identify necessary conditions, which may be overlooked in individual case studies. But these conditions may not be sufficient and political entrepreneurs of violence, who mobilise both grievances and the resources to pursue the conflict, often play a crucial role. In a number of cases, the conflict was only ended with the death or capture of such entrepreneurs. For instance, it was only the death in February 2002 of Jonas Savimbi of UNITA which bought the long war in Angola to an end. The war had other dimensions. It dated from the national liberation struggle against Portugal, the colonial power, from the 1950s. At independence in 1975, there were three rival nationalist groups. The MPLA, the Portuguese initials of the Popular Movement for the Liberation of Angola, became the government; UNITA, the National Union for the Total Independence of Angola, led by Savimbi, became the insurgents; the third, the FNLA, the National Liberation Front of Angola, dropped out. The government was supported by Cuba, which supplied troops, and by the Soviet Union. UNITA was supported by South Africa and the US. Ironically, the government deployed Cuban soldiers to protect US-owned oil-installations, from attack by US-financed UNITA forces. The revenue from the oil-fields financed the Cuban troops and Soviet arms; UNITA financed itself by diamonds. With the end of the Cold War and the transformation in South Africa, there was a peace initiative in 1992, but the conflict only ended with the death of Savimbi. Other conflicts have also been ended by the removal of the entrepreneur. In Peru, the capture in 1992 of Abimael Guzman, the leader of Sendero Luminoso, Shining Path, led to the demoralisation of the insurgents and a reduction in violence.

Given the central role of charismatic leaders in many conflicts, one might consider how to remove them. They can be removed by bribing, capturing or killing them. The policy of offering senior figures in the insurgency large rewards to defect can be effective; the difficulty is identifying the seniority of the defector. It pays low-level defectors to pretend to be high level to collect the reward. Capturing or killing senior figures can be difficult. The US made a number of unsuccessful attempts to kill Fidel Castro and, at time of writing, has yet to kill or capture Osama bin Laden. There is also some dispute about the consequences; if, for instance, the attempted assassination of Hitler in 1944 by disaffected German Generals had succeeded. Such counterfactual questions face the difficulty that we can never know what would have happened if Hitler had been assassinated or if President Kennedy not been assassinated. If we try to draw conclusions from large numbers of cases we face the difficulty that relatively few leaders are assassinated and they may be atypical, not like the vast majority of leaders that are not assassinated. Jones and Olken (2007) try to get around this difficulty by looking at assassination attempts. Whether the attempt succeeded or failed is partly a matter of chance; there was an element of luck in the fact that President Reagan survived being shot, while President Kennedy did not. Their data set included 298 assassination attempts, over the period 1875–2004, of which 59 resulted in the leader's death. They note:

> Analyzing the effect of assassination is difficult. While some assassinations may be associated with historical turning points, the direction of causation is difficult to establish, especially since assassination attempts often occur (as we will show) in times of crisis, such as during war. To overcome this problem, we employ a large set of assassination attempts and use the 'failures' as controls for the 'successes'.

They found that assassinations of leaders in autocratic regimes produced substantial changes in the country's institutions, while assassinations of leaders of democratic regimes did not. A move to democracy was more likely following the successful assassination of an autocrat than following a failed attempt. There are, of course, the usual difficulties of measurement, interpretation and identifying causality.

Let us return from the leaders to the conflicts and how long they last. While the motivation for the insurgency is rarely purely economic, the means required to pursue the struggle are always economic: fighters need to be fed and armed; an army marches on its stomach. Thus an economic surplus that can be used to finance conflict is a necessary though not sufficient condition for war. Running a war, like running a business, requires that income is greater than expenditure. This applies to both sides. Sources of easy loot such as drugs, diamonds, minerals and oil have been the focus of attention; but other, more traditional sources of income may be important, such as taxing trade and peasants.

As the conflict proceeds, division of labour sets in; some specialise in fighting and some specialise in financing the fighters. Incentives then become important. Quite apart from their grievances, it can be the case that some actors have economic motives for continuing the conflict. This raises the policy issue: how do you construct alternatives for the combatants that are better than continuing fighting? These alternatives may be positive (a child soldier may think school is better than taking his or her AK47 back into the bush) or negative (the warlord finds that money laundering regulations mean that he has to stay in the bush rather than spend his loot in Monte Carlo). Changing incentives can be difficult and there are practical problems of implementing and enforcing what may appear obvious policy responses. This partly helps explain why conflicts can be so persistent.

Oil

The most common greed-based explanation in modern international relations is oil. Many see oil as a driving force in international politics and conflict, particularly in the Middle East. It is clearly an important factor: Saddam Hussein would probably not have invaded Kuwait in 1990, had Kuwait not had oil. But, it is far from a complete explanation: the 'it is all about oil' response is usually over-simple, as is any mono-causal explanation. For instance, if the US did invade Iraq in 2003 because of its oil, it seems a stupid thing to do. Oil prices would probably have been lower without the invasion, which added a geo-political risk premium to the price, and oil production higher. Oil also matters to the military because they are heavy users of it; tanks and fighter aircraft are not optimised for their fuel efficiency, so the oil price influences the defence budget.

Different communities tend to focus on different aspects of the oil market: supply, demand or prices. Strategic analysts tend to focus on supply. If you like frightening yourself, as many strategic analysts do, this is an easy way to do it; since most of the supply and potential supply is in potentially politically unstable regions of the world. Five Gulf states control 60 per cent of known oil reserves, governments control 75 per cent and many sources of supply are potentially unstable. Many of the new sources of oil, such as the Caucasus, Central Asia or the Arctic, are areas of geo-political tension, with unstable governments and actual or potential border disputes. These tensions pose risks for the negotiation of exploration agreements, the oil production itself and the transmission of oil to market when the pipelines go through neighbouring countries. Europe is heavily dependent on Russian oil and gas with the risk that the Russians may use this leverage for political purposes. The Venezuelan president, Hugo Chavez, used oil to gain political leverage and the classic use was the OPEC embargo and price increase following the 1973 Israel–Arab war. Oil revenues have played a role in financing a number of wars, including Angola and Colombia.

For oil producing states, the surplus of price over the marginal cost of production provides them large rents which they can use for political purposes. This makes government revenues less dependent on taxation, which requires a degree of political consent. The instability in the oil price can leave producer governments vulnerable: low oil prices undermine their economic and political base. Expropriation of these rents is a potential source of conflict, in particular how it should be divided between states and the oil companies that develop the production. Although the oil companies in many countries, like Saudi Arabia, are state owned, they are dependent on multinational companies for the development technology. Without this technology, which only comes at a price, production starts to fall, which has been the case with a number of producers.

On the supply side, there are two marginal production costs that matter. The short-run marginal cost is what is required to get oil out of existing reserves; the long-run marginal cost is what is required to develop new reserves. The short-run marginal cost differs between oil fields, but can be very low. It is estimated to be $15 a barrel in Saudi Arabia. This leaves a large rent available to be fought over. The long-run marginal cost is much higher but very uncertain, perhaps around $80. It appears that there are diminishing returns. The easy reserves have already been exploited. New reserves are deeper, in more hostile environments or require more expensive refining; all of which raises marginal cost. However, if the oil price stays high enough for long enough it may still be profitable to develop these expensive sources. Given the geological constraints, some suggest that the world is close to peak oil: the point in time beyond which world oil production will fall each year rather than rise. The International Energy Agency estimates that output from existing fields will fall at about 9 per cent a year and increases in oil production will depend on the development of new fields.

Strategic analysts, particularly in the US, tend to present the supply position as an existential threat, which requires thinking the unthinkable and taking extreme, possibly military, measures. However, the unthinkable possibilities that they consider have rarely extended to a sharp increase in the US federal tax on gasoline; to an economist, if not a US politician, the obvious solution. OPEC as a supply-side cartel has an interest in maintaining high prices. However, as OPEC has found, international cartels are difficult to maintain, the price collapses in 1985 and late 2008 being examples. There are always incentives for some producers to increase production, under-cutting both the price and the cohesion of the cartel. Probably the only successful, sustained, international cartel is the De Beers' monopoly of diamonds; there is little indication that oil producers can be as effectively organised as diamond producers.

Environmentalists tend to focus on the demand side. Rich countries are profligate in their use of oil, and rapid growth in large poor countries, like China and India, is also boosting demand for oil. This demand depletes a non-renewable resource; causes environmental damage when extracted from fragile ecosystems like Alaska and the Arctic; and generates carbon-dioxide and other greenhouse gases which increase global warming, raising further geo-political threats. From this perspective, high oil prices are a good thing: they reduce demand. Economists measure the sensitivity of demand to price, by the price elasticity of demand: the percentage reduction in demand that follows a 1 per cent increase in price. Goods where the elasticity is greater than 1 (a 1 per cent increase in price causes a more than 1 per cent reduction in demand) are called price-elastic. Goods where the elasticity is less than 1 are called price-inelastic. Economists also distinguish between the short-run elasticity and the long-run elasticity. In the long-run people can replace their gas-guzzling cars with more fuel-efficient vehicles, reducing their demand. Oil demand is inelastic in the short-run, but can adjust quite a lot in the longer run. Estimates of the medium-run elasticity are around -0.3. A doubling of the oil price, a 100 per cent increase, will reduce oil demand by around 30 per cent. In the long-run with technological substitution to more fuel-efficient equipment and the use of alternatives to oil, the effect may be larger, though it is difficult to estimate. Where the price mechanism tends not to work on demand is within the oil producers. These often subsidise domestic oil products, because they can afford to and because it provides political benefits. Even for an oil producer, the opportunity cost is what could be got on the world market. Being a producer provides no economic reason to provide cheap oil to your population, though it may provide a political reason. Because the effects of price on the demand and supply are rather small, it is sometimes said that the price mechanism does not work in this area. Rather it is that prices have to work harder, with bigger movements to balance demand and supply.

Developing new oil-fields, alternative energy sources or new fuel-efficient equipment requires large investments. Whether these investments seem profitable depends on the expected future oil price; but it is very difficult to predict oil prices. The best statistical model of oil prices seems to be a random walk: tomorrow's price equals today's price plus a large unpredictable positive or negative shock. In the long-run fundamental factors, such as the long-run marginal cost of production, must matter. But the long-run can be very long and the long-run cost of production is very uncertain. Without faith in fundamentals, markets do not know what the price should be; so prices can become volatile, jumping around wildly. In 2008 oil prices started below $100 a barrel, rose to $147 in mid-July, then falling back dropping below $100 again in September. Prices then jumped from $90 to $130 in a week, before falling below $40 in late 2008. The late-September spike reflected a financial factor, called a short squeeze. You are long on a commodity or stock if you hold it in expectation of the price rising; you are short, if you sell it in expectation of the price falling. Many traders had gone short on oil. Expecting prices to fall they had sold oil forward, for delivery in the future. They did not own the oil when they sold it, expecting to be able to buy it more cheaply just before the delivery date. When the delivery date arrived they had to buy the oil to cover their contracts, driving the price up and making their short sales unprofitable. Short selling has a long history. Like most financial innovations it seems to have originated in the Netherlands in the 1600s and the dangers of it were captured by the 19th-century US financier Daniel Drew: 'He who sells what isn't his'n, must buy it back or go to prison.'

Normally the solution to high prices is high prices. High prices tend to reduce demand and increase supply, putting downward pressure on prices solving the problem. The effect on demand is discussed above.

Short-run supply adjustments, increasing output from existing wells, are relatively straightforward, but there is the complication that a price increase may be taken by producers as signalling the start of a trend towards steadily increasing prices. In this case, they have an incentive to leave the oil in the ground so that they can sell it at the expected future higher prices. Thus there may be a perverse supply response, because of expectations. Long-run supply responses depend on the development of new fields. These will be developed if the expected long-run price is greater than the cost of development, which usually involves large fixed costs and political negotiations. If prices are very volatile, like oil prices, or if the politics are very unstable, which they often are in potential oil producing countries, oil companies may not have any confidence in their estimate of long-run price and costs. Without confidence they may be unwilling to risk the investments in new fields. From an environmental point of view, high and volatile prices are a good thing: they depress demand but do not encourage the expansion of supply.

Oil is clearly an important factor in military economics, but it is a very random and unpredictable factor. Economists are often accused of being complacent about problems such as resource depletion. They are seen as complacent because they argue that the system will adjust through various economic processes, such as changing relative prices, the introduction of new technologies and national and international changes in the level and distribution of income (impoverishing people reduces the demand for oil). Economists point to previous scares that did not materialise. Thomas Malthus at the beginning of the 19th century predicted that population would outstrip food production. William Stanley Jevons at the end of the 19th century predicted that the world would exhaust its coal reserves. The 1972 *Limits to Growth* book and the Club of Rome report predicted rising prices of primary products and constraints on growth before the end of the 20th century. Perhaps a better charge against economists than complacency is political insensitivity. Probably, as in the past, the system will adjust through the usual process of creative destruction; but economists tend to forget that people do not like creative destruction, find adjustment very unpleasant and may find preparation for war preferable to the usual economic process of adjustment.

Arms races and arms control

Preparation for war often involves an arms race. A country may increase its military expenditure in the hope of raising its security against a potential enemy, but if its antagonist raises its military expenditure in response, this security benefit is nullified; both countries are spending more but neither has increased their security. This is a particular example of the more general security dilemma: the steps you take to make yourself secure make others insecure. An arms race can easily escalate if both countries want to have more arms than the other; something which is mutually impossible, but may drive continual growth. Even if they do not want superiority, over-estimating their antagonist's capability can lead to the same effect. Arms races – enduring rivalries between pairs of hostile powers, which prompt competitive acquisition of military capability – appear to be a pervasive phenomenon. From the Cold War competition between the US and USSR, to regional antagonisms, such as those between Greece and Turkey, China and Taiwan or North and South Korea, arms races remain a matter of continuing concern. The case of India and Pakistan is discussed in the next chapter.

Arms races cause concern because they consume scarce resources; because they can have repercussions for the whole international community, particularly when the arms are nuclear; and because of the danger that they may increase the probability of war. Whether arms races do increase the probability of war or whether they deter war is a hotly debated topic. The classic mathematical model of an arms race is due to Richardson (1960b). This is a mechanical action reaction pattern, in which each side tries to have more than the other side, subject to some fatigue effects as the cost of arming slows acquisition. Despite a vast literature, the statistical evidence for a mechanical Richardson-style arms race is quite limited (Dunne and Smith 2007); but at a more qualitative level there is considerable evidence for the existence of arms races, as the list above indicates. Arms races are usually seen as a bilateral interaction between two countries; but the decision to arm is usually taken in a wider strategic context and the behaviour of third parties can often have considerable influence on the dynamics of arms acquisition.

An arms race can take various forms. Until the East–West arms race of the Cold War, most arms races were naval; while armies were labour-intensive, navies were capital-intensive. Before World War I, Britain had a policy of maintaining a fleet of warships that was as large as that the next two largest fleets combined. When Germany tried to construct a fleet that was as large as Britain, this gave rise to a typical Richardson-type reaction function. This arms race was quantitative, numbers of battleships, and symmetric, both acquired the same weapons. The nuclear arms race between the US and the USSR was partly a quantitative symmetric arms race, in numbers of missiles and warheads, and partly a more qualitative technological arms race. A qualitative and asymmetric arms race was that between fortifications and siege trains in the late mediaeval period, where there were evolutionary improvements in the technology of both, until the advent of gunpowder changed the balance between besiegers and fortifiers. The current increasing returns to scale in military technology leads to a virtual monopoly of military force by the US. This gives its opponents, including terrorists, incentives to choose asymmetric warfare and an asymmetric arms race. Data on preparations by terrorist groups, as distinct from actual attacks, are limited. The 9/11 Commission estimated that the cost of preparing the attack by the four planes was between $400,000 and $500,000, tiny compared to typical military expenditure numbers.

A common game theory model for many strategic interactions is called the prisoners' dilemma. If neither side arms, both are better off, they are secure and have saved the money. However, if one side arms and the other does not, the side that arms gains a great advantage. Thus the incentives are for both sides to arm, gaining no more security but at great cost. The interest of the game is that under this sort of pay-off the rational strategy is for both to arm (defect), whereas they would both be better off not arming (cooperate); but there is no way that they can ensure this. This little model has been very fruitful in a range of areas. Dixit and Nalebuff (2008) provide an introduction to game theory.

Although the prisoners' dilemma model has been widely used, the game depends on rather special circumstances. The participants are isolated, unable to communicate; the game is one-off, not repeated; and there are no external sanctions, no punishment of cheaters. If the game is repeated, the position is somewhat different. In stylised games the strategy 'tit-for-tat' does well. This strategy is to cooperate in the first period, then subsequently copy what the other actor does. This is 'do unto others as they have done to you' rather than the golden rule: 'do unto others as you would have them do to you'. As a strategy tit-for-tat is clear, nice (it starts by cooperating), easily provoked (responds immediately to non-cooperation) but is forgiving (it switches back to cooperating as soon as the other person does). It is vulnerable to misperception, mistakes about whether the other person has cooperated or not. Since the strategy never accepts defection without punishing it, an initial misperception of defection can generate long-standing feuds of repeated mutual retaliation. In this sense, it is too easily provoked and too unwilling to conciliate. Long sequences of mutual retaliation are characteristic of many conflicts, such as Israel–Palestine.

Robert Axelrod (1984) uses tit-for-tat to discuss the evolution of cooperation and analyses (1997) the complexity of cooperation.

One response to arms races is to try and establish arms control measures. Arms control aims to reduce the probability of war; to reduce the adverse consequences of war should it occur; and to reduce the cost of military preparations. Schelling and Halperin's *Strategy and Arms Control* (1962) is a classic text. Arms control measures are also seen as confidence-building measures to establish trust between the two parties. But for arms control measures to work, the two sides have to trust each other, which adversaries may not. This tension has been the basis of a criticism of the whole idea of arms control, by Colin Gray (1992) among others. The difficulty is that when arms control is possible, because the two sides trust each other, it is not needed; and when it is needed it is not possible, because the two sides do not trust each other. In 1817 the US and Britain agreed to limit naval vessels on the Great Lakes and Lake Champlain, but because subsequent relations between the countries were good, compliance was never an issue. However, the Washington Naval Agreements of 1922 were widely evaded (Craft, 2000). The agreements focussed on the number of battleships over 10,000 tons allowed for each of the participating powers. These limits could be evaded by switching to alternatives to battleships, such as aircraft carriers, or constructing technologically advanced warships, pocket battleships, below the 10,000 ton limit.

Arms control works best when: there are a small number of parties involved, then it is easier to negotiate a deal that provides benefits to all parties; there is an identifiable object, such as a particular type of equipment, that can be easily monitored; that object has an unambiguous military purpose (which is often not the case with nuclear installations); and control of that object restricts destabilising military capability.

4
Military Spending: How Much Is Enough?

Military spending, the defence budget, is the first element in the value chain producing security. In principle, governments should determine how much is enough by adjusting military expenditure to the point where the marginal security benefit of a little more military expenditure is equal to the opportunity cost. The opportunity cost is what could be gained if the money was used for other government expenditures, like health and education, or used to reduce taxation, which would allow higher private consumption. While this is a useful framework, reality is more messy, partly because of the difficulty of measuring the marginal security benefits and partly because states are not unified rational actors that could make such decisions. Instead decisions arise from competition between groups. Some, like the arms manufacturers and the military, may have an interest in higher military expenditure and in presenting the threats as more pressing than they are. Others, like the general public, may have little interest in strategic calculation or awareness of potential dangers.

This chapter begins with the difficult measurement issues involved in determining how much is actually spent on the military. There is then a general review of the motives for arming. Our main explanation of military expenditures emphasises the interaction of resource constraints, ability to pay, with strategic perceptions, as mediated through various interest groups. There is however an alternative explanation which emphasises the economic rather than strategic functions of military expenditure. This explanation has been most popular in the US and it is discussed in the third section, in the context of the evolution of US military expenditures. Even if countries have decided how much is enough, they have hard choices about the broad allocation of the money between manpower and equipment. The fourth section discusses these choices using the UK and France as examples. Arms races were discussed in the last chapter and the fifth section uses India and Pakistan as an example. The chapter ends with two important, but rather more technical, issues. The first is defence inflation: how to measure military prices. The second concerns stocks and flows. Military expenditure is a flow of money that buys new equipment and pays for troops. The equipment lasts, so at any time military capability depends on the stock of equipment, the military assets available, not just the current expenditure. Just as firms have balance sheets which measure their stock of assets and their liabilities, one can construct military balance sheets. The final section examines these.

Military budgets

The institutional process for determining military budgets differs across countries. In democracies the usual pattern is for the executive arm of the government to propose a defence budget and for this to be debated and perhaps amended by the legislature which approves the final budget. The degree of detail that is given in the budget differs substantially between countries as does the freedom of the legislature to amend the budget. There are usually specialised committees of the legislature that oversee the budget and specialised agencies, like the GAO and NAO, that conduct the detailed auditing. In some countries, this process provides considerable detail on the composition and use of the defence budget. In other countries, there is little information.

The main source for comparable international data on military expenditures is the Stockholm International Peace Research Institute (SIPRI). They publish an annual yearbook which provides figures on military expenditure as well as many other aspects of the military such as arms production and the arms trade. They estimated that in 2006 world military expenditure totalled $1204 billion, of which 46 per cent was by the US, which is a relatively secure society, and less than 1 per cent was by sub-Saharan Africa, which is very insecure. Between 2006 and 2007 global military expenditure increased by about 6 per cent in real terms. There are substantial variations over time. Between 1986 and 1999 it is estimated that global military expenditures dropped by about a third, while procurement spending on weapons and employment in the arms industry halved. The estimates come from Michael Brzoska (2007, p. 1179) who discusses the economic adjustments to this long decade of disarmament and the conversion of military resources to civilian uses.

Although these estimates are probably the best available, as SIPRI emphasises, these figures are not straightforward and they should be interpreted with caution. Their appendix to the military numbers on sources and methods is an excellent introduction to the issues. They emphasise that there are problems of reliability (different sources give different numbers), validity (exactly what is being measured) and comparability (the numbers can mean different things in different countries). Validity relates to the purpose for which the data are used. Military expenditures measure the resources devoted to defence; they are input measures, not output measures like forces available, military capability or security.

Countries differ in what spending is included in military expenditure. There are variations in the treatment of the intelligence services; paramilitary forces like the Gendarmerie in France and the Guardia Civil in Spain; nuclear or space research which has civil and military applications; and pensions of retired members of the armed forces. Definitional differences can be large and cause differences between sources even within one country. For instance, the figure for defence spending in the budget approved by the legislature for the defence ministry may be different from the figure in the national income and product accounts because the coverage differs. This is prior to the problem that not all countries are honest in reporting how much they spend on the military.

The spending figure is initially presented in current prices in local currency. To remove the effect of inflation, it is converted to constant prices, or real terms, deflated by some price index. The choice of price index is problematic, a question we return to. In practice, one of the various general price indexes is used. To compare military spending across countries, the local currency figure is converted to a common currency, usually dollars. This conversion produces a measure that can be compared over time and countries: military expenditure in constant US dollars. The conversion to dollars can be done using either market exchange rates or purchasing power parity (PPP) exchange rates. Military expenditures at market exchange rates can fluctuate not because the military expenditure changed, but because floating exchange rates can be volatile. PPP exchange rates allow for the fact that relative prices are very different in different countries: labour is very cheap in poor countries and expensive in rich countries. In rich countries only the very rich can afford personal servants, whereas in poor countries the middle classes take them for granted. The world total above uses market exchange rates. For poor countries the choice of exchange rate measure – market or PPP – makes a very large difference. In the 2007 SIPRI yearbook

China's military expenditure in 2006 was estimated at about $50 billion when converted at market exchange rates, but about $190 billion when converted at PPP exchange rates. SIPRI uses World Bank estimates of PPP exchange rates and in 2008 the World Bank issued new estimates based on better price data. In particular, it took account of the first detailed survey of prices in China. This led to the estimate of the Chinese PPP rate being reduced by about 40 per cent with a similar reduction in the estimate of Chinese military expenditure at PPP rates.

The problem of inflation and exchange rates can also be avoided by expressing military spending as a percentage of gross domestic product (GDP). Being a percentage, the share of military expenditure in GDP is comparable across countries. This share of military spending, sometimes called the military burden, is a measure of the priority given to defence, the share of output devoted to the military, not military power or the absolute level of military expenditure. If the growth rate of military expenditure is greater than the growth rate of output, the share will rise.

GDP measures the total output, incomes or expenditures of the whole economy. All three should be equal: if you spend to buy something, it has to be produced and the producers have to be paid income, wages or profits. GDP covers only marketed goods, so non-marketed output like domestic labour in the home is excluded. Expenditure is made up of consumption, plus investment in capital goods, plus government expenditure on goods and services, plus exports, minus imports. Imports are subtracted because the imported part of consumption or investment is not produced in the country. Not all government expenditure is included. Transfer payments, such as pensions or debt interest payments, do not create a demand on the output of the economy until they are spent on consumption and investment, where they are counted. Nearly all military expenditure is a demand for goods, like weapons, or services, like those provided by the armed forces; so it is included in GDP. There is another measure, gross national product (GNP). Domestic measures production within a country's border, whether by citizens or foreigners; national measures the production by the citizens of the economy, wherever it takes place. The difference between GDP and GNP, net property income from abroad, is quite small for most countries. The ratio of the current price GDP series to the constant price measure is a price index called the GDP deflator. These national accounts measures were developed in the middle of the 20th century, but economic historians have made estimates for earlier times. Angus Maddison (2007) gives a history of national accounting and estimates back to 1 AD.

Estimates of the GDP of the Roman Empire are inevitably subject to some uncertainty.

Military expenditures can change quite rapidly. On SIPRI figures the combined military spending in the South Caucasus by Armenia, Azerbaijan and Georgia in 2007 was five times what it had been in 1998. Since countries also differ in the size of their populations, military expenditure figures are also expressed in per capita terms, per head of population. Table 4.1 gives some SIPRI measures for the dozen largest military spenders, who account for about 80 per cent of world military expenditure. The first column gives estimates of total military expenditure in 2007 measured in US dollars at 2005 prices converted using market exchange rates. The second column gives the per capita figure, military expenditure divided by the country's population. The third column gives military expenditure as a percentage of GDP. The fourth column gives total military expenditure converted to dollars using PPP exchange rates. The Chinese and Russian figures are estimates with potentially large errors.

Table 4.2 gives some figures for 1985 towards the end of the Cold War when military expenditures peaked. These come from a different source, *World Military Expenditure and Arms Transfers*, a publication of the US government which has not been published since 2000. The table

Table 4.1   Military Spending in 2007

Country	Spending MER(2005$bn)	Spending per-capita	Per cent of GDP	Spending PPP(2005$bn)
US	547.0	1799	4.0	547.0
UK	59.7	995	2.6	54.7
China*	58.3	44	2.1	140.0
France	53.6	880	2.4	47.9
Japan	43.6	339	1.0	37.0
Germany	36.9	447	1.3	33.0
Russia*	35.4	249	3.6	78.8
Saudi Arabia	33.8	1310	8.5	52.8
Italy	33.1	568	1.8	29.6
India	24.2	21	2.7	72.7
South Korea	22.6	470	2.5	29.4
Brazil	15.3	80	1.5	26.7
Total	963.5			1149.6
World	1214.0	183	2.5	

* Estimate. MER: Market Exchange Rate. PPP: Purchasing Power Parity. Spending figures are in US$ at constant 2005 prices and exchange rates.
Source: SIPRI Yearbook.

Table 4.2 Military Spending in 1985

	M	YPC	POP	AF	M/AF	M/Y	AF/POP
Argentina	7673	6627	30.4	129	59.5	3.8	4.2
Brazil	4172	3718	136.8	496	8.4	0.8	3.6
China	53470	1040	1052.9	4100	13.0	4.9	3.9
Egypt	4289	677	49.5	466	9.2	12.8	9.4
France	48990	22330	54.9	563	87.0	4.0	10.3
Germany, West	54000	27670	61.0	495	109.1	3.2	8.1
India	6883	252	771.7	1260	5.5	3.5	1.6
Israel	10650	12870	4.1	195	54.6	20.2	47.6
Japan	37550	31880	120.8	241	155.8	1.0	2.0
Korea, South	8919	4380	40.8	600	14.9	5.0	14.7
Nigeria	1038	935	74.7	134	7.7	1.5	1.8
Pakistan	2480	402	99.1	483	5.1	6.2	4.9
Saudi Arabia	29240	9769	13.2	80	365.5	22.7	6.1
South Africa	4282	3394	33.4	95	45.1	3.8	2.8
Soviet Union	379900	10410	278.9	3900	97.4	13.1	14.0
Spain	10060	10810	38.4	314	32.0	2.4	8.2
Sweden	5904	23800	8.4	69	85.6	3.0	8.2
Syria	7445	3258	10.5	402	18.5	21.8	38.3
Turkey	4890	2100	50.7	814	6.0	4.6	16.1
UK	45850	15800	56.6	334	137.3	5.1	5.9
US	353800	24140	238.5	2244	157.7	6.1	9.4

M military spending million 1995$
YPC per capita GDP 1995$
POP population, millions
AF number in armed forces, thousands
M/Y share of military spending in GDP per cent.
Source: WMEAT 1996.

also provides some ratios of the variables that might be useful for certain purposes. Military expenditure per member of the armed forces, M/AF in the table, is a rough measure of the capital intensity of the military. Military expenditure per capita, M/POP, given in Table 4.1 is a measure of the cost per person in the society. Armed forces as a proportion of the population, AF/POP in Table 4.2, gives the proportion of people that have to serve in the armed forces. One can link these ratios; for instance, the second ratio, M/POP, divided by the third ratio, AF/POP, gives the first ratio, M/AF.

The high shares of military expenditures in the Middle East, Egypt, Israel, Saudi Arabia and Syria are noticeable, though the measurement problems should be emphasised and the Saudi figure is probably inflated by weapons deliveries and the high oil price, prior to 1985. The shares of military expenditure are generally higher in this period than they are in

2007 and the degree of militarisation varies more substantially. China, despite having 20 times the population of the European countries like France, Germany and the UK, has very similar military expenditures because its per capita income is so much lower.

Adam Smith said, 'Among the civilized nations of modern Europe, it is commonly computed, that not more than one hundredth part of the inhabitants of any country can be employed as soldiers, without ruin to the country which pays the expenses of their service.' In crisis, the military may take a much larger proportion, but trying to sustain such higher proportion for a long period will bankrupt the country. Azar Gat (2006) gives various historical examples which suggest that this 1 per cent estimate of the sustainable proportion of the population devoted to the military was about right. In Table 4.2, values of AF/POP greater than 10 correspond to armed forces which are greater than 1 per cent of population. Israel and Syria were both about four times Smith's limit. The 1 per cent in the military need to be fed and equipped and if this took two other workers, 1 per cent of the population in the military would require military spending of about 3 per cent of GDP. Rich countries can substitute capital for labour and devote a much higher share of output than 1 per cent to the military. During both the Civil War and World War II about 15 per cent of the US population were enrolled in the armed forces. But whereas military expenditures took about 17 per cent of GDP in the Civil War, they took over 40 per cent during World War II. There seems to be very little evidence on whether some limit like that suggested by Smith operates today.

Table 4.3 shows the distribution of shares of military expenditure for the countries for which there is data for 2005 in the 2008 SIPRI Yearbook. The modal (most common) share is between 1 per cent and 1.9 per cent and over half the countries have shares of less than 2 per cent. Shares tend to be rather higher in the Middle East than in other regions and the Americas have 82 per cent of the countries with a share below 2 per cent, the other regions except the Middle East have around 60 per cent below 2 per cent. Although it is a relative judgement overall in 2005, there was not much variation in shares of military expenditure in GDP between countries. Of course, average shares were lower in 2005 than in earlier periods when more countries were involved in conflicts, including during the Cold War. Shares of military expenditure were around 50 per cent in the UK and US during World War II.

Table 4.3 Distribution of Shares of Military Expenditure in GDP, per cent, by Region 2005

	Number of countries					
	Africa	Americas	Asia & Oceania	Europe	Middle East	Total
0–0.9	7	11	2	6	0	26
1–1.9	20	7	15	21	1	64
2–2.9	10	1	5	13	1	30
3–3.9	4	1	3	3	2	13
4–4.9	2	2	1	0	4	9
>5	1	0	0	0	5	6
Total	44	22	26	43	13	148

Source: SIPRI Yearbook, 2008.

Motives for arming

The primary factor determining a country's military expenditure is its GDP, what it can afford. As the data above indicated, the share of GDP devoted to the military varies less between countries than the levels of military expenditure. What share is thought appropriate depends on the perceived threat and foreign policy goals. The perceived threat will reflect the danger of armed conflict, enduring hostilities, and domestic political factors which shape perceptions, such as militaristic traditions. Other foreign policy goals may include provision of peacekeeping troops or the felt need to acquire military indicators of international status. History and inertia also matters: the bureaucratic baseline budget tends to be the amount spent last year.

There is a considerable quantitative work on explaining the levels of military expenditure in different countries. The other side of the coin is explaining why countries do not spend on the military and disarm or not arm. However, the sample of countries that chose not to arm and have zero military expenditure is small. It includes Iceland, whose contribution to NATO was hosting a large US military base; Costa Rica, which abolished its army in 1949 after a Civil War; and Panama, which has only paramilitary forces. There are few political parties around the world who advocate zero military spending. An exception was the Danish Progressive Party in the 1980s, which wanted to abolish taxation; their defence policy was said to be an answer machine that said 'We Surrender' in Russian. Most countries tend to spend about 1 per cent of their GDP on the military, even when there are no threats.

Consider a decision with more zero observations, having nuclear weapons. Most countries have armies, why not nuclear weapons? Initially the spread of nuclear weapons was almost linear, one every five years: US 1945, USSR 1949, UK 1952, France 1960 and China 1964. In the 1960s, optimists hoped this linear pattern would continue so that there would be about 15 nuclear powers by 2000. Pessimists, looking at supply-side capabilities, noted that followers could acquire nuclear weapons more easily than pioneers and that the expansion of civil nuclear power would also provide weapons capabilities. They guessed that around 30 countries would have the capability to build a bomb by 2000 and assumed that everyone who could build a bomb, would build one. In terms of capabilities their estimate was a bit low: it did not allow for the rapid growth of the Asian Tigers and some other countries. By 2007 probably most of the 45 members of the Nuclear Suppliers Group (NSG) had the capability to build nuclear weapons. In addition a number of non-members of the NSG had the capability to build nuclear weapons, and non-members, India, Pakistan and Israel, did build nuclear weapons.

Although there are probably about 50 countries that could have nuclear weapons, the vast bulk of them have chosen not to do so, often as in the case of Sweden and Japan after serious consideration. Since 1965 only two countries have publicly joined the nuclear club: India and Pakistan. There is some question as to whether two other nuclear states, Israel and South Africa, carried out a test and North Korea did carry out a test in 2006 but its low yield reinforced doubts about their ability to reliably manufacture a deliverable nuclear weapon. South Africa denuclearised before the African National Congress (ANC) came to power. The three former Soviet Republics of Belarus, Ukraine and Kazakhstan also denuclearised. Brazil is reported to have been preparing a test explosion when the programme was stopped in 1990. Other countries, including Libya, started to try to build them and decided not to. Had you forecast in 1965 that there would be only eight nuclear powers in 2007, not 30 or 40, and that four powers would have denuclearised, few would have believed you.

In his Nobel Prize Lecture, Thomas Schelling (2006) wrote, 'The most spectacular event of the past half century is one that did not occur. We have enjoyed 60 years without nuclear weapons exploded in anger.' He quotes C.P. Snow saying, in 1960, that unless the nuclear powers drastically reduced their nuclear armaments, thermonuclear war within a decade was a 'mathematical certainty'. Now with 11,530 operational (capable of being delivered) nuclear warheads and about 26,000 in total, the risk is still there; but the taboo against their use is well established. Not only was there no use, but there was much less ownership or proliferation than many feared. Some supply-side initiatives may have helped including the nuclear non-proliferation treaty, but it was primarily demand-side factors that mattered: most countries that were capable of building nuclear weapons decided, often after some consideration, that it was not in their interests to do so. The arguments that persuaded so many states not to acquire nuclear weapons seem to have been that they are expensive and dangerous. Owning nuclear weapons made one more likely to become a nuclear target, because of the strong incentives for a pre-emptive strike against a nuclear opponent. Inadvertent war is another danger. Many scenarios for nuclear use during the Cold War were of accidental or inadvertent launch or becoming locked into pre-committed responses, as had the generals before World War I, with their mobilisation timetables. The political flashpoints which led to nuclear mobilisation included the Korean War, the Cuban Missile Crisis and the 1973 Arab–Israeli war. There were also instances where the US had received false alarms of Soviet attacks. With the end of the Cold War Soviet equivalents became known, such as the case in 1983 where a Soviet satellite malfunction led to signals that there had been a sequence of US missile launches at a time of political tension.

This raises the question: why do countries choose to have armies but not nuclear weapons? The obvious justification for military expenditure is threats, internal or external. But this can easily be self defeating. In the case of external threats the spending may just provoke a response by the other side and in the case of internal threats, Paul Collier (2007) suggests that post-conflict military spending increases the probability of conflict recurring. Non-military measures may be a better way to increase security. Examples are the use of economic integration in the case of France and Germany after World War II or the abolition of the armed forces by Costa Rica after a Civil War. But when there are no real threats what is the explanation? Status and prestige are certainly important: to be a proper state is thought to require armed forces. Certainly in the case of the UK and France considerations of status and prestige, or *grandeur*, motivated the decision to acquire nuclear weapons. Supply-side forces, such as a powerful military–industrial complex, can also be an explanation for military expenditures. Even if there is no immediate threat countries may want to be able to project power to reassure allies and stop threats developing.

The military often have a range of more general functions. Troops may be useful in natural disasters and emergencies, what in the UK is called 'aid to the civil power'. The coast guard usually provides functions like search and rescue, towing stranded vessels, dealing with oil spills and more general police type functions like preventing piracy and enforcing fishing controls. These essential activities may, in many cases, be efficiently provided by the military, since they have relevant training and equipment. But they could be provided in other ways, if there were not a military. Providing them by the military does raise the danger that they may be neglected or starved of resources should the military emphasise their central war-fighting role relative to these peripheral civilian roles. The UK switched military helicopters from civilian search and rescue to Afghanistan in 2008. Troops may be used abroad in peacekeeping operations and UN payments for this can be a useful source of income to some poor countries. Even when there are no apparent threats, there may be a general concern for insurance: one never knows what may come up, so it is useful to have some military forces just in case.

The arguments that appeal to a government's interest in not having armed forces are essentially the same arguments that appeal to its interest in not having nuclear weapons, arguments that persuaded so many states not to acquire nuclear weapons: they are expensive and dangerous. When large armed forces face each other minor miscalculations can have major consequences, as the war between Russia and Georgia in August 2008 over separatist element in South Ossetia and Abkhazia indicates. Changing the status quo, acquiring nuclear weapons or giving them up, is more difficult than maintaining the status quo. Similarly, giving up armed forces is a big political step; but given a history of civil war, as in Cost Rica, it may be appealing, particularly as a way of signalling commitment by the government not to renege on agreements. In some cases it may be necessary to provide an independent security guarantee as insurance. Iceland though without armed forces did have a large US base in the country and when that closed had to consider other arrangements for its defence, given its strategic position in the North Atlantic.

Having armed forces can be dangerous because they may provoke neighbours into arms races and make internal measures that may increase security more difficult, just as military build-ups after civil wars seem to increase rather than reduce the risk of conflict resuming. They are also dangerous to their governments in that, statistically, a major threat to the survival of a government comes from its own armed forces through military coups. This should be a real concern in poor countries though it tends not to be of much concern to rich countries today, though Thailand and Turkey, where there have been military coups, are quite rich. But it was of concern to developed countries in the past. Until late Victorian times British policy towards the army was influenced by the memory that during the Civil War the army had taken over the country and beheaded the king. The French attachment to conscription was influenced by similar fears and more recently in the 1960s members or ex-members of the French military tried to kill the President, de Gaulle, on a number of occasions after he withdrew from Algeria.

That leaves the expense argument and often cuts in military expenditure are driven by financial crises: finance ministers can be effective disarmers. However, their leverage is often reduced by 'separate tracking', the fact that different people deal with international economic issues than with international security issues, so economic criteria are sometimes not applied to security decisions.

Economic functions of the defence budget and US military spending

Figure 4.1 below shows the US share of National Defence Expenditures in GDP 1929–2007, cut off at 15 per cent, for clarity. The share was less than 2 per cent of GDP during the inter-war period; then rose with the

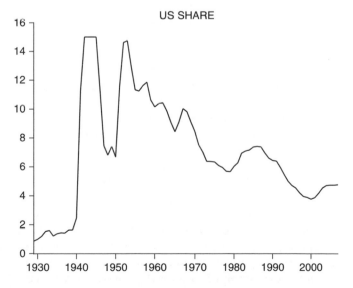

Figure 4.1 Share of military expenditure in the US, per cent of GDP 1929–2007 (cut off at 15 per cent)

war, peaking at just over 40 per cent of GDP in 1943 and 1944 (though this is not shown). With the end of World War II, the share fell sharply to around 7 per cent, rising again to almost 15 per cent in 1953, with the Korean War. Subsequently the share trended downwards, jumping upwards in the late 1960s with the Vietnam War, reaching a peak of 10 per cent in 1967. The share then resumed its downward trend till 1979, falling to 5.7 per cent. With the Soviet invasion of Afghanistan, the election of President Reagan and worsening relations with the Soviet Union, the share rose, peaking in 1986 at 7.8 per cent. As the Cold War thawed and then ended, the share fell, reaching a new low of 3.8 per cent in 2000. The 1991 Gulf War, Desert Storm, is not obvious on the graph; it was not expensive and was partly financed by allied contributions. The Global War on Terror, after 2001, increased the share to just over 4.5 per cent. By US post-war historical standards this is still quite low; military expenditure had accounted for over 5 per cent of US output in every year from 1941 to 1994.

There is a long tradition of explaining military expenditures not by their strategic functions but by their economic functions: that they are necessary to maintain growth and profitability. This type of explanation has been particularly popular for US military expenditures. Part of the context for this explanation is the high unemployment of the inter-war period. Despite the passage of time the causes of this great depression that followed the 1929 US stock market crash remain a matter of controversy, though it was worsened by the widespread adoption of protectionist measures which led to a large drop in world trade. The slump was widely interpreted as an inability of capitalism to generate enough effective demand, consumption or investment, to maintain full employment. Keynes argued that there was a role for the Government to maintain demand. Some Marxists and others argued that under-consumption, an inability to generate demand, was a systemic and unavoidable feature of capitalism. Many forecast that World War II would be followed by a slump like that following World War I. This did not happen; the period from the end of World War II until the crises of the 1970s was one of low unemployment that, in retrospect, was labelled a golden age of capitalism. Some argued that military expenditure was the source of the extra effective demand that stopped capitalism sinking into depression, since the US and UK devoted a much higher share of output to the military than their previous peacetime norms. The most influential exposition of this view was Baran and Sweezy (1966). This argument, sometimes labelled military Keynesianism, was developed by various other authors, particularly with reference to the US.

They suggested that military expenditure was used to offset the tendency to stagnation and unemployment and adjusted to stabilise the economy. Thus military spending was driven by its economic functions, not its strategic functions and that it was a blessing for capitalism, allowing it to grow, rather than a burden.

While this book is largely about the importance of economics to military matters, in this case the economic explanation does not seem convincing. I am partisan in this dispute, having written a paper, Smith (1977) 'Military Expenditure and Capitalism' which criticised the military Keynesian, under-consumption, arguments from a Marxist perspective. There are various problems with the military Keynesian argument. It is not clear that either Marxist or Keynesian theory actually predicts such under-consumption and Keynes certainly did not. The strategic explanations, concern with the threats from communism and the wars in Korea and Vietnam, seemed more important explanations of military expenditures than economic justifications. It is relatively straightforward to tell a strategic story to explain the graph of the share of military expenditure in the US, as was done above. It is very difficult to tell an economic story. Although World War II, the Korean Wars and the peak of the Vietnam wars were periods of relatively full employment in the US, the strong downward trend in the share of military expenditure is not marked by any corresponding upward trend in unemployment. The shares of military expenditure and the unemployment rate in the US are given in Figure 4.2.

The communist threat may have been exaggerated but it was certainly perceived as real. While economic factors were certainly important at a micro level (weapons projects and base locations), they seem less so at a macro level. Military expenditure would be a very bad fiscal regulator because of the lags before it comes into effect: it takes too long to plan and implement to be an effective stabiliser. Many countries with low military expenditure, in particular Germany and Japan, showed lower unemployment and faster growth than the US and UK, though it could be argued that they benefited from the spill-overs from UK and US military Keynesianism. There are other explanations for the golden age and why it came to an end in the 1970s. Dunne and Smith (1990) conduct a detailed quantitative analysis of the relationship between military expenditure and unemployment in Organisation for Economic Cooperation and Development (OECD) countries and find no relation. Subsequent experience has not provided any more support to the view that high military expenditure is needed to maintain low unemployment. When the Cold War ended, the UK and US cut their military

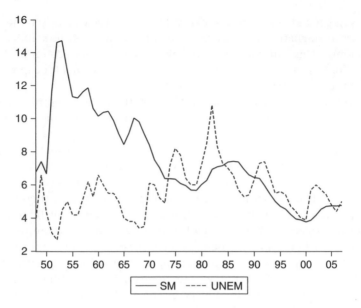

Figure 4.2   Share of military expenditure and unemployment in the US, per cent 1948–2008

expenditures substantially and rather than sinking into unemployment both grew rapidly, benefiting from the peace dividend. The cuts in military expenditure reduced government deficits, which allowed lower interest rates boosting investment in the technology boom of the 1990s.

Hard choices: UK and France

The UK and France provide a revealing case study of military choices. Both were once Great Powers, who show both similarities and differences in how they balanced strategic aspirations with financial resources.

There are long runs of data available for the UK. Figure 4.3 gives UK military spending as a share of GDP since 1830, again cut off at 15 per cent for clarity. In the period before World War I, there are two noticeable spikes. The first is for the Crimean War 1854–1856, when Britain and France fought with Turkey against the Russians, followed in 1857 by what the British call the Indian Mutiny and the Indians the First War of Independence. The second spike is for the Boer War, 1901–1903, fought in South Africa. Although it is not obvious from the figures, during the 19th century Britain fought various small and

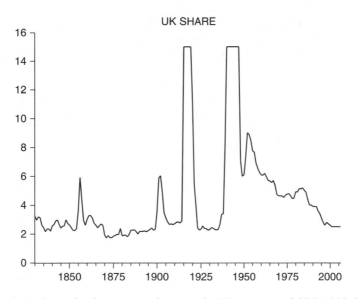

Figure 4.3   Share of military expenditure in the UK, per cent of GDP, 1830–2006 (cut off at 15 per cent)

medium sized wars and expanded its empire out of a peacetime budget of around 2.5 per cent of GDP. Saul David (2006) provides a history of Queen Victoria's Wars. Britain could do this in the 19th Century because it did not need to maintain expensive standing armies to defend its borders like the continental powers; naval forces provided a relatively cheap form of power projection; and the colonies, in particular India, shouldered a lot of the military burden of empire. India prior to the mutiny of 1857 had been run by the East India Company and so was not a burden on the British government. After the company was abolished, Britain financed the military expenditures in India out of its own budget for a few years before they were taken over by the colonial government of India.

During World War I the share jumped to around half of GDP, then dropped back to peacetime levels until rearmament for World War II, when it again rose to over half of GDP. After World War II, the usual pattern of the share dropping back to its historical peacetime level was interrupted by the Korean War rearmament of the early 1950s and the higher though declining Cold War level. There was then a fairly steady downward trend in the share. This was interrupted by increases following the 1977 NATO target to raise defence spending by 3 per cent more than inflation from 1979, which was accepted by the Labour

Government and implemented by Mrs Thatcher. This was reinforced in the early 1980s in response to a perception of an increased Soviet threat after the invasion of Afghanistan. This increase was similar to that in the US. The Falklands War of 1982 and the Desert Storm recapture of Kuwait in 1991 hardly disturbed the trends. Recently the share has stabilised close to the peacetime average of around 2.5 per cent. This share is higher than that in most continental European countries other than France.

Shares of military expenditure give only a very broad brush picture, since they do not show the political context and the composition of military expenditures. Since World War II Britain and France have had similar populations, GDP and military expenditures. Both have spent a higher share of GDP on the military than most European countries, though less than the US. Economic constraints and domestic political pressures made financing their defence budget difficult. They are geographically close, with similar strategic positions in the post-World War II world. Historically, their strategic positions differed because Britain was an island and France a continental power; thus the relative roles of their armies and navies were different. Since the successful French invasion of Britain in 1066, the British have repeatedly worried about the threat of further French invasions. Their closeness meant that historically they have alternated between being allies and enemies and they tend to have difficulty remembering, at any particular time, what their current relationship is supposed to be.

Britain and France were both colonial powers who had to decolonise and who have maintained close links with at least some of their ex-colonies. Both are permanent members of the UN Security Council and acquired nuclear weapons. During the Cold War, both were dwarfed by the superpowers and were thus extremely sensitive about their status: their grandeur as the French put it, or their seat at the top table as the British put it. Both valued the ability to project force internationally, which they did on various occasions; sometimes jointly, as in their joint invasion of Suez in 1956 and their joint participation in the 1991 Gulf War to retake Kuwait from Iraq. Their similarity in position made co-operation between them attractive in principle, but the dissimilarity in their interests, including rivalry over dominance in Europe, made it difficult in practice. Though there was some collaboration in weapons procurement, such as the Anglo-French Jaguar aircraft, they often found it easier to collaborate with other European countries than each other. A late Cold War comparison is provided by Boyer, Lellouche and Roper (1989). Despite the title *Franco-British Defence Co-operation:*

A New Entente Cordiale, the papers in the collection tend to bring out the difficulties of co-operation. Keith Hartley (2008) discusses recent European defence collaboration.

There are also interesting differences. For France the large wars in Indochina and Algeria made decolonisation more traumatic than for Britain. Although the partition of India after the British departure was a bloody affair, Britain was not directly involved in the conflict. France withdrew from Indochina after the defeat at Dien Bien Phu in 1953. War started in Algeria in 1956 and by 1958 a large part of the French defence budget was directed to North Africa. The acquisition of power by General de Gaulle in 1958 was followed by withdrawal from Algeria, a progressive reduction in the defence effort and an improvement in the economic situation. Between 1964 and 1969 equipping the armed forces took priority with capital expenditures taking over half of the budget with nuclear expenditure reaching 52 per cent of procurement in 1967. The period after 1966 is marked by stability in military expenditures relative to the variations before. This is apparent in Figure 4.4 below.

Although France has some terrorism and internal unrest, such as in Corsica, it had nothing comparable to Britain's long war in Northern Ireland. Britain, after Suez, maintained its very close 'special relation-ship' with the US and strongly supported NATO. As a consequence of

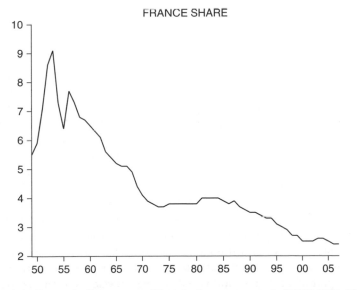

Figure 4.4 Share of military expenditure in France, per cent of GDP 1949–2007

this it got its nuclear weapons systems relatively cheaply, bought or copied from the US. France insisted on its independence from the US and left NATO's integrated military command in 1966. Financing its independent nuclear forces (force de frappe or force de dissuasion) was expensive and at the expense of conventional forces. Brauer and van Tuyll (2008) discuss this choice. Britain announced the end of conscription in 1957; France maintained conscript forces till 2001. Throughout the period France adopted a more labour-intensive military expenditure than Britain. As Table 4.2 shows, for very similar military expenditures France had 563,000 in the armed forces compared to the UK with 334,000. Even by 2008, after the end of conscription, again with very similar military expenditures France had 255,000 in the armed forces plus 99,000 paramilitaries, compared to the UK's 181,000. However, the French 2008 Defence White Paper planned substantial cuts in the number of personnel.

The defence budget is usually split into various sub-totals: these typically include the wages of the military and defence civilian employees; running and support costs for the weapons systems (operations and maintenance) including fuel; procurement of new weapons systems; research and development; and construction of military bases and housing for troops. Good international data on these sub-totals is very difficult to get, but they appear to differ substantially between countries. The cost of military personnel is less than a quarter of the US budget, and total personnel costs around a third, because it has a relatively capital-intensive military. In the UK personnel costs are just over 40 per cent of the budget, rather higher in France. By international standards these are rather low proportions; personnel costs can be between a half and three quarters of military budgets in countries that adopt more labour-intensive military postures, as most do. France tried to develop its defence industry by the arms trade. Britain privatised almost the whole of its arms industry; France retained a considerable degree of state ownership. Ownership does not imply control and at times it appeared that state ownership in France meant that the arms industry was controlling the state rather than the state controlling the arms industry.

The relationship between the state and the military sector was rather different in the two countries. In France a tight symbiotic relationship existed between the procurement agency, the Delegation Generale pour l'Armement (DGA), and the largely nationalised arms firms. The DGA acted as a patron for the industry, using procurement and export promotion as part of a coherent industrial strategy developed over decades, in which defence firms, mainly state-owned, had considerable freedom to develop weapons they thought would sell abroad (Kolodziej, 1987). The armed forces and politicians were marginalised by technocrats trained at the Ecole Polytechnique who moved between the arms firms and the DGA. French foreign policy was often driven by the desire to export arms and that equipment was designed in the light of perceived foreign demand rather than French military needs, prompting complaints by the armed services. The British approach was rather different, particularly after Mrs Thatcher privatised the arms firms and introduced competition under Peter Levene, the head of defence procurement, during the 1980s. This commitment to competition was given credibility by occasional purchases of foreign weapons. As in France foreign policy could be driven by arms exports, in particular the Al Yamamah programme of arms exports to Saudi Arabia. The contract, initially signed in 1985, was worth about £40 billion over two decades and is still continuing today as Project Salam. G.C. Peden (2007) reviews the interaction of technology, resources and strategic goals in the evolution of the UK budget.

An arms race: India and Pakistan

Examples of contemporary arms races usually include India and Pakistan. As noted in Chapter 3, while arms races are usually seen as bilateral they happen in a wider strategic context. Thus whereas in strategic contexts India was once usually juxtaposed with Pakistan, it is now as likely to be juxtaposed with China, both rapidly growing Asian powers with large populations. This wider context needs to be kept in mind while we consider the interaction between India and Pakistan.

On independence in 1947, British India was partitioned along religious lines into India and Pakistan. Partition was a bloody affair with large movements of people. Partition left the position of Kashmir disputed. This was a Muslim state with a Hindu ruler which was separated along the Line of Control into Pakistani-administered and Indian-administered parts, which remain a source of conflict. Pakistan is an Islamic Republic; India, though predominantly Hindu, has a large Muslim minority and a secular constitution. The Congress Party which ruled for long after independence was explicitly secular but lost ground to the Hindu Bharatiya Janata Party (BJP). Pakistan alternated between civilian and military governments; India remained democratic except for a period of a year-and-a-half of emergency imposed in June 1975 by Indira Gandhi. Pakistan was initially separated into Eastern and Western sections on opposite sides of the sub-continent. West Pakistan gained its independence with Indian help in a 1971 war and became Bangladesh. India and Pakistan fought fairly small wars in 1947 and 1965 over Kashmir, in 1971 over Bangladesh and an unofficial war in the mountainous Kargil district of Kashmir in 1999. Periods of tension followed the 2001 attack on the Indian Parliament and the 2008 attacks in Mumbai. In both cases India believed that the attacks had been organised in Pakistan. India and China fought a small war over disputed border areas in 1962. Pakistan borders Iran and Afghanistan as well as India and China, so is in a geo-political hotspot. Its role in the Afghanistan conflicts since 1979 has given it international strategic importance.

Neither India not Pakistan signed the nuclear non-proliferation treaty. India conducted a test of a 'peaceful' nuclear explosion in 1974 and conducted full-scale weapons tests in May 1998, followed within a couple of weeks by Pakistan. China had provided considerable aid to Pakistan in developing its nuclear weapons and Pakistan, through the A.Q. Khan ring, aided other aspiring nuclear powers. China, India and Pakistan initially all adopted policies of planning that were inimical to growth. The Chinese take-off into rapid growth began with the reforms of 1978; India's reforms were much later dating from 1991. Pakistan has still not taken off. The patterns of Indian and Chinese growth were quite different, China relied on export of manufactures, exploiting its supply of low wage labour; India emphasised services, particularly software, exploiting its supply of highly educated English speakers.

Figures 4.5 and 4.6 show levels and shares of military expenditure in India and Pakistan taken from SIPRI. SIPRI currently only give data from 1988. Estimates for earlier years come from old Yearbooks, though SIPRI advises against chaining series in this way. The Indian figures do not include spending on military nuclear activities and the Pakistan figures are only for current expenditures, excluding capital expenditures on equipment. So both are likely to be underestimates, but they are the best estimates available. Figure 4.5 shows shares of GDP devoted to the military in the two countries. After a jump at the beginning of the period, the Indian share was relatively stable at between 3 and 4 per cent, falling just below 3 per cent towards the end of the period. The Pakistani share was higher and more volatile but coming down towards the end of the period.

India is a much larger economy than Pakistan and towards the end of the period was growing considerably faster than Pakistan, so it was expensive for Pakistan to match India's military spending. As Figure 4.6 shows, in terms of levels of military expenditure, measured in millions of 2005 US dollars, Pakistan spending was dwarfed by Indian spending.

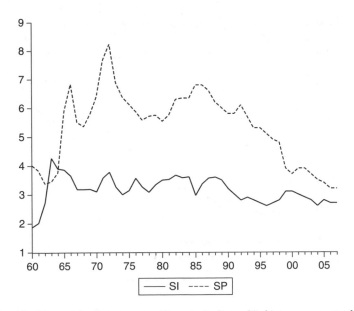

Figure 4.5 Shares of military expenditure in India and Pakistan, per cent of GDP 1960–2007, India: SI, Pakistan: SP

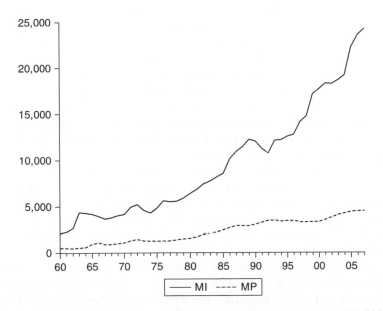

Figure 4.6 Levels of military expenditure in India and Pakistan 1960–2007, (2005 $m): India, MI, and Pakistan, MP

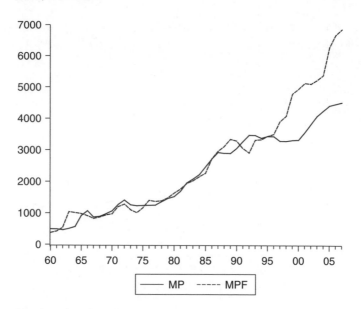

Figure 4.7   Actual and predicted military expenditures in Pakistan 1960–2007, Actual: MP, predicted: MPF

For a long time there seemed to be a stable relationship between Indian and Pakistani military expenditure. Pakistani military spending seemed to stay about 30 per cent of Indian military spending, though of course this relationship might hold only for reported, rather than actual, military spending. This is illustrated in Figure 4.7, which shows predicted Pakistani military spending based on the 30 per cent of India rule as the dotted line and reported Pakistani military spending. It is noticeable that they move together very closely until about 1995, when they diverge. Subsequently, Pakistani military expenditure is well below what would be predicted on the basis of the historical relationship with Indian military spending. There are various possible explanations. The fact that both became nuclear powers may have reduced the need for Pakistan to match India in conventional expenditures. The economic constraints imposed by its lower growth rates may have meant that Pakistan was unable to finance the required growth in expenditures to match the historical relationship with India.

There are divergent views on the issue of whether both India and Pakistan becoming explicit nuclear powers should be regarded as a positive or negative development. The people of the two countries seem to regard it as a good thing, giving them protection and extra status.

Military expenditures may be lower if cheap nuclear weapons substitute for expensive conventional ones. Some regard the possession of nuclear weapons as reducing the probability of war, since the consequences of a nuclear war would be so disastrous. The US and Soviet Union took some time to learn to manage mutual assured destruction, though India and Pakistan may be able to benefit from the superpower's Cold War experience. Should deterrence fail and war happen, the severity of the destruction is likely to be increased by the use of nuclear weapons. There is also concern about the security of the command and control of the weapons, the effectiveness of the systems for preventing unauthorised or inadvertent use, and concern that future governments may be less responsible than current ones.

Military prices

In the national accounts, aggregates such as GDP are expressed both in current and constant (adjusted for inflation) prices. The constant price measure gives an estimate of the real output of the economy. The ratio of GDP at current prices to GDP at constant prices is an index of the price level called the GDP deflator. This is probably the most general price index for a country, but there are a large number of other prices indexes which measure prices in different sectors of the economy. Consumer price indexes, which measure the cost of living, are probably the most familiar since they are widely used for many purposes. This raises the issue as to how we should measure military prices, or defence inflation, to get an estimate of the real output of the military sector. There are three different aspects to defence inflation.

First, there is cost escalation between generations of a particular type of weapons system, such as fighter aircraft. Over time the growth in real unit production costs, after allowing for general inflation, between generations of different system has been on average about 8 per cent per year. As a result each new generation of tank, aircraft or ship costs a lot more than the unit it replaces. Part of this is not pure inflation but reflects performance enhancement and improved capability: Typhoon can do more than Tornado, the F35 is more capable than the F16. Separating cost changes into their price and performance elements is difficult. The average 8 per cent growth reflects a set of vicious circles, or positive feedback loops, driving up costs. The effectiveness of a military system does not depend on its absolute technical performance but its performance relative to an enemy. There tend to be diminishing returns to technology, so that adding an extra 5 per cent to performance may double the cost of a system. Because it is relative performance that matters in combat, countries are in the position of the Red Queen in Lewis Carrol's *Alice Through the Looking Glass*: 'It takes all the running you can do to stay in the same place.' This Red Queen effect is important in evolution, which is also driven by relative fitness.

Since costs between generations grow faster than the budget, one can only afford smaller numbers of units in each generation. This reduction in numbers means that fixed costs are spread over a smaller number and the benefits of economies of scale and learning curves are lost, raising the unit production costs. Learning curves come from the experience gained in production, causing costs to fall with the total number of units produced. Economies of scale depend on the rate of production, the number produced in any period of time. There also appears to be a tendency for fixed costs, such as software and networks to support the system, to grow relative to variable costs, the production cost of each unit.

Rising costs increase the temptation to keep the systems longer, making the gaps between generations bigger: many military platforms, like the US B52 bombers, are very old. The capability of the platform is maintained by updates and the insertion of new avionics, electronics, sensors and weapons. But the long gaps between generations add to the uncertainty and cost of building the replacement. The vicious circles interact. Technological competition for relative performance causes cost escalation, which causes smaller numbers produced with longer gaps between generations, which increase the cost escalation.

The second aspect of defence inflation is cost escalation on individual projects, which often cost a lot more than initially estimated. To a certain extent these forecast failures reflect the 'conspiracy of optimism' by which military and industry have incentives to collude in underestimating costs to get the project accepted and included in the planned budget. Project cost escalation is discussed in detail in Chapter 5. On long projects, the agreed initial price is often indexed to allow for inflation: the agreed price is increased each year in line with some price index. There are many possible indexes and one needs to choose among them. The contractor for the UK EH101 helicopter, IBM, suggested one index; MoD insisted on another index. NAO (1993) concluded that MoD would have saved £70 million if they had accepted the index IBM suggested. This got very little publicity or political attention at the time the NAO reported, probably because politicians and journalists, like my students, tend to find that discussion of price indexes sends them to sleep. The difference between the indexes was that the one suggested by IBM was a price index and the one MoD insisted on was a cost index. Costs tend to grow faster than prices. Productivity growth means that even if input prices, such as labour and material are growing, improved efficiency means that the items can be produced for less, so that the growth in prices is less than the growth in costs. For the UK on average this difference is about 2 per cent a year. In particular areas, such as electronics, the rate of productivity growth is much faster. For many firms, despite high inflation in input costs like wages and raw materials, they are selling higher quality goods at lower prices, because of technological progress and productivity growth.

The third aspect of defence prices is the rate of inflation for the whole budget. This can be measured in terms of the cost of inputs to defence or the price of defence output. Some input costs are reasonably easy to measure: wages tend to grow at the same rate as the economy as a whole; fuel prices tend to move with oil prices; and defence benefits from being an intensive user of the inputs whose prices have fallen most rapidly: electronic and IT equipment. In the US, defence prices indexes are largely input based. On the output side, inflation, the rate of growth of output prices is equal to the rate of growth of input costs minus the rate of growth of productivity (output per unit input). To measure prices you need a measure of the output or productivity of defence. Measuring defence output is difficult, though it is being attempted in the UK in order to construct a measure of defence inflation, to match existing output figures for health and education spending. To get a good defence inflation estimate would require making the appropriate adjustments for quality and productivity improvements to get a measure of the real output of defence. This presents formidable difficulties. In the past the UK did try to control public expenditure in real terms, but this just provoked disputes between the Departments and the Treasury about the appropriate way to measure inflation in particular areas of public expenditure, like defence.

Military accounts and balance sheets

Military expenditure is a flow of money each year, some of which goes to pay troops and other personnel, some to operate existing weapons and some to buy new weapons. Military capability depends not on the purchases of weapons in a year but the total stock of weapons, most of which were purchased in previous years. This stock of military assets (guns, ammunition, planes and ships) depreciates. During peace equipment wears out, becomes obsolete or is lost in accidents; during war munitions are used up in combat, equipment is destroyed by enemy action and wears out more quickly through heavy use in operations. The Humvee vehicles used by the US in Iraq need to be replaced after two years rather than the usual 13 years because of heavy wear.

Commercial firms summarise the value of their assets (what they own, including machinery and property) and liabilities (what they owe others) in a balance sheet, which together with their income and expenditure and profit and loss accounts makes up their financial statements. Governments tend to focus just on the cash flows, the income and expenditure accounts. There has usually been fairly limited information on balance sheet items, such as military stocks, except where they can be easily counted, such as the number of warships or missiles. The UK is somewhat unusual in having a military balance sheet. After some trial years, in 2003–2004 Resource Accounting and Budgeting (RAB) was introduced for public sector accounts. This makes interpreting UK defence spending somewhat more difficult. Previously, the budget was a relatively straightforward measure of cash spent; now there are extra accounting adjustments. Under cash accounting, costs are counted when the money is actually spent; under accruals accounting, costs are counted when they are incurred. There are also various balance sheet adjustments, including the cost of capital and depreciation. Cost of capital is equivalent to interest paid on the assets valued on the balance sheet. The interest rate used to calculate this is largely notional and was reduced from 6 per cent to 3.5 per cent in 2003/2004. Depreciation and impairments to those assets is also charged as a cost. For most government departments these are rather minor adjustments; but MoD has £90 billion of assets, £34 billion of that being Single Use Military Equipment, which does not have a civilian use. That makes the cost of capital and depreciation big numbers for MoD, about £10 billion in total. Adjustments to these figures can make significant differences to the reported budget. There are also various other adjustments, relating to nuclear liabilities and to Private Finance Initiatives (PFI) for instance. RAB also has incentive effects, because of which totals are controlled; not all of them are desirable.

For commercial firms there are three ways to value an asset, such as a piece of machinery: on the basis of its historical cost, its market price or its going concern value. The historical cost of an asset is what the firm paid for it adjusted for depreciation, which is usually calculated on some conventional basis, such as estimating a lifetime for the asset and allowing for it to be written off over its lifetime. This is the usual book value of an asset. The market price of an asset is what someone else would pay for it. For some assets, such as mobile construction equipment, market prices can be discovered relatively easy; for others there is no obvious market. The going concern value of an asset is the present value of the future profits that would accrue to the firm from owning and using the asset. A lot of financial management involves adjusting to discrepancies between these three measures. If the market price of the asset is greater than its going concern value, it is worth more to someone else and you should sell it. With financial assets there is dispute about the extent to which they should be 'marked to market', constantly revalued in the light of possibly volatile market prices.

Valuing military assets presents difficulties. Historical costs are usually available, but some equipment is very old and it is not clear what rate of depreciation should be used. Sometimes one can determine a market price, for instance the UK MoD sold Chelsea Barracks in central London to a property developer for a lot more than its book value. But in most cases there is no well-defined market price for assets that have no non-military use. The people who would pay the most for your advanced fighter aircraft are usually people that you would usually rather not sell them to, since they may use them against you or your friends. Valuing fighter aircraft on a going-concern basis is equally difficult since there are no monetary equivalents for the services they provide in the future. Valuing MoD assets for RAB took some creative accounting.

The assets may not be owned by the government, in which case they are 'off balance sheet' not incurring cost of capital and depreciation charges. Under PFI, the assets may be acquired by a private consortium and leased to the military as required. An example is the Future Strategic Tanker, which is urgently required to replace the old 1960s VC10s and Tristar in-flight refuelling aircraft. The project is estimated to cost £13 billion over 27 years. The replacement is to be provided by a consortium, involving the manufacturer, which owns the aircraft. It leases them to MoD and can use the aircraft, for private air-freight contracting, when the MoD does not need them. This alternative use of the aircraft reduces the cost to the MoD, though there are issues as to whether the US would regard the aircraft as commercial or military, subject to restrictions, in this alternative use. Such a leasing arrangement gives the manufacturer an incentive to make the aircraft reliable and cheap to maintain, since it operates the aircraft itself rather than just selling it to MoD. Negotiating such contracts can be difficult because of the uncertainties involved in financing and sharing risks. One risk is whether MoD will need a refuelling aircraft in 10 years time. By 2008 the UK had spent almost a decade negotiating prices and conditions, which had cost the taxpayer about £47.5 million. The firms had also incurred heavy costs in the negotiations. Unlike the US case, discussed later, there was no doubt about the aircraft chosen: a converted A330 Airbus produced by European Aeronautics, Defence and Space (EADS). The PFI consortium borrows the money to acquire the assets. Private firms usually have to pay higher interest rates than the government, because of default risk, and this raises the cost. The spread or excess over the government borrowing rate depends on circumstances. During most of the negotiations this spread was quite small, but then there was the credit crunch of August 2007. This raised the spread to 100 basis points over LIBOR, the London inter-bank offered rate, at which banks lend to each other. A spread of 100 basis points is 1 per cent, so if LIBOR was 5 per cent, they would pay 6 per cent interest. Normally LIBOR is very close to the base rate, which the Bank of England controls and the Government can borrow at. But the credit crunch, and the lack of trust between banks, caused LIBOR to diverge sharply from bank rate, increasing the cost. PFI schemes are often big with large early uncertainties. If the contractors can successfully surmount these early risks, the operation phase can be very profitable indeed. If the contractors cannot surmount the risks, they may be bankrupted. Because they are long-term contracts PFI schemes may commit a large proportion of future budgets.

The usual reported UK defence budget is called the total Department Expenditure Limit (DEL), which is the resource DEL (current spending plus depreciation and cost of capital) less depreciation plus the capital DEL. Since capital expenditure is added in, depreciation is subtracted, to stop double counting. Actual cash spending is about £3 billion lower than the reported budget mainly because the cost of capital does not require any cash spending. Clearly the government, like any firm, must manage its assets; but managing military assets should be driven by military needs not accounting conventions.

Accounting procedures can reduce transparency in ways not related to RAB. For instance the NAO 2007 Major Projects Report notes how 62 per cent of the reported cost reductions by MoD had been achieved by reallocating expenditure to other projects or budgets. Operations such as those in Iraq and Afghanistan (including any urgent operational requirement (UOR) for equipment) are funded outside the defence budget from the Government's general reserves. The US has a similar system of supplemental appropriations for expenditure on operations which are outside the normal budget. The UK Winter Supplementary for 2007–2008 estimates costs for Iraq and Afghanistan of £1.9 billion, but noted that the need for UORs may require additional provision.

The actual figure is proving much higher, perhaps £3 billion. There are also complications like the costs of peacekeeping operations in the Balkans are included in the Foreign Office Estimates rather than the MoD estimates. Some of the equipment provided under UORs represents a response to new threats that appeared in operations, but the bulk of it represents operational equipment that was identified as necessary but not funded due to budgetary constraints, squeezed out as the large equipment projects running over budget forced economies elsewhere. Both in the US and UK, the military may try to finance what they cannot get in the regular budget through such UORs and supplementals.

The accounting issues are complex and I have only given a simplified picture; it is said that economists are people who are good with numbers, but not creative enough to be accountants. Budgeting for defence is inherently difficult; the difficulties are compounded if the budgetary system itself is not transparent and the senior managers do not understand the numbers. In the UK, complexity is introduced by the treatment of depreciation, capital consumption, balance sheet adjustments, contractual PFI terms and operations financed outside the budget. This complexity creates scope for financial engineering, may confuse planners and can distort incentives.

5
Force Acquisition I, Demand: The Biggest Bang for a Buck?

There are two dimensions to force acquisition and they will be covered in separate chapters. The first is demand, what troops and equipment are wanted, examined in this chapter. The second is supply, the arms industry and the arms trade that provide the weapons, examined in the next chapter.

Entrepreneurs face a standard economic problem: how to acquire labour and capital (workforce and means of production) and choose a technology to produce a product that will thrive in the competition of the market. The military entrepreneur faces a similar problem: how to acquire labour and capital (armed forces and weapons) and choose a technology to produce military capability that will thrive in the competition of war. Military entrepreneurs can solve these problems in ways not always available to their commercial comrades. Joseph Kony, who established the Lord's Resistance Army in Uganda, which promised to rule by the Ten Commandments, recruited by abducting and indoctrinating children who were provided with AK47s. Child labour was traditionally used by civilian employers, and in some countries still is. But with some exceptions, such as naval midshipmen who usually started at an early age, children tended not to be used in the military because they did not have the required strength. With modern military technology this limitation is removed, so children can be used.

In more conventional circumstances, how many forces you get for your budget involves a range of microeconomic issues. It depends on the state of the labour market (national wage rates and unemployment); the nature of the product market (the efficiency of the defence industry in building the weapons and the cost of other inputs, such as fuel and food); the use of technology; and the efficiency of the public sector (the size of the non-fighting bureaucracy and the effectiveness of the expenditure and acquisition process).

If the share of defence in GDP is constant, defence budgets grow with GDP, in the US and UK about 3 per cent a year on average, though it fluctuates from year to year. The wages of volunteer armed forces and defence civil servants also tend to grow at the same rate. Planners need to determine the capital intensity of their defence provision, the balance between spending on personnel and weapons. Given that they have decided on the size of the armed forces, this determines the share of the budget devoted to personnel and the remainder can be spent on operating the existing weapons and buying new weapons.

Weapons can be developed and produced within a country, developed and produced collaboratively by a group of countries, produced under license from the country that developed it, or imported. The fear that other countries might not re-supply spares and munitions in time of conflict prompts countries to prefer domestic supply from a 'defence industrial base' (DIB). However, the cost of developing major weapons systems is so great that few can afford to be self sufficient. We defer these issues to the next chapter and here emphasise the choices involved in acquiring troops and weapons and choosing the appropriate technology.

Labour

Throughout history, the supply of suitable labour, usually young men, has been a constant concern to the military. Troops may be forced to join or they may want to serve their country or to fight for a cause they believe in. The travel and adventure may seem attractive, and the military may offer better pay and more secure employment than the alternatives available to them, so the military often recruit in areas of poverty and high unemployment. The troops may acquire useful skills and education and the military may look after them better than their community and even provide a pension. Petty criminals were once given the choice of jail or army. The troops may be coerced into joining through press gangs or conscription. Even without coercion the decision may not be fully considered. In the past, recruiting sergeants would try to get potential candidates drunk enough to sign up; now the armed forces rely more on advertising. Historically, whereas the infantry could use relatively unskilled recruits, the navy needed skilled seamen. In the age of sail, not only were landlubbers useless, they could be a danger to everybody else on board and skilled sailors had usually been at sea from an early age. N.A.M. Rodger (1997, 2004) describes the recurrent difficulties of the Royal Navy in recruitment and training. As always, it is the opportunity costs that are important. Conditions that are perceived by some as the appalling hardships of military service may be seen by others as quite pleasant relative to their previous circumstances.

A major question is the relative advantage of volunteers and conscripts. There is no unique answer; it depends on the size and type of the forces required, the ease of recruiting volunteers relative to the ease of evading conscription and the relative military effectiveness of volunteers and conscripts. The UK announced the abolition of conscription, national service, in 1957. The US abolished conscription, the draft, and moved to all volunteer forces (AVF) in the 1970s. Conscription still remains the norm in many countries and was almost universal among continental European countries during the Cold War. France announced the end of conscription in 2001, Italy in 2005, but Germany still retains conscription. Some countries rely on reserves. Switzerland has 18 weeks of compulsory service and then seven refresher training courses of 3 weeks until the age of 30. The Swiss also allow reservists to keep weapons at home; other states tend to be more hesitant about arming their citizens. Conscription has been controversial in Russia, with the military arguing for maintaining a large conscript army, mainly, some have suggested, to justify jobs for the large number of generals. The size of the Russian armed forces has reduced from about 3 million to about a million in 2008; the length of service for conscripts has been reduced from two years to one year and there are attempts to establish core forces of longer term volunteers.

At first sight conscripts appear cheaper than volunteers, since conscripts are paid much lower wages than would be required to recruit the same number of volunteers. But this is partly illusory, since there is a real opportunity cost, the lost output those conscripts would have produced had they not been in the military. Conscription is a tax which falls most heavily on young men. It is a tax that is relatively easy to collect, which is one of the attractions, though there are fixed costs in setting up effective conscription systems. During major wars there is usually no alternative, the wages required to attract large numbers of volunteers would be too high and those that volunteer may be taken away from work that is crucial to the war effort. During the early part of World War I, the UK was able to recruit volunteers very easily. The famous poster of Kitchener pointing out above the message 'Your Country Needs You' was very effective. But the recruitment disrupted the economy, volunteers left jobs that were crucial to the war effort, and eventually conscription was introduced. Conversely, when only small forces are required and only a proportion of the age-cohort are conscripted, it can seem very inequitable on those that are chosen, even when chosen randomly, as in the US draft.

There is also a large cost in training. Learning about modern weapons and tactics can absorb a large part of a conscript's tour of duty, so despite very large flows through the military there is a relatively small force of experienced troops. Much smaller AVF forces can provide the same level of capability. As with weapons one must distinguish between the stocks, the number of trained personnel available, and the flows, the numbers recruited or leaving. Training times differ between infantry and fighter pilots, for instance. Training issues can often shape forces. From the 1500s guns displaced bows and arrows not because guns were militarily more effective. A skilled archer could fire more rapidly, with greater accuracy, over a greater range, with a greater penetrating power than a soldier with a gun, well into the 19th century. But becoming a skilled archer took a lifetime of training, whereas soldiers could learn to use a gun relatively quickly. In some societies the acquisition of military skills was part of ordinary life. John Keegan (1993) notes how nomadic pastoralists, moving with their herds of animals, learn to kill and select for killing as a matter of course. Their mobility, their ability to live off the land and their tactical skills of movement, gained through herding their flocks, could all be used against their enemies. This made pastoralists like the Huns and the Mongols dangerous neighbours for both Eastern and Western powers.

AVF forces may also be more highly motivated than unwilling conscripts. Conscription does provide a trained reserve that can be mobilised in time of war and this is important to countries like Israel. Maintaining operational reserves can be expensive in terms of lost output to the economy, since reserves have to regularly leave work to train. It can be politically difficult to use conscripts in some operations as the US found in Vietnam. Conscription may provide training and socialisation that contributes to society; but conscription may not be the most effective way of providing it. While some believe that young thugs would be straightened out by a spell in the military, it may only produce fitter, better-organised, more dangerous young thugs, able to handle weapons.

Some argue that conscription establishes closer links between society and the military and that it may be a constraint on military interventions in politics. However, most military coups have been conducted with conscript armies; largely because military coups are more prevalent in poor countries and poor countries tend to use conscription, not having the tax capacity to pay for volunteer forces. Whether, when one allows for the level of development, conscription increases or decreases the risk of military coups is unclear because there are so many other factors at work. Thailand and Turkey, relatively high income countries with large conscript armies, have had military coups or threats of them in recent years, but that is not conclusive. The labour market issues overlap with the wider issues of the relationship between the armed forces and civil society, such as the role of the warrior ethos and the treatment of gays, women and ethnic minorities in the armed forces. For the military (as for teachers, doctors, nurses and police) the public sector is both the main buyer of their services and the main provider of them through training. The government has to decide how many to train now in the light of their expectation of the future demand for their services, which can be often difficult to foresee.

Most military organisations are strongly hierarchical and make a sharp distinction between officers and enlisted troops with further stratification among the enlisted troops: the non-commissioned officers (NCOs), having considerable power. Such clear stratification used to be common in companies and government organisations but has largely disappeared elsewhere. One possible function is to prevent promotion on ability. If promotion on ability operated freely, all the very capable people would be promoted to command jobs behind the lines and front line positions would be filled only by the young and inexperienced or the old and incapable. Having a barrier means that capable experienced NCOs are leading front-line units and advising the nominal commander, usually a very junior officer. In the age of 'the strategic corporal' where the decisions even of junior NCOs can have major repercussions, this is important. Of course, the barriers are not completely impermeable and some do rise from the ranks to become officers and attain senior positions. This tends to be more common in war. Within the military, promotion is largely internal and unlike commercial firms, recruitment to top posts from outside the organisation is rare. There are usually 'up or out' rules (get promoted or leave) and age limits on service so that even in an AVF people leave the military to go on to other jobs.

Recruitment and retention issues play a large role in an AVF and there is an economic literature on such military personnel issues, surveyed in Asch, Hosek and Warner (2007). In the US the military have provided education, most notably through the GI Bill after World War II, which made a major contribution to US human capital. The education benefits have attracted recruits to the US military. The US military has also been seen as a profession where African-Americans and Hispanics can

get ahead. While there may be externalities for society in military training, the recruitment and retention effects are probably more important:
people will be more willing to join and stay in the military if they are
acquiring skills that will enable them to get good jobs when they leave.

There are other possibilities than national conscripts or volunteers.
One can hire mercenaries, like the Italian Condottieri, and some countries have extensively used foreign recruits, such as the UK Gurkha
troops from Nepal and the French Foreign Legion. In recent years private
military companies have increasingly been used for logistics, security
and other military tasks, though there has been controversy over their
role. Governments that want to provide covert, deniable support to one
side in a conflict, may release their military for a time to serve with a
private military company that will actually provide the support.

While much of standard personnel economics associated with recruitment, training and retention apply to the military, motivating the willingness to kill and be killed raises somewhat different, non-economic,
issues on which there is a large sociological literature.

Weapons procurement

Buying military products is hard and, as a result, military projects tend
to be late, over-budget and fail to meet performance targets. The Government Accountability Office (GAO) in the US, the National Audit
Office (NAO) in the UK and their counterparts in other countries regularly report on the progress or lack of progress of the development of
major weapons systems. Regular reports are *Defense Acquisitions: Assessment of Selected Weapons Programs* by the GAO and *Ministry of Defence
Major Projects Report* by the NAO. As usual there are pessimistic and optimistic perspectives. Pessimists are dismayed by the failures. Optimists
are pleasantly surprised that the military have any working weapons,
given the difficulties involved in meeting time, cost and performance
targets.

As an example, the UK MoD ordered 14 Chinook helicopters in 1995.
The Chinook is a widely used, heavy-lift helicopter, introduced in 1962
and produced by Boeing. Six standard Mk2a were delivered satisfacto-
rily; the other eight were modified to Mk3 for special-forces operation.
These eight cost some £259 million and MoD took delivery in 2001.
Although Boeing met its contractual obligations, the MoD could not get
access to the source code, to ensure that the avionics software met UK
airworthiness standards. Despite a desperate need for helicopters, particularly in Afghanistan, the helicopters had still not flown on operations

by June 2008, when NAO (2008) reported. They may be available for use in 2011, though at considerable extra cost.

The UK problem of ageing air-to-air refuelling tankers was discussed above; the US has similar problems. In 2002 the Air Force offered a $23.5 billion leasing contract to Boeing for military refuelling tanker aircraft. It was then discovered that Darleen Druyun, the top Air Force acquisitions official for tankers, had held illegal job negotiations with Boeing while negotiating the contract. She and the Boeing finance director, Michael Sears, got prison sentences for violating conflict of interest laws. The competition was reopened and the European company European Aeronautics, Defence and Space (EADS), in conjunction with Northrop Grumman, won the contract for 179 tankers, based on the Airbus A330 aircraft, in February 2008. In June 2008, a GAO enquiry found flaws in the process choosing EADS and the competition was again reopened. In September 2008 the Pentagon postponed restarting the competition, to allow a 'cooling-off period', despite the urgent need for new tankers. By this stage the contract was worth about $35 billion.

Procurement means to purchase or acquire, but it tends to be used in a narrower sense: the purchase of a one-off or customised product or service, where there is usually asymmetric information between buyer and seller; risk and uncertainty; concerns about the quality of the product provided; an inability to write a complete contract; and the possibility of renegotiation. Nearly all these problems arise when a family hires a builder and they are common in large IT systems, big infrastructure projects and pharmaceuticals. Failure in procurement is common to both public and private sector. Products that are bought regularly, in volume, from a large market raise different issues of supply chain management, just-in-time supply, transactions costs and logistics. The military can make mistakes even with low-tech commodity products. The UK army boot proved inadequate during the Falklands War of 1982 and the consequent trench foot caused more British casualties than Argentina (Frost, 1983).

Principal–agent or contracting problems are central. A principal, with certain objectives, employs an agent, with the necessary skills and information, to achieve the objectives. However, the agent's objectives are different from the principal's. The principal's problem is to construct a set of incentives to ensure that the interests of the principal and agent are aligned, so that the agent acts in the principal's interest. The principal can rarely observe the agent's actions, including the agent's effort, only the final outcome; so the principal cannot tell whether the agent was not trying or was merely unlucky. This sort of relationship is common. It occurs when people hire lawyers or owners of a firm appoint managers and is prevalent in procurement.

As an example of the principal–agent problem, every UK procurement review from the 1960s to the present (Zuckerman, Downey, Learning from Experience, Smart Procurement) concluded that on the typical complex project the MoD should spend about 15 per cent of the development budget on early research prior to full development, to demonstrate the feasibility of the technology and conduct pilot programmes to reduce risks. This is almost never done and the amounts spent on de-risking tend to be small. While the value of such up-front research is recognised, there are strong incentives against doing it, since it may reveal major problems that would cause the project to be cancelled. Neither the military, wanting the project, nor industry, wanting the profits, want the project cancelled. They would rather proceed and hope that they can resolve the difficulties later, albeit at the expense of time, cost or performance. To the senior manager, trying to fit the project into the budget, the extra early research does not seem to produce anything, so money will be saved by cutting it. The early research looks particularly wasteful if its only function is to cause the project to be cancelled.

There is not just one principal and one agent in defence procurement; there are agency problems all through the system. Politicians employ civil servants and the military; the civil servants and military employ industry; the top-level decision makers employ specialists to implement the decisions, and so on. The incentives of the various groups differ substantially: military and civil servants want promotion; politicians want good publicity; bureaucrats want a quiet life; industry wants to make profits. There is nothing wrong with these objectives in themselves but they constrain the way the system operates.

Solutions are proposed, reforms implemented but the problems remain, so the system cycles, alternating between approaches. There is a vast literature. Recent UK examples are: Chin (2004) in the aptly titled *British Weapons Acquisition Policy and the Futility of Reform*; Kincaid (2008), which reviews recent reforms; and DEG (2005), based on a course by the Defence Engineering Group at University College London which examines the process of defence acquisition. Procurement is hard because of the interaction of a range of elements, which is why reform programmes which try to fix one aspect in isolation rarely work. To capture this interaction we will look first at the questions that military procurement organisations have to address and then at the economic problems that make answering them so hard. The agency problem is that there is no single organisational answer, since the organisation is made up of conflicting groups with different answers to each of these questions.

Procurement: The difficult questions

What do we want? Requirements are vague, change and evolve over time and differ between stakeholders. It may be difficult to get input about needs from final users, such as troops on the ground, until too late. The requirement changes over time as one resolves uncertainties in technology, through work on the project, and as the perceived threat changes. US and UK combat experience in Afghanistan and Iraq showed that the threat from improvised explosive devices (IED) was more serious than expected and equipment had to be adapted rapidly to take account of this new threat. There is a choice between presenting requirements as a set of 'cardinal points', the general objectives of the system, or very detailed requirements about how it should meet those objectives. There may be disagreements about other objectives, such as how to trade off getting best value for money with promoting competition or maintaining a DIB. In areas where the government is the only buyer, such as warships, its procurement determines national industrial structure by default. Trying to achieve multiple objectives, like trying to hit two targets with a single missile, can be a recipe for disaster and it may be better to do one thing (buy weapons) properly, than two things (buy weapons and promote an industrial policy) badly. In practice, determining what is wanted is complicated by industrial issues, political accountability, budgetary uncertainty, compatibility with other systems and compliance with complex regulations.

There are hard trade-offs between the elements of time, cost, performance and risk. An important one is between a standard and a customised solution. The standard Chinooks worked well; those customised for special-forces caused difficulties. There is often an apparent trade-off between efficiency and competition. Economies of scale and scope and learning curves make a single supplier look cheaper, but competition can force down prices. Both effects are difficult to quantify and there has been considerable controversy in the US about having a second engine supplier for the JSF F35 aircraft. Nobody but the US could even consider this choice, given the cost of the investment and information transfer required to second source jet engines.

There is an issue as to who should make the decision about what is wanted. Buyers know more about their demand; the sellers know more about the potential of technology and materials. Lack of clarity in objectives may be worsened by poor communication or lack of knowledge. It is said that an 'intelligent customer' knows the right question to ask; an 'informed customer' understands the answer; and an 'expert customer' does not need to ask the question, already knowing the answer. The cost of becoming a better customer increases very steeply. To be an informed customer may require research labs; to be an expert customer may require being able to produce the product.

How do we get it? Equipment may be imported; produced under license from a design developed elsewhere; designed and produced in collaboration with other countries; or designed and produced domestically. Collaboration promises great benefits: fixed costs are shared, longer production runs bring the benefits of learning curves, economies of scale and inter-operability. The use of common equipment between countries aids maintenance, training and logistics. In practice, the compromises required to get agreement, the inefficiencies associated with work-sharing arrangements and the lack of centralised control and coordination mean that these potential benefits are rarely realised. Wood and Sorenson (2000) present a set of case studies on military collaboration. In the commercial field, Airbus had difficulty coordinating German and French elements in the development of the A380 jumbo and Boeing in coordinating its suppliers in the development of the 787 Dreamliner; both aircraft are about two years late and over-budget. Procurement problems are not confined to the military.

Military goods or services may be provided in various ways. Equipment may be government owned, used and produced in government arsenals or it may be produced in government-owned facilities operated by a private contractor. Equipment may be leased from the producers, as with Private Finance Initiative (PFI), and services may be provided by private military companies. Equipment may be specifically developed for the buyer or purchased as either commercial off-the-shelf (COTS) or military off-the shelf (MOTS). Commercial suppliers, such as Microsoft, may be unwilling to provide the guarantees or information that the public sector contracts traditionally required, such as access to source code. This may also be a problem with military suppliers, as in the Chinook case; either where there are issues of intellectual property rights (IPR) or where governments restricts access to foreigners by, for instance, 'blackboxing' code. This has been an issue between the US and UK over the F35. Availability of suppliers may vary over the cycle as contractors substitute between public and private work.

On what terms? Contracts vary between fixed-price and cost-plus. Fixed-price contracts usually follow a competitive tender won by the lowest bidder. Cost-plus contracts are usually part of a partnership arrangement where a preferred supplier is paid cost of production plus a profit margin. There are many intermediate cases where any difference between initial estimate and final cost is shared by buyer and seller, perhaps with some inflation adjustment. The price bid in a competition and the cost of production are not fixed numbers; they will be determined by the form of the contract. The profit rate used in cost-plus contracts is usually the average rate of return in industry. This may not be appropriate, since the industry average embodies a risk premium (firms may not sell the product), whereas cost-plus contracts are safe. Cost-plus requires the buyer to be able to audit the costs of the supplier and this may be difficult, allowing the supplier to attribute unnecessary costs to a project. Under cost-plus, the contractor may have incentive to make components in-house, on which there is a profit margin, rather than buy-in, on which there is not.

Fixed-price and cost-plus each have advantages and disadvantages. With experience, decision-makers learn the disadvantages of the current system and are tempted to switch to the other, so the UK government has cycled between the two approaches over periods of 15–20 years. Contracting for quality raises difficulties. At the end of the project, the equipment will be evaluated with trials, exercises and simulations, before it is accepted. But it can only be rejected on the basis of criteria that are specified in advance, otherwise the supplier would not know what to provide, and that can be tested, otherwise one cannot judge whether it meets the criteria. In practice, important characteristics, such as performance in combat, cannot be tested. Contracts also have to cover allocation of IPR and responsibility for failure.

Competitions can be very expensive, both for buyers who have to evaluate many complex bids and for the suppliers who may invest millions in bidding. Partnerships, with bidding restricted to suppliers with established reputations, are safer and allow cost savings and quality improvements; but they restrict entry, reduce competition and limit the range of solutions proposed. Collusion among the bidders in a competition is always a danger and more transparency may increase the probability of collusion, allowing price-fixing cartels to detect cheating by members more easily. Although the market may appear competitive, it may be very dependent on a single specialist subcontractor who supplies all the competitors.

What will it cost? There are various measures of cost; from purchase price, the cost of acquisition, to through-life cost including operation. Estimation of costs, particularly through-life costs, is difficult. There is an optimism bias, by both buyer and seller, to get the programme approved. The operation of this bias in the UK is discussed in Kincaid (2008). There is also the 'winners curse': the firm that wins a competition tends to be the one that bid too low, unaware of the problems that the other bidders took into account. There is the tendency, discussed above, to spend too little on de-risking the project during the assessment phase. Problems can also result from the overlapping of production and development and integration between systems. In IT and defence, systems integrators often take responsibility for making all the elements work together, not always successfully. There are parametric cost estimation procedures. These use past information on how costs are related to characteristics of the system, such as cost per kilogramme of aircraft delivered, to provide estimates. They are approximate, but quite useful, particularly in identifying where some break in trend is assumed in the cost estimate.

When do we want it? Time may be of the essence. In combat, an expensive piece of equipment, which only just meets the requirement, but is now available, may be of much more value than a cheaper more effective alternative that will be available in the future. Military equipment cycles are long. In the UK, the cycle is known as CADMID: concept, assessment, demonstration, manufacture, in-service, disposal. Procurement covers the first four stages. The Eurofighter-Typhoon design dates from the early 1980s, it came into service in the mid-2000s and could be operating for another 30 years, a CADMID cycle of half a century. Commercial and public sector heritage IT systems can be 50 years old, as are the B52s that are the backbone of US bomber command. Buildings and infrastructure can last even longer. In-service and operating costs, which are influenced by reliability and maintenance, are a large element of through-life costs. Small investments in reliability early on can produce large savings later on. But these are often cut to keep the initial cost low.

Procurement tends to be divided between normal budgeted procurement and requirements needed rapidly in war. In the US the latter are called 'emergency supplemental funds' and in the UK 'urgent operational requirements' (UORs). Normal procurement processes are slow (average 7 years), formalised, taking account of many objectives, trying to build compatibility with the rest of the system to minimise maintenance costs and maximise interoperability and usually require research and development (R&D). UORs are fast (usually less than 6 months), informal, focus on a single objective, may be incompatible with the rest of the system (creating fleets within fleets) and largely use off-the-shelf components.

In the normal budget procurement, the distribution of expenditure on projects is highly skewed, dominated by the large projects, which can become black holes, absorbing money. It can then be difficult to get small valuable projects into a constrained budget dominated by the big projects. In 2006 the distribution in the US and the UK was very similar with the two largest projects accounting for half the expenditure, with each succeeding project, ranked by size, being about half the size of the previous one. Flexibility can be bought by writing contracts that make it easy to change specifications and cancel projects, but this can be expensive and involve penalties.

Given the uncertainties, moral hazards and large expenditures involved, it is tempting to construct elaborate 'rational' decision-making procedures. These tend to emphasise process rather than outcomes and it is not clear that they produce better decisions. Excessive regulations can cause more problems than they solve and those involved in procurement regularly complain that they are 'drowning in process', as Bill Kincaid (2008) reports. The best projects seem marked by unified authority, sharp trade-offs and flexibility, characteristics that formal processes do not provide. Projects are easier if there is a single objective. This may be a performance goal, as with the Manhattan Project to build the atomic bomb; a time goal, as with UORs; or a cost goal, where price is treated as an independent variable and specified in advance. The problem with most projects is that they have multiple goals, which have to be traded-off.

Economic problems

Risk aversion is important, because of the size of the project and the consequences of failure. There are military, political and financial risks. The public sector may be risk averse because of the political fall-out from failures. The firm may be risk averse because the project is large relative to the firm. Rolls Royce went bankrupt with the RB211 fixed-price civil engine project and had to be nationalised in 1971. Suppose firms are risk averse and eventual cost is subject to uncertainty about technology. The MoD, pooling over a number of projects is better able to absorb this risk, so should be risk neutral, acting as an insurer. Insuring the producer with a cost-plus contract reduces the risk premium that MoD has to pay and uninsured, fixed-price, contracts may not be credible if enforcement would drive the firm into bankruptcy leaving MoD without the project. Bailing out firms, like bailing out banks in a financial crisis, is likely to be optimal for MoD and this will be anticipated by firms making the bids, creating moral hazard. Whatever the contract says renegotiation cannot be credibly precluded. Given that the uncertainty on military contracts is large, so is the risk premium that suppliers have to build into fixed-price bids.

Moral hazard problems arise because costs and quality are determined by the effort of the seller, which the buyer cannot monitor. Greater insurance, by cost-plus contracts, gives the seller less incentive to reduce costs. Under fixed-price contracts, the firm has incentives to minimise costs. However, if quality cannot be easily monitored fixed price gives it incentives to economise on quality. Changes to the contract can be very expensive on fixed-price project, because the firm can use the leverage from the existing contract. Corruption and bribery also raise issues of moral hazard.

Adverse selection arises under competitive bidding because the buyer cannot discover information private to the selling firm and may select the wrong supplier. The firm that makes the lowest bid may not be the lowest cost producer, but merely the firm that is most ignorant of the difficulties involved and thus subject to the winners curse. With large number of competitors, bidders should build a premium into their bids to protect them from the winners curse. If costs are higher than the winning firm's bid, this would just be a transfer from firm to buyer. But a large transfer may not be credible and the buyer may have to bail out the firm to get the project completed. Since firms know this, they have incentives to bid low to get the buyer to commit to the project, knowing that once committed the buyer will have to complete. Because of the conspiracy of optimism, the buyer may be happy to collude in this, to get the project onto the budget. Selling to the government may open up other markets or act as a signal of the quality of the product. Thus it may be worth a firm under-pricing to the government to get the contract, if it can exploit the subsequent monopoly elsewhere, for instance in exports. Firms may bid low on early stages to get the contract, then use learning curves and acquired tacit knowledge to establish a monopoly position, which they can exploit later. US defence firms tend to bid low on development and make their money on production.

Monopoly is common and while a single supplier can have great power this power is reduced if the monopolist is facing a single buyer, a monopsonist, as is usual in the defence market. The relative bargaining strength of monopolist and monopsonist will depend on factors such as the cost to each of not coming to an agreement. Information rents can be extracted under fixed-price contracts by monopolists with private information about costs who can bid high and still get the contract. With cost-plus the monopolist has to reveal their costs. Even where there is not a global monopoly, a single national supplier may gain monopoly power from the political unacceptability of buying abroad.

Incomplete contracts and renegotiation are common because not every contingency can be specified in the original contract and changes in technology and buyer needs mean the contract may have to be rewritten. Cost-plus contracts can accommodate design changes easily; renegotiating fixed-price contracts gives the firm great bargaining power, since it has the option of insisting on the original contract. Failure by the firm to meet a fixed-price contract also prompts renegotiation. In 1997 the UK MoD signed contracts with GEC-Marconi to build a set of Astute class, hunter-killer submarines in the Barrow shipyards for delivery in 2005 on a fixed-price contract. GEC was taken over by BAE and there were big cost overruns on the submarines. In 2003 BAE and MoD had to renegotiate the contract and BAE had to write down its profits by £750 million because of the penalty. BAE said that it would never accept fixed-price contracts again. In 2008 the first of the class was still running late relative to the renegotiated schedule and was planned to enter service in 2009. The budget increased from an initial £2.58 billion to an estimated £3.79 billion in 2008. EADS faces similar issues with the A400M military transport aircraft that it is producing for Germany, France and the UK, under a fixed-price contract. It has incurred about €2 billion in extra development costs primarily because of problems with the propulsion system and the in-service date is delayed. Media reports in 2008 indicate that EADS hopes to be able to renegotiate the contract.

Technology

Technology can be crucial in combat. The Maxim gun, which could fire at 600 rounds per minute, was a major improvement on the earlier hand-cranked multi-barrelled Gatling gun. In the battle of Omdurman in Sudan in 1898, the British killed 10,000 Dervishes for the loss of 48 of their troops. The machine gun also transformed warfare in World War I, when advancing troops were mown down. In many cases the technology is introduced before armies know how to use it and there is a long period of painful learning and military reorganisation before the technology is successfully integrated into military doctrine. This was the case with self-loading rifles, tanks and nuclear weapons. Thus there was always a substantial evolution in any revolution in military technology. In the 1990s, it was proposed that there was a new 'revolution in military affairs' which would follow from the networking of sensors, command, control, communication and weapons into an integrated system. As yet, the reality of 21st warfare has not conformed to that model.

Many issues in the technology literature are common to both military and civilian applications. It is often useful to distinguish invention, the idea; innovation, turning the idea into a useful application; and diffusion, the spread of the technology. In 1620 Francis Bacon identified the three innovations that created the modern world: gunpowder, ocean navigation and printing. All were Chinese inventions; the magnetic compass in the case of ocean navigation. But it was in Europe that the process of innovation, diffusion and adaptation made each of them disruptive technologies that transformed society. Evolutionary innovations continue an established technological trajectory; disruptive innovations change how a technology is organised and applied. Some military technologies concentrate power, like the expensive armour and horses required by the mediaeval knight; others disperse power, like relatively cheap guns that can be used by anyone. Innovations can be in the product, like a new type of tank; or in the process, like a new way of producing armour; or in organisation, like Blitzkrieg, a new way of combining technologies. Military technologies are sometimes divided into offensive or defensive, but this does not seem a useful distinction. Attack is often the best form of defence and certain defensive technologies, like castles and anti-ballistic missiles (ABM), are perceived as offensive. The 1972 ABM treaty restricting their use, from which the US withdrew in 2002, was seen as reducing the incentives to strike first.

Given a fixed budget, there is a choice between the quality and quantity of weapons: a few, technologically advanced, highly capable, units; or many, less capable, units. The balance between quality and quantity will be chosen to maximise force effectiveness, which depends both on the number of units and the capability of each. This quantity–quality balance is often described by Lanchester Laws, after Frederick Lanchester who in 1916 developed mathematical models of the relative power of opposing forces. The choice of the number of units also has implications for the number of armed forces required to operate and maintain them. It may be possible to maintain a Hi-Low mix as the US did by combining small numbers of the expensive F15 aircraft with large numbers of the cheaper F16. The F16 being a relatively cheap aircraft was also very successful in export markets and over 4000 have been produced. There may also be choices between investing in new systems and upgrading old systems. Upgrading, by technology insertion, may be attractive when military effectiveness depends not on the characteristics of the platform – aircraft, ship or tank – but on what it carries – sensors, weapons or electronics – which can be upgraded within the old platform.

Chapter 4 discussed the vicious circles that tend to drive up weapons systems prices: the technological arms race in relative performance against an opponent; the reduced numbers of units in each generation; and the longer gaps between generations. Technology escalation differs over time and weapons. Military technology remained largely stagnant from about 1700 to about 1850 before starting to escalate again. Assault rifles have remained very similar since the AK47 was developed in 1945. Innovations, such as night vision equipment, have increased the effectiveness of the rifles, but the AK47 remains the market leader. Despite the lack of a catchy name or multinational marketing, the AK47 has become an iconic brand; it appears on the Mozambique national flag. Mikhail Kalashnikov with Elena Joly (2006) provides a personal account of the development of the rifle, which was designed to be simple – even child soldiers can use it – reliable and easy to repair. It is widely produced, partly because the Soviets did not patent it, though the quality varies between producers. The Taliban are said to pay more for an Iranian AK47 than a Pakistani one. Its wide use makes it familiar, reducing training costs, and makes ammunition abundant. Availability of ammunition is often more of a constraint than availability of weapons. Wide use also creates barriers to entry, making it difficult for competing brands to establish themselves. Quality has many dimensions and the AK47 does have disadvantages relative to competitors, including low range and accuracy and a lack of user safety features.

Phillip Killicoat (2007) analyses the market for assault rifles. Small arms are estimated to be responsible for between 200,000 and 400,000 deaths a year, between 10 and 25 per cent of these occurring in conflict settings. Of the approximately 500 million firearms available worldwide, approximately 100 million belong to the Kalashnikov family, three quarters of which are AK47s. He has 335 observations, from 117 countries, on AK47 prices, over the period 1986–2005. The average price is in the range \$450–\$550, with prices in Africa being about \$200 lower and prices in Western Europe being about \$400 higher. He attributes the low African prices to porous borders that allow more trade and more efficient markets; though in this context, many would see an efficient market as a bad thing. A legacy of conflict in the country and higher military spending by neighbouring countries both seem to increase available supply and reduce the price of AK47s. A number of other possible determinants of price do not seem important. The collapse of the Soviet Union, which was thought to have increased supply, does not seem to have reduced prices.

There are two dimensions to the quantity–quality trade-off; in design and in production. Arms manufacturers get paid for the numbers produced. To meet their production targets at minimum cost, they have incentives to take short cuts that compromise the quality of their products. Military buyers try to prevent this by monitoring the quality of the products, rejecting those that do not meet specified standards. Quality has two aspects: how the product performs in battle and how it meets the technical criteria specified in the contract. It is only the latter that can be monitored and used as a basis for rejection, though the military hope that the technical criteria will be related to battle performance. During war the choice is harder: do the military accept sub-standard weapons or reject them, getting fewer or no weapons?

Even autocratic command economies, where draconian penalties can be imposed for non-compliance, face this dilemma. Using recently released files, Markevich and Harrison (2006) examine how the Soviet Union, under Stalin, responded to this choice. Soviet manufacturers of particular types of weapons were largely monopolists. Their prime objective was to meet the production quotas specified in the plan and had strong incentives to cut quality to meet quotas. The military responded by putting military agents, often quite senior officers, in the factories. These agents had the power to accept or reject the weapons produced. But, since the military needed weapons, particularly once the war started, the agents could not reject everything that was sub-standard or they would get no weapons at all. The compromise that resulted was that a lot of low quality output was produced and sent into service; but the danger of rejection resulted in average quality being higher than it would have been otherwise and higher than the quality of products supplied to civilian buyers. Interestingly, the authors find no evidence that the arms producers bribed military agents to accept sub-standard product. As the authors point out, no evidence of bribery is not evidence of no bribery; the files dealing with bribery may not have been released. However, it is plausible that bribery was uncommon; being a military agent was an attractive job, certainly relative to serving on the front, and the risk of losing it could have outweighed the benefit of the bribe.

The value to civilian society of spin-offs from military technology is discussed in Chapter 8; here the issue is how the military gets the technology it needs. Increasingly, the military gets the technology from commercial sources, spin-in. This COTS procurement can cause problems because of the difference between military and commercial time-scales. An average military procurement takes 7 years; so by the time the weapon system enters service, not only are the electronic components in it obsolescent, they are often no longer even being produced. Since military systems may be in service for 30 years or more, obtaining spares and replacements can be difficult. The US DoD has established a facility to produce obsolete electronic chips, no longer in commercial production but still in military use.

Some have seen a technological imperative which drives the elaboration of weapons along a particular trajectory. The interactions seem more complex. A detailed account of the interactions in the development of guidance systems for submarine-launched ballistic-missiles is described in *Inventing Accuracy* (MacKenzie, 1990). The driving force here was inter-service rivalry: the navy wanted their own nuclear delivery systems. Submarine-based missiles had many advantages, such as being less vulnerable to first strike attack, but their main disadvantage was lack of accuracy. This arose because of the difficulty of pinpointing the position from which the submarine fired its missiles. The problem was solved by breaking from the established technological trajectory of guidance systems and introducing the quite different stellar guidance methods. Near the top of its trajectory a little window would open and the missile would use the stars to check its position. This was also culturally more acceptable to the navy, where there was a tradition of using starts to establish position, than it was to the more traditional guidance community.

Guidance has been transformed by the Global Positioning System (GPS), a military satellite-based system. This has enabled 'dumb' bombs to be transformed into 'smart' or precision-guided weapons. During the 1991 Gulf War, 9 per cent of the ordnance dropped by the US was smart. In Kosovo in 1999, the figure had risen to 29 per cent, though cloud cover hindered employment of laser-guided munitions. In the invasion of Afghanistan in 2001, between 60 and 70 per cent were smart, a large proportion of which were dumb bombs with strap-on guidance kits. In the 2003 invasion of Iraq, over 90 per cent were smart. The two main strap-on kits (the GPS-guided joint direct attack munition (JDAM) and the wind corrected munition dispensers (WCMD)) were cheap in military terms because they used more commercial development programmes and components. It was estimated that under a traditional acquisition programme each JDAM would cost $68,000. A mandated maximum price was used and the final cost was about $18,000, though with volume, competition and dual sourcing this fell to about $12,000.

Since there were a large number of dumb bombs to be fitted with guidance kits, these could be produced in volume.

Innovation involves integrating technology into culture and this can be difficult. The problems with replacing cavalry by tanks are an example, but then tanks themselves became cultural symbols. Tanks are usually evaluated on three performance characteristics: protection, firepower and manoeuvrability. In a US competition for new tank designs during the Cold War, the US Defence Advanced Research Projects Agency (DARPA) entered a dune buggy fitted with a missile. On the specified performance criteria it won. It had high protection because it was small and not easily visible by sight or radar; the missile gave it effective firepower against tanks; and it was fast and manoeuvrable. But despite winning the competition on the specified performance criteria, it was not adopted by the army, because it was not a tank; though it was used by special forces. The army's instinctive preference, irrespective of the specified performance criteria, was for something that looked like a tank: a powerful macho machine with lots of armour and a big gun. While this preference may be criticised, the performance criteria did reflect a specific scenario: tank-on-tank battles in fairly open country. The lack of armour would make the dune buggy little use in urban warfare against concealed insurgents using IED, where a traditional tank has advantages. Preferences about technologies can matter and unfashionable technologies can have difficulty in being accepted without powerful product champions. An example of an aircraft that met resistance is the A10 Thunderbolt II. US experience in Vietnam showed the limitations of both fast jets and helicopters in providing close air support to infantry. The solution was a slow, heavily armoured, aircraft designed for endurance and survivability. Although very popular with ground troops, initially it was not welcomed by the US air force. Their view, that a slow ugly jet was not the sort of weapon they wished to be seen flying in, is reflected in its usual name: the Warthog or Hog.

6
Force Acquisition II, Supply: Merchants of Death?

Arms can be developed and produced domestically; developed and produced collaboratively with other countries; produced domestically under license from the foreign firm or government that developed them; or by importing a finished weapon that was developed and produced elsewhere. Importing tends to be the cheapest, domestic development and production the most expensive. Because they are concerned with security of supply, governments foster a defence industrial base (DIB), a domestic arms industry. Governments fear that foreign producers may not be willing to re-supply in time of conflict or may charge high prices for spares and munitions once the importer is committed to the system. Protected by a preference for domestic supply, the national arms industry can become a political actor in its own right, a military industrial complex (MIC). Despite the preference for self-sufficiency, the vast cost of domestic development and production of major weapons systems means that countries often have no choice but to import, so there has developed a large trade in arms. International law and the UN charter give states rights to self defence and thus the right to import arms for their defence. This right means that there is nothing inherently unethical or immoral in the arms trade itself. Nonetheless, the arms trade does have an unsavoury reputation, hence the widespread use of the term 'merchants of death'. Because arms sales are a politically sensitive component of international trade, with implications for security, economics and technology transfer, they are subject to regulation by national governments and intergovernmental organisations. Arms sales, whether domestic or international, are always both economic and political.

The arms industry: DIB or MIC?

Maintenance of a DIB that can supply current, future and emergency military requirements is a central objective of any defence ministry. In the US, the Deputy Under Secretary of Defense (Industrial Policy) makes judgements on the number of suppliers needed in particular areas. The policy instruments available include acquisition strategy; structuring procurement competitions to determine the number of players; funding research and development (R&D) to encourage innovation and entrants; regulating mergers; allocating industrial resources; controlling arms exports; and regulating investment by foreign firms. The UK Defence Industrial Strategy of December 2005 carefully considered 'which industrial capabilities we need to retain in the UK to ensure that we can continue to operate our equipment in the way we choose to maintain appropriate sovereignty and thereby protect our national security'. In other countries, such as France, state ownership of arms firms extends the instruments available. These powerful levers give the defence ministry effective power over the number of firms in the domestic industry. In 1993 a US merger wave was stimulated by the 'last supper' when the Pentagon Deputy Secretary Perry told a dinner of defence industry executives that they were expected to start merging. It ended when the Pentagon decided that it had gone far enough and blocked the merger of Lockheed Martin with Northrop Grumman in early 1997. The merger wave was not confined to the US. Surveys of the arms industry can be found in Brauer (2007), who emphasises developing countries, and Hartley (2007), who emphasises industrial countries.

The image of a national arms industry can be misleading, since it is increasingly internationalised. As yet, the arms industry is not as concentrated or dominated by multinationals as comparable high-technology industries. For instance, the large civil aircraft market is dominated by two companies, Boeing and Airbus, while the smaller civil aircraft market is dominated by two different companies, Bombardier and Embraer. The lack of concentration in the hands of multinational companies largely reflects the desire of governments to protect their national champions for strategic reasons, particularly security of supply. However, the arms industry is not completely immune to more general trends in both concentration and internationalisation. BAE Systems, once called British Aerospace, may sound British but over half its 2008 revenues came from abroad; it sells more to the US DoD than it does to the UK MoD. Rolls Royce's defence division got 45 per cent of its

2008 revenue from the US and 20 per cent from the UK; the remaining third came from the rest of the world. European Aeronautic Defence and Space Company (EADS) is explicitly multinational, a merger of French, German, Spanish and, initially, British interests with headquarters in the Netherlands. Airbus, produced by EADS, competes with Boeing in large civil airliners and EADS is the second largest European arms company after BAE. The US firms are equally internationalised; Boeing maintains a large range of partners and overseas operations. Equipment tends to be identified with a country, but an F16 aircraft, apparently of US origin, will contain components from all over the world and may have been assembled in Taiwan, Turkey or Korea.

From a commercial point of view the arms industry is not a particularly attractive market for large, legitimate commercial firms and their share prices and profits tend to reflect this, being very volatile. The eventful history of BAE since privatisation, where bankruptcy loomed on more than one occasion, is an example. The large firms that produce major weapons systems sold legitimately are located in relatively few countries. There is a large, less legitimate, market for small arms and light weapons (SALW). Production for this market is dispersed over many more countries and there is a rather different industrial structure. The large producers depend on purchases by their own government and changes in government policies and personnel can have an adverse impact on sales. The export market is made highly competitive by the excess capacity that results from government's attempts to maintain national DIBs. Wars and armaments booms boost demand and profits, but survival in the slumps can be difficult. The Brazilian arms industry profited from the Iran–Iraq war, but then collapsed, though one of its companies, Embraer, subsequently managed to establish a dominant position in regional passenger aircraft. Even when there are potential export markets, government regulation may stop companies meeting the demand through arms embargoes and controls. Selling arms requires a range of specialist skills, particularly the ability to influence the buying government, which may require bribes and other corrupt tactics. While the use of such tactics is normal in this market, it can have adverse effects on the reputation of the companies with an impact on other activities. BAE suffered such reputation effects over the alleged bribery associated with the Al Yamamah sales to Saudi Arabia. Since the contract was between the UK and Saudi governments and both governments seem to have been aware of the payments, it is not clear that the company, as distinct from the governments concerned, was responsible for the corruption. The corruption associated with the large

South African arms deal has played a major role in the politics of that country.

Bidding for arms export contracts can be an expensive business: setting up subsidiaries in the buying country, demonstrating the technology, providing specialist advice and entering competitions. This investment is wasted if the contract is not obtained. Contracts are complicated, involving not merely the supply of the weapons, but training, spares and munitions, which can be more profitable than the main sale. In 2008, the value of the initial order of 72 UK Typhoons by Saudi Arabia was put at £4.3 billion; armaments and weapons systems added £5 billion, and maintenance training and support added another £10 billion. This sale required US approval because the aircraft contained US technology. The sales are often financed through export credits, provided by the country of the supplying firm. The contracts may also involve offsets, promises by the supplier to locate production in the buying country, and counter-trade, payment in kind or barter. There are large technological risks and it can be difficult to forecast product performance, in particular how well the weapon will work in combat. Technological spin-offs from military development to commercial products does not seem to be an important source of competitive advantage, though there are exceptions. Conversion from military production to civilian production is often hazardous since different skills are required in the two markets. For instance, technological advance is given much greater weight than cost-minimisation in military markets, in contrast to civilian markets.

SIPRI (2007) lists the top 100 arms companies (outside China, for which there is little data). Of these 40 were American accounting for 63 per cent of total sales, 32 were Western European accounting for 29 per cent of total sales. The top five, each with arms sales of between $20–30 billion accounted for 47 per cent of the market. All the top five, except BAE Systems at number 4, were from the US. There has been a rapid increase in the concentration of the arms industry since the end of the Cold War. In the 1990 SIPRI list, the five largest firms accounted for 22 per cent of the global market; by 2006 the five largest firms accounted for 47 per cent of the market. However, this is still quite a low degree of concentration relative to other high-technology markets. It seems likely that major weapons systems would be a very concentrated market, like civil airliners or pharmaceuticals, had not national governments inhibited the growth of multinational firms to protect their DIB. Until the 1970s government procurement rules in many countries restricted the purchase of telecommunications equipment from foreign suppliers and determined the number of firms. Easing of procurement rules led to very rapid concentration in the world telecommunications industry, which is what we might expect to happen if governments ceased to care about market structure in the arms industry.

Determining the appropriate DIB is difficult. The ministry must decide the number of different types of systems required and the quality and quantity of each; the extent to which it can trust allies to collaborate in production or to provide imports, in particular whether they would supply in conflict; the potential export market for the systems; the degree to which exports are taxed or subsidised; and the security consequences of those exports. All these judgements have to be made subject to a budget constraint, the amount they can afford. In fact for most countries, their budget constraint is such that they cannot afford the massive R&D required to develop and produce major weapons systems. There are a few large producer countries and the remainder import all their major weapons systems. Even the largest producer, the US, has to import some systems. For instance, the US has used UK short/vertical take-off and landing technology in the AV8B, a Harrier derivative used by the Marines, and in JSF. The UK had a classified list of four types of system for which it had to maintain domestic capability. In a reported version of the list, the first three, nuclear weapons, cryptography and chemical and biological systems, are natural candidates; these are systems where it was highly unlikely that it could rely on its allies; the fourth, warships, seemed more a matter of heritage. From 2005 the UK had a more explicit, though equally heritage sensitive, defence industrial strategy.

Producer governments regulate arms exports and choose domestic procurement prices. There has been a long, though rather unhappy, tradition of collaboration in arms production in Europe, but it is also becoming more common in the US. The F35 Joint Strike Fighter (JSF) involves collaboration with a number of other countries, including the UK which intends to put the short take-off version on its planned aircraft carriers. Developing the aircraft required collaboration, not only with other countries, but between the US air force, navy and marines which was also problematic. The estimated price of JSF has doubled and there have been disputes about the US reluctance to share crucial technical information that the UK regards as essential for the effective operation of the aircraft. The UK has contingency plans to acquire an alternative aircraft for the carriers should the collaboration not work.

Throughout this book two visions of the state exist in uneasy conjunction. One is of the state as a rational actor that can make decisions about issues such as the maintenance of a DIB. The other is of the state as an arena for conflict among competing interests subject to standard operating procedures. In defence one of these interests can be an alliance of the military, the arms industries and members of the legislature, to promote defence spending. This alliance was labelled the military industrial complex (MIC) by Dwight D. Eisenhower, the Republican US President (1953–1961) and Supreme Commander of Allied Forces in Europe during World War II. In his farewell speech to the nation in 1961 he warned the US to guard against the acquisition of influence, whether sought or unsought, by the MIC. Although it has since gained left-wing associations, he had a very conservative concern: the danger that coalitions of vested interests could exploit the special nature of decision making about military matters to shape choices against peaceful goals and national security interests in order to extract funds for their own purposes (unproductive rent-seeking). These coalitions could include members of the armed services, of the civilian defence bureaucracy, of the legislature, of the arms manufacturers and their workers. These are the transmission mechanism by which perceptions of the threat and the economic opportunity costs are translated into particular budgets or systems. These operate not just nationally but internationally and their power varies.

The arms trade

It is common to classify military products into weapons of mass destruction (WMD) (nuclear, biological and chemical); major weapons systems (such as tanks, fighter aircraft and warships); SALW; services (those provided by private military companies in Iraq and elsewhere have become increasingly important); and dual-use systems, which have both a civilian and military function. Much military technology is dual use, including the nuclear, biological and chemical technologies and this poses problems of classification. Definitional difficulties and secrecy make measuring the trade difficult, particularly for small arms. Over the period 2000–2004, SIPRI estimates that exports of major weapons systems were around $20 billion a year, in 1990 prices, with the US and Russia accounting for around half the exports. Using a somewhat different definition and measurement procedure, the US Congressional Research Service estimated 2004 agreements to export arms at $37 billion, in 2004 prices, and deliveries at $34 billion, with about 60 per cent going to developing countries: China, India and Egypt being large importers. China is also a significant exporter.

In economic terms, an arms trade of about $40 billion is not large, but it has significant political implications. Trade is a small proportion of total military expenditure of about $1200 billion, a much smaller share of demand than for most products. The world trade in arms has also grown more slowly than world trade in other goods. The factors determining the demand for arms imports are very similar to those determining military expenditure, ability to pay and perceived threat, though shaped by domestic arms production capability. As with military expenditure, richer countries can afford more. Arms importers are often oil exporters: Venezuela is estimated to have spent $4 billion on arms imports, mainly from Russia, over the period 2005–2007. Since ability to pay matters, price also matters, and even quite rich countries can be priced out of the market for major weapons systems. Factors that raise prices, such as monopoly, reduce demand; factors that reduce prices, such as subsidies, increase demand. As with military expenditure, the perceived threats, as interpreted by domestic interests, matter. The former Soviet republics in the Caucasus, including Georgia, which faced both internal and external threats, were big arms importers in the years up to 2008. As income and military expenditures grow there is a non-linear relationship with arms imports. Small poor countries cannot afford to import major weapons systems and the conflicts they are involved in tend not to require major weapons systems. As countries get larger in economic and military terms their arms imports at first increase; but then as they develop their own arms industries, imports decline replaced by domestic substitutes. Smith and Tasiran (2005) provide a quantitative analysis of the demand for arms imports and some evidence that price matters, though the limitations of the data mean that the conclusion must be tentative. Price is always relative to quality, but quality can have many dimensions from quantitative performance to how good it looks in annual parades. Where performance in combat matters, weapons that have shown their capability in battle tend to command a premium price.

The UN introduced a register of conventional arms transfers in 1992, but not all countries report fully and it covers quantities not prices. Figures on the arms trade may refer to orders, quantity of arms delivered or payments. These differ in timing; and orders may be cancelled or deliveries not paid for; so the three measures can differ substantially. Figures may measure the quantity of arms transferred or the value, which can differ because some transfers are heavily subsidised while others generate high rates of profit. SIPRI measures the quantity of arms transferred using trend indicator values which may not correspond to payments. In the early 1990s a large part of the East German navy was transferred almost free to Indonesia; this appears as a large quantity transferred but a small payment. The standard US figures measure the value of the payments associated with the transfer.

Because ownership of more advanced weapons gives an advantage to potential adversaries, restriction on their transfer has been common: in the 8th century Charlemagne declared the death penalty for Frankish merchants selling swords to Vikings. Organised arms production on a large scale, such as naval dockyards and royal arsenals, has a long history; but the modern arms industry dates from the mid-19th century and from the beginning it was global. Alfred Nobel's dynamite and cordite, both dual-use systems, were produced in subsidiaries around the world. Technological developments in metals production in the second half of the 19th century were rapidly applied to arms by Krupp in Germany and Armstrong and Vickers in Britain, all of whom relied heavily on foreign sales. Sir Hiram Maxim, an American operating in Europe, sold his guns all over the world. By the beginning of the 20th century there was a dense multinational network of interlinked arms firms and specialised arms merchants, who emulated Krupp, Armstrong and Maxim. George Bernard Shaw's play of 1905, *Major Barbara*, addresses the issues of international arms manufacture as perceived in the early 20th century. Anthony Sampson (1991) provides an account of the history of the arms trade.

Before World War I, the thriving international arms trade was largely unregulated, but subsequently many blamed these 'merchants of death' for the war itself. In the inter-war period there were a series of intergovernmental initiatives to restrain the arms trade and individual countries began to pass laws regulating arms exports. These were of limited effectiveness. During World War II there were vast arms transfers particularly from the US to the UK, initially under lend-lease, and from the US to the Soviet Union. After World War II, the arms trade was shaped by the Cold War, in three dimensions. Each side tried to prevent military technology flowing to the other. In the West this was organised by the coordinating committee for multilateral export controls (COCOM) which tried to restrict the transfer of arms and dual-use technologies to communist countries. Each side wanted to ensure that its allies were well armed, because this improved the quality of defence. Each side hoped that by providing arms to non-aligned countries they could be aligned a little more closely. The driving forces at this stage of the development of the market were largely political and transfers were often heavily subsidised.

In the later 20th century, commercial factors became more important. Selling nations hoped to use arms exports to maintain their DIB in the face of fluctuating domestic demand and spread the large fixed R&D costs of developing major weapons systems over more units. This was particularly a feature of French policy, where systems were designed with export markets in mind, rather than the needs of the domestic armed forces. Countries importing arms also hoped to acquire technology; agreements by the exporter to offset the arms sale by purchases from the importer were a common feature of contracts. Arms export contracts are complicated packages that include not just the weapons-systems themselves, but munitions, spares and training. They are often paid for by counter-trade, barter (the UK Al Yamamah arms export package to Saudi Arabia was paid for in oil); have associated offsets (such as the seller promising to set up production in the buyer country); and may be financed by soft loans from government-supported agencies like the UK Export Credit Guarantee Department. The US has a large Foreign Military Sales programme. The UK had the Defence Export Services Organisation to facilitate sales, and in 2008 its functions were transferred to the Defence and Security Organisation in the UK Trade and Investment department. Evidence on the financial details of arms contracts is scarce. The contract is usually part of a long-term relationship since the weapons will need munitions, spares and upgrades in the future. A crucial part of the relationship will be whether the exporter is willing to continue supply in time of conflict.

Because the market is so competitive, the profitability of arms sales is questionable. The companies make money, they would not make the sales otherwise, but this may reflect subsidies by the supplier government. In 2003 the French government instructed arms suppliers not to offer products at prices below production cost in order to win contracts. The $3.4 billion 1993 order for 436 Leclerc tanks from the UAE resulted in a loss of $1.2 billion for France. In the UK there has been dispute about the costs and benefits of arms exports to the economy. A team of two MoD economists and two academic economists collaborated to examine this topic. Their conclusion, reported in Chalmers et al. (2002), was that the economic costs and benefits of arms exports were small and that export decisions must be based on non-economic criteria.

Because the US has the largest military R&D budget, its weapons tend to be the most technologically advanced. The large number produced, such as over 4000 F16s, gives them a cost advantage. However, the US also tends to impose extra-territorial restrictions on technology transfer and on the use or transfer of US-built equipment. Thus other suppliers may appear more attractive to importers who fear political and technological dependence on the US. Foreign companies also try to ensure that they do not include US components in their military systems to avoid the complex US export control regulations.

Arms exports are almost universally regulated by national governments on the basis of certain criteria. The economic issues are reviewed in Garcia-Alonso and Smith (2006). A typical set of criteria are given in the 1991 guidelines agreed by the five permanent members of the UN Security Council. These indicate that restrictions on exports are required where the transfer would be likely to prolong or aggravate an existing armed conflict; increase tension in a region or contribute to instability; introduce destabilising military capabilities; contravene embargoes or other relevant internationally agreed restraints; be used other than for the legitimate defence and security needs of the recipient state; support or encourage international terrorism; be used to interfere with the internal affairs of sovereign states; or seriously undermine the recipient states economy. Exports may also be restricted if the transfer has an adverse effect on national security of the exporter or other countries; facilitates internal repression or breaches of human rights; or encourages the proliferation of weapons of mass destruction. These criteria are quite vague and involve subjective judgements. For instance, the European Union (EU) imposed an arms embargo restricting deliveries to China after the 1989 Tiananmen Square massacre. During 2003–2004 there was a substantial dispute among EU members about whether the embargo should be lifted. Those in favour of lifting it argued that it would help to engage China in dialogue, those against argued that China had not shown sufficient improvements in human rights. In any event, when the embargo was imposed no list of items covered by the term 'arms' had been agreed. Deciding what was covered by the embargo was left to individual EU states, who differed in their interpretation. In addition to national regulation there are various informal multilateral transfer control regimes by supplier countries. These include the Nuclear Suppliers Group, the Australia Group (chemical weapons), the Missile Technology Control Regime, the Wassenaar Arrangement (conventional weapons) and the EU Code of Conduct on arms transfers. There are also more formal agreements like the Treaty on the Non-Proliferation of Nuclear Weapons.

Controls over arms transfers may have unintended consequences. States subject to embargo or control, or who fear that they may be subject to embargo in the future, may develop their own arms industry to produce the weapons that they cannot import. Apartheid South Africa developed its own arms industry in response to embargo and the French embargo increased the Israeli desire for domestic self sufficiency. States subject to embargo may also develop weapons of mass destruction, again Israel and South Africa are examples. As in any industry, the high prices and restricted supply produced by an embargo encourages new entrants. States that are tightly coupled into the international community may be deterred by the reputational cost of illegitimate transfers. But where the international community has little leverage over a state, it may become a major source of illegitimate supply as did North Korea which became a major source of missiles. Embargoes invariably prompt the development of embargo-busting networks which add to the large illicit and poorly documented trade in SALW. There is also an international market for military scientists, particularly those with nuclear expertise. The transnational dimensions of arms sales, and of arms traffic are likely to remain a matter of continuing concern.

7
Military Capability: How to Win?

Military forces are acquired to provide military capability, the ability to fight and prevail in combat against actual or potential opponents. This capability may be used to attack, defend, deter or maintain peace. The military capability provided by the forces depends on how they are used and what they are used for. How the forces are used involves all the military skills of leadership, strategy, tactics, training, logistics, morale and infrastructure. The elements of the infrastructure are often grouped under the heading C4ISTAR: command, control, communications, computers, intelligence, surveillance, target acquisition and reconnaissance. What the forces are used for involves the aims of the operation; military forces are used for a very wide range of different purposes and the different purposes have different criteria for success. The how and what interact. Forces organised and trained for war-fighting may be counter-productive when used for peacekeeping, their heavy-handed interventions provoking more conflict. The reverse can be true: a force trained and equipped for peacekeeping, with narrow rules of engagement, may not be able to deliver the required robust response to stop a conflict escalating. Casualty rates that are thought acceptable for one purpose may be unacceptable for another.

The economic perspective leads to a focus on the material factors such as budgets and forces. But the non-material factors, what Carl von Clausewitz called the moral factors, are usually more important. We will look at how the forces are employed, motivated and supplied. Then we will look at the use of military capability for a very specific security objective, peacekeeping.

Force employment

Military capability will be treated as the probability of achieving military objectives in particular sorts of combat. The emphasis on objectives is important. Members of the military in Germany in 1918, France in Algeria in 1958 and the US in Vietnam in 1968 claimed that they had won a military victory but suffered a political defeat. This shows a misunderstanding of the instrumental functions of war, to achieve particular objectives. The emphasis on probability is also important. In peacetime, military capability is unknowable and overestimation of their military capability by both sides can be a cause of war. Sometimes capability is used to describe the ability to do certain things: keep an air defence system at full readiness, transport a battalion between specified points in a certain time. But these are better regarded as aspects of force structure; actual capability is performance in combat. These overlap, maintaining air superiority is a mixture of the ability to do things and combat performance. Much of the economic analysis uses a conflict success function in which the probability of winning is a function of the numbers and quality of forces on each side. This is useful in certain circumstances but does not seem to capture important aspects.

Voltaire commented that 'God is on the side of the big battalions'. If so, God's help does not always seem to have been an asset: it is very often the case that the small battalions win, particularly when those smaller forces fight in ways that surprised the big battalions, so called asymmetric warfare. The US withdrew from Lebanon in 1983 after a suicide bomber killed 241 troops and in October 2000 two suicide-bombers, using a small boat in Aden harbour, incapacitated the US navy destroyer USS Cole, killing 17 sailors. Ivan Arreguin-Toft (2005) examines 200 wars between 1800 and 2003 and estimates that the weaker side won 57 times. As with all quantitative work, one can argue over what counts as a war; what counts as being weaker (in terms of quantity or quality); or what counts as winning (a military victory may be a political defeat). However, it does appear that while strength helps, it is not enough. He argues that when the weaker side follows the same approach to fighting as the stronger side, they are likely to lose. However, when they adopt an opposite approach, which does not allow the stronger side to use his forces effectively, they can win. History is full of examples of powerful armies humbled. The Roman army of Crassus was defeated by Parthian horse archers in 55 BC, who did not allow the Romans to get close enough to exhibit their military superiority in close quarter battle. At Isandlwanda in 1879, Zulus were able to defeat a British column, killing over a thousand soldiers, including 850 Europeans. The defeat, which was partly the result of British failures in command and logistics, was the prelude to the British defence of Rorke's drift, the subject of the film *Zulu*.

The transformation of forces to capabilities, the ability to win, depends on all the standard military virtues such as training, logistics, leadership, morale, tactics and strategy which determine force deployment. Luck also matters. The element of chance, the vagaries of weather and war, makes the transformation of forces to capabilities a very uncertain process. Benjamin Franklin noted that 'fortune favours the prepared mind' and luck may be a matter of having made the right preparation to take advantage of the opportunities of war; hence Napoleon's advice to hire lucky generals. Preparation requires plans, but no plan survives contact with the enemy. A good plan allows for various contingencies, exit strategies and fall-back positions and provides insurance, typically by maintaining adequate forces in reserve.

Good military leaders will also use surprise, deception and various tactics to outwit the enemy. The Mongols repeatedly used a very simple tactic, the feigned retreat, with great effect. A token force attacked the enemy, then seemingly beaten would retreat. The enemy would follow, often for a considerable distance, being drawn into a trap where the main forces could attack the flanks of the enemy, while the token force wheeled round and attacked from the front. Although simple, this tactic took considerable skill, training and co-ordination to implement. Even if aware of the tactic, the enemy commander rarely had sufficient control of his troops to stop them pursuing an enemy who seemed to be fleeing.

Tactics describes the way that individual military units are deployed, the manner in which they actually fight. Strategy is the way that the whole battle or war is fought, how all the forces are deployed in the theatre of conflict to achieve the military objectives. Some wars may involve many theatres. World War II involved the Western Front, initially the Germans against the French and British; the Eastern Front, the Germans against the Soviets; and the Pacific War, Japan against the US. The term 'grand strategy' is often used to describe the process of integrating strategies in different theatres with economic and diplomatic means. There is also an operational, or theatre, level between strategy and tactics. All these distinctions, while useful, can be vague: use of a tactical nuclear weapon would almost certainly be a strategic decision.

Over the years weapons technology has advanced and the destructiveness of weapons, such as artillery, has increased many fold, but casualties in battle have not increased correspondingly. Increased destructiveness of weapons is countered by changes in deployment. For instance, troops spread out and the lower density of dispersed troops means that fewer are within range of an artillery explosion. With changes in deployment, military organisation must also change. If soldiers were side by side in massed ranks they could not easily desert; if they were widely dispersed, skirmishing forward under cover, they could. Dispersed troops need to be motivated and trained quite differently from troops in massed ranks. With changes in the nature of war the ratio of civilian to military casualties also changes. Eric Hobsbawm (2007) notes

> The contrast between the First World War and the Second is dramatic: only 5 per cent of those who died in the former conflict were civilians; in the latter, that figure increased to 66 per cent. It is generally supposed that 80 to 90 per cent of those affected by war today are civilians.

However, earlier wars, like the Thirty Years War in Europe, also caused massive civilian casualties.

Dispersal is only one aspect of the adjustment. Stephen Biddle (2004, p. 3) describes how armies adjust to increased lethality.

> The modern system is a tightly interrelated complex of cover, concealment, dispersion, suppression, small-unit independent maneuver, and combined arms at the tactical level, and depth, reserves, and differential concentration at the operational level of war. Taken together, these techniques sharply reduce vulnerability to even twenty-first century weapons and sensors. Where fully implemented the modern system damps the effects of technological change and insulates its users from the full lethality of their opponents' weapons.

He points out that the modern system is difficult to master because it is complex and poses painful political and social trade-offs.

Morale

The old adage 'if it is not measured, it is not managed' is unfortunately often true. It is unfortunate both because the most important factors that need to be managed are often not measurable and because there is a temptation to try to manage by using measurable targets that relate to the real objectives only indirectly, if at all. Use of such quantitative targets, the body counts in Vietnam being an example, can distort the incentives of those in action and mislead the top decision makers. One of the most important characteristics that cannot be measured with any precision is morale. Morale is crucial to combat. Having confident, motivated, adaptable troops that are willing to continue fighting can make the difference between defeat and victory. Confidence comes from the troops' trust, sometimes misplaced, in their training, equipment and leaders. Motivation comes from their belief in what they are doing and enables them to risk their lives and take casualties in achieving their objectives. Adaptability comes from giving them responsibility and enabling them to flexibly respond to the vagaries of war. Although high morale can be recognised and there are various indicators, it cannot be directly measured because it covers so many dimensions. During the Cold War, Western analysis of the Soviet army indicated severe morale problems, such as bullying new conscripts and widespread alcoholism. However, historians pointed out that Russian soldiers had defeated Napoleon drunk; defeated Hitler drunk; and might well defeat NATO drunk. Napoleon said that in war three quarters of what matters is morale, the relative strength of troops only matters one quarter. But he did not indicate how to calculate the respective proportions.

There is clearly an economic dimension to morale – unpaid, poorly fed troops are likely to be less effective – but other dimensions are likely to be more important.

Morale is a complex mix, which involves leadership, training and all the factors that produce tribal loyalties and group cohesion: soldiers tend to fight for their buddies, not to let down their mates, rather than for their country. Motivating people to be willing to be killed, which is central to effective fighting, is more difficult than motivating them to kill. Leadership is fundamental, but difficult to characterise. An appraisal of a British officer, probably apocryphal, said of him, 'he is a born leader, his men would follow him anywhere; mainly out of curiosity about what he will do next'. Leaders need followers and military training emphasises the importance of knowing the members of the team and what they can do, looking after their interests and enhancing their skills.

Logistics

Most of the components of military capability, like strategy, leadership and morale, are ones in which economists have no special expertise. However, one crucial component has a large economic dimension since it involves balancing supply and demand by the constrained optimisation of resources. To be able to fight effectively you have to get your troops to the right place and keep them provided with the food, water, fuel and ammunition they need to carry out the plan. The ability to do this, logistics, has determined many conflicts. There is a military saying: amateurs talk strategy, professionals talk logistics. Because it is less exciting than battles, logistics tends to get forgotten in military history. But many perplexing decisions can often be explained by logistics. The fact that a general retreats after a series of victories is more likely to be explained by a lack of supplies than a lack of nerve. *Supplying War* by Martin van Creveld (1977) is the classic account.

For much of history, more military were killed by disease, climate and malnutrition than enemy action. Often all that was required was to keep the opposing army engaged while disease killed them off. Supplying an army can mean facing mountains, mud, lack of roads and various other obstacles to supply. As you advanced, this gets more difficult because the lengthening supply lines are more vulnerable to attack, particularly by guerrilla enemies, and the suppliers have to carry their own supplies and protection. A mule that carried a 200-lb load of fodder, eating 12 lb a day, could go for about 16 days before starting to starve, without having delivered any useful supplies. Its effective range was 4 days out, delivering half its load, and eating the remaining quarter of its load on the way back. This range could be extended a little if you had enough mules to allow them to be eaten when they arrived at the front. The ratios are rather better with motorised vehicles or airlift. But modern transport can be almost as temperamental as mules, require a large team of specialists with spare parts to maintain them and cannot be eaten when they stop working.

With the industrialisation of war, the efficiency of transport and supply has increased; but the amount required to be supplied has tended to grow faster than the capacity of the supply lines, making logistics a continuing constraint. Modern weapons use ammunition at a very rapid rate, so troops can quickly exhaust their supplies. The capacity of the supply lines often depends on some critical point or bottleneck. The bottlenecks are often interfaces between modes of transport, where supplies are transferred from ship, rail or air to road for instance. Marc Levinson (2006, chapter 9) describes how the military build-up in Vietnam from 1965 was initially disrupted by the lack of either suitable ports, railways and highways to supply the US forces deployed there or a co-ordinated logistical system. The problem was eventually solved when the US military adopted containers, then a recent innovation, and constructed new container ports. The success of the 1991 Gulf War was as much a matter of logistics as of strategy and the general responsible for the logistics, Gus Pagonis, then went on to apply those skills to business.

Apart from, perhaps, the Mongols who carried everything with them and could live off the land, supplying war has always been a crucial factor. Even the Mongols needed to ensure that they had adequate grazing land for their animals and planned their campaigns to exploit available grasslands.

Peacekeeping

Military capability can be used not merely to make war but also to make peace and SIPRI estimates that there were 61 peacekeeping operations in 2007, with roughly 170,000 people involved, all but 20,000 military. About 40 per cent of the peacekeepers were located in Africa. There are two dimensions to peacekeeping, demand and supply: the situations that demand foreign intervention and the willingness to supply that intervention by other states. Peacekeeping missions are mainly sponsored by the UN, but are also conducted by individual countries, by NATO and by regional organisations, like as the Organisation for Security and Co-operation in Europe (OSCE), which had observers in Georgia, and the African Union, previously called the Organisation of African Unity. The top 20 contributors listed in Table 7.1 provided just under 70,000 troops to the UN. All except Italy, France and Spain, which are well down the list, are poor countries, for whom the payments for contributing troops to peacekeeping missions can be a useful source of revenue.

Although peacekeeping is not specifically mentioned in the UN Charter, a distinction is made between actions taken under Chapter Six of the Charter (Pacific Settlement of Disputes) and actions taken under Chapter Seven (Action with respect to threats to the peace, breaches of the peace, and acts of aggression). The latter, which involve the direct use

Table 7.1 UN Peacekeeping: Top 20 Contributors of Uniformed Personnel to UN Peacekeeping Missions March 31 2008

Country	Number	Country	Number
Pakistan	10629	Senegal	2558
Bangladesh	9047	China	1978
India	8964	France	1924
Nigeria	5415	Ethiopia	1828
Nepal	3667	South Africa	1771
Ghana	3312	Morocco	1562
Jordan	3077	Benin	1345
Rwanda	3008	Brazil	1277
Italy	2873	Spain	1251
Uruguay	2589	Egypt	1230

of force, are sometimes called peace enforcement. The US and its allies fought the Korean War as UN forces under Chapter Seven, but that was unusual since the Soviets had boycotted the meeting and not vetoed the action. Normally one or more of the five permanent members of the Security Council, the P5, would veto such actions. The 1991 War after the invasion of Kuwait was also carried out under Chapter Seven, during a short interval when the P5 were on good terms. The distinction between Chapter six and Chapter seven actions is not clear-cut and there are references to Chapter six and a half missions. The traditional peacekeeping mission was installed with the agreement of both parties, for instance, to monitor a border after a cease-fire, and if the conflict resumed the mission would withdraw. With the end of the Cold War more robust missions were attempted. The role of a mission is defined by the mandate agreed by the UN and the rules of engagement (RoE) which define when and how the mission is allowed to use lethal force. Rules of engagement under Chapter Six tend to allow the use of force only for the self-defence of the mission, whereas under Chapter Seven, force may be used on the basis of a reasonable belief in hostile intent, either to the mission or to the local population.

In either Chapter Six or Seven missions, one needs clear objectives, the means to achieve those objectives and rules of engagement that are consistent with those objectives. The relationship to local security forces is often a difficult issue. Part of the mandate may involve training or reforming the police and army of the state being supported. Such security sector reform (SSR) is more difficult when you are simultaneously fighting an insurgency and when the police or army are the main perpetrators of the crimes against the local population. Trying to impose typical western army and police structures may not mesh well with local patterns and cultures, particularly where there are powerful militias with local loyalties.

The UN reviewed its peacekeeping after a series of failures. These included Somalia in 1992, the basis of the film *Black Hawk Down*; Rwanda, in 1994, where UN forces were unable to prevent genocide; and Srebrenica in 1995, where UN forces withdrew allowing the Bosnian Serbs to conduct a massacre. The 2000 report by Lakhdar Brahimi highlighted the need for the UN to integrate various elements in its peacekeeping including the military, political, legal and humanitarian resources. Getting 'the boots and suits' to work together can be a problem.

A larger, more aggressive, peacekeeping force in Rwanda or Srebenitza may have stopped the subsequent massacres. General Romeo Dallaire

(2003) provides an account of the difficulties of being force commander of the UN Assistance Mission for Rwanda from July 1993 to September 1994 and his inability to stop the genocidal extermination of Tutsis by extremist Hutus after the Rwandan President's plane crashed on 6 April 1994. Generals hope that they will be given the means required to meet specified military objectives, in order to achieve some political purpose. In Rwanda the UN and international community did not provide the mission with means, objectives or purpose.

There have also been a large number of peacekeeping successes, though in some cases they were by individual countries, with particular interests in the conflict zone, working under UN auspices. Examples of these are the Italian intervention in Albania, the Australian intervention in East Timor and the UK intervention in Sierra Leone in support of UN troops. Because these interventions were largely by rich countries in poor countries that had once been colonies, they could be presented as forms of neo-imperialism. In Sierra Leone after the British intervention, there were even people within the country who advocated making it a British colony once more. Collier, Hoeffler and Soderbom (2008) provide quantitative evidence suggesting that UN expenditures on peacekeeping are cost-effective in stopping conflicts restarting. Doyle and Sambanis (2006) conduct a detailed analysis of the factors contributing to success or failure of peacekeeping interventions.

Patrick Cammaert (2008) provides a commander's perspective on peacekeeping. He served in Cambodia, Bosnia-Herzegovina, Ethiopia-Eritrea and as General Officer commanding the Eastern Division of the UN Mission in the Democratic Republic of the Congo 2005–2007. He argues strongly that peacekeepers must be impartial rather than neutral. Neutrality cedes opportunity, initiative and advantage to others; impartiality allows the seizing of all three. Peacekeeping requires logistics, often heavy airlift since roads are bad and insecure, engineering to provide infrastructure such as roads and bridges both for forces and for local population, as well as basic necessities like water and electricity which may not be available. Budgets are needed for local projects, to pay for intelligence and access to satellite imaging and communications intercepts. Secure communication for the mission is also required as is integration of the military, political and economic dimensions.

An attempt to try and learn the lessons from recent peacekeeping and peace-building experience is the Tswalu Process Protocol in Mackinlay, McNamee and Mills (2008). The process involved getting people from various backgrounds who had been involved in peacekeeping operations, mainly in Afghanistan and Africa, to try to share the lessons. These are summarised in a six-page document, which sets out in short lists the shortcomings of past interventions; the principles that should govern the international response; the priorities in successful peace-building (security, development and governance); the hard choices that are involved in implementing those priorities and the steps needed towards operational coherence. The hard choices involve issues like peace versus justice; reliance on formal law versus customary law; and working with or working around the state. As they recognise there can be no general answers to these choices, it depends on local circumstances.

Peacekeeping involves all the elements examined in this book. There is a security objective, establishing peace, and to attain that objective requires military capability to complete certain tasks. To provide that capability requires forces with the appropriate training, weapons and logistic support. There has to be an adequate budget to finance those forces and some decision-making structure for command and control. The same basic question arises for such a multinational operations as for a national state: should the decisions produced by this structure be regarded as those of a rational actor or the outcome of the interaction of competing interest within a framework of standard operating procedures?

8
Economic Choices: Swords or Plowshares?

Military expenditures have opportunity costs: the other activities that are given up to provide the military resources. In the literature, this is often referred to as the choice between guns or butter or swords and plowshares. The latter choice comes from the Bible. Isiah 2:4 says 'They will beat their swords into plowshares and their spears into pruning hooks. Nation will not take up sword against nation, nor will they train for war anymore.' However, the less quoted, Joel 3:10 says 'Beat your plowshares into swords and your pruning hooks into spears. Let the weakling say, "I am strong".'

In having opportunity costs, military expenditures are no different from other sorts of government expenditures and one can apply standard public finance theory. In most cases, there is nothing special, in economic terms, about military expenditures and the money spent on it is an appropriate measure of its opportunity cost. There are exceptions. When there is conscription, the expenditure underestimates the opportunity costs. In planned economies or in times of war, when there are very high levels of military expenditure and non-market mechanisms, like price controls and rationing, the expenditure may again underestimate the opportunity costs. It is often thought that there are specific economic externalities, positive or negative, that are associated with military expenditure, which give it distinctive effects and a distinctive role with macroeconomic consequences for the whole economy. Clearly its use is different from health or education, but it is not clear that it has special economic effects that require a different treatment from other sorts of expenditure. For most purposes, the usual economic theories of public expenditure can as easily be applied to defence as they can to other categories of public expenditure. With current shares of military expenditure, less than 5 per cent of GDP, the macroeconomic effects of military expenditure are probably small and decisions about defence budgets should be taken in terms of threats and opportunity costs, not macroeconomic effects. There are more effective macroeconomic policy instruments than the defence budget.

There is one respect in which military expenditures are quite different from other categories of government expenditure. No other category of government expenditure goes through such large changes as the increases in military expenditure at the beginning of a large war or reductions at the end. The special issue with military expenditures is how to manage very large adjustments. In both world wars UK military expenditure rose from around 3 per cent of GDP to around half of GDP and then fell back by similar amounts after the wars; thus war financing does raise special economic issues.

Budget constraints

The money flows that a government has to balance are called the government budget constraint. The government surplus or deficit, the difference between revenue and expenditure (military and non-military), must be matched either by changes in the money supply or by changes in government assets and liabilities. Thus an increase in military expenditure must be financed by some combination of reductions in other government expenditures; increased taxes; printing more money; borrowing by issuing more debt; or selling assets. The UK partly financed both world wars by selling foreign assets. Many countries finance their military expenditures from taxes on resource rents, like oil revenues.

The government may borrow from its own population, in domestic currency, or it may borrow from abroad, with the debt denominated in foreign currency. These have different implications. Payments on domestic debts are just transfers within the country and so not a cost to the country as a whole. They may have distributional consequences if the government taxes the poor, to pay debt interest to the rich. Interest payments on foreign debts transfer money out of the country and are thus a cost to the country as a whole. Governments control their own currency and can pay their domestic debts by printing money or debasing the coinage. Paying foreign debts requires foreign currency, which they cannot produce so easily. Printing money may cause inflation, reducing the real value of the debt, effectively defaulting on part of it. Inflation has distributional consequences, reducing the wealth of those who lent to the government. The political and economic consequences of default on domestic and foreign debts may be different. In both cases, creditors are less likely to lend to a government that defaults and this loss of future credit may be a large cost. Defaulting on your citizens may provoke riots and political instability, defaulting on foreigners may provoke other sorts of political action. In more robust days, defaults provoked lenders to send gunboats to ensure repayment, as was done with Egypt and Turkey in the 19th century. With both citizens and foreigners, the consequences of default depend on the degree of organisation of the creditors and their capacity to retaliate, both political issues.

Revenues come largely from taxes, either direct taxes on incomes or indirect taxes on expenditures, such as import tariffs or sales taxes. There are usually political obstacles to raising tax rates; but these may be less in times of war. Wars have tended to be times of fiscal innovation, when governments have found new ways to raise revenues. Income taxes were introduced in the UK during the French Revolutionary Wars, in 1798; abolished after the war in 1816, but reintroduced in 1842; and expanded substantially during World War I. US income taxes were introduced in 1861, during the Civil War, rescinded after the war and then subsequently reintroduced. Taxes may have economic as well as political effects: income taxes may reduce the incentive to work and high tax rates may cause evasion.

Expenditures also include debt interest and it is sometimes useful to look at the primary deficit: revenues less expenditures other than debt interest. If a government is running a deficit which it finances by issuing debt, this tends to add to the deficit in the following periods since expenditure to pay the debt interest is increased. The effects of financing by printing money or issuing debt are rather different. The government can use its ability to issue money to extract resources: people give it valuable goods in return for cheaply produced pieces of paper. The profits from this activity are called seigniorage, the difference between the value of money and the cost of producing it, and can be an important source of government finance. On an international scale the US has benefited substantially from the willingness of the world to exchange expensive goods for cheap pieces of green paper. However, there are limits. If the government pays by printing money, that puts money into the hands of those it purchased from. They can then spend the money adding to the demand for goods and services in the economy. If there is a shortage of goods and services, the increased demand tends to increase their price, causing inflation: too much money chasing too few goods. If this process accelerates into hyperinflation, there comes a point when inflation destroys the value of money and people are not willing to accept money from the government in payment for goods. Many wars, including the US revolutionary war of independence, have ended in hyperinflation. To stop inflation, governments often try to control prices. Sometimes this works, but it can also create distortions and black markets.

Inflation is normally seen as a problem of paper money, but it can also happen with gold and silver money. After the conquest of the new world, Spain paid its bills with gold and silver that it had shipped from the Americas; this caused a general European inflation resulting from the increase in money supply. Governments that issue gold and silver coins are also tempted to debase the currency by increasing the proportion of base metals in the coins. When this happens people tend to hold on to the older, good, coins with a higher proportion of gold and pass on the new, bad, coins. This is summarised in Gresham's law: bad money drives out good. Sir Thomas Gresham was a 16th-century financier and adviser of Queen Elizabeth I of England. As with most laws named after people, it is not clear that he originally formulated it.

When the government issues money to finance the deficit, people tend to spend the money; but when it issues debt, the people who lend cut their spending to buy the government bonds. Thus when the government issues debt, there is matching savings, reduced demand for goods and services, which there is not when the government prints money. Government bonds are promises to pay interest at regular intervals and to repay the principal, the amount lent, at a particular time. Governments can only borrow, sell bonds, if lenders have confidence in the ability of the government to repay. Governments that lose wars are usually unable to repay their debts. Those who bought Confederate bonds, during the US Civil War, lost their investment. During the 18th century the national debt was described as Britain's secret weapon in war. Following the establishment of the Bank of England in 1694, an innovation copied from the Netherlands, Britain had a well-organised way of raising money. Unlike most continental monarchs, Britain did not default; therefore it was able to raise money relatively easily, on good terms and low interest rates. It could thus borrow to finance its wars, often subsidising continental allies to do the fighting. In *The Cash Nexus*, Niall Ferguson (2001) argues that it was finance, as much as firepower, that decided wars and that wars were a major source of financial innovation over the period 1700–2000. There is a positive feedback. If you have good credit, you can borrow to finance wars. This money makes it more likely that you will win the war and be able to pay back your creditors, raising your credit further.

Behind the monetary flows are the real flows of goods and services, which one can think of as the output–expenditure balance. The total output of the economy, all the goods and services produced, is equal to the total expenditure of the economy. The expenditure goes on consumption; investment, the construction of new capital goods; government demand for goods and services, military and non-military; and exports. Some of this expenditure is produced not at home but abroad, so imports are subtracted from this total to give production. In preparing for war, the government must consider where the resources to meet the demand for military expenditure can come from. It will first try to raise output. If there are unemployed resources these can be used; in World War II the UK and US increased their labour forces substantially by calling on women who had not worked in peacetime. Table 8.1 gives US GDP in 1939 prices in 1939 and 1944. Over this period real GDP grew by 90 per cent, military spending grew massively from under $2 billion to over $75 billion, but real non-military expenditure also grew by almost $10 billion, so it was not a pure displacement of non-military by military expenditures. The data come from the Bureau of Economic Analysis, National Income and Product Accounts and the military expenditure total is the national defence component of government consumption and investment. The table assumes that military and non-military prices grew at the same rate. Using different price indexes for the two categories would change the numbers, but not the basic story: much of the military expenditure in the US for World War II was financed by an expansion of real GDP rather than merely displacement of non-military expenditure. This can only be done if there are unemployed resources that can be utilised.

Raising output is rarely enough and the government will try to cut consumption, either by higher taxes, higher prices (which cut real wages) or rationing. The government will try to direct investment to projects necessary to prosecute the war and it will cut government expenditures that do not contribute to the war. It will also try to increase

Table 8.1 US Financing of World War II

Billions of Dollars 1939 prices			
	1939	1944	Change
GDP	92.20	175.18	82.98
Military	1.50	75.33	73.83
Non-Military	90.70	99.85	9.15

imports, to the extent that it can. During World War II, Britain was very dependent on US imports, under schemes like 'lend lease' and in both world wars sold foreign assets to pay for imports.

To pay for war, governments can rely on market mechanisms and borrowing or use planning and rationing. Wartime governments differ in their effectiveness at mobilising resources. In World War II, German economic mobilisation seems to have been less effective than the UK, US or USSR. In major conflicts, direction of labour and conscription is usually necessary. While output in general may be adequate, shortages of particular specialised resources may be a bottleneck and societies search for substitutes. In World War II UK, production of aircraft was constrained by shortage of metal and metal workers, so aircraft, such as the successful Mosquito fighter-bomber, were made out of wood, using workers from the furniture trades. Military products can only be rapidly produced by civilian factories when the technologies are similar and development times are short. In the 1991 Gulf War the US and UK forces needed a large number of GPS sets, but since there was a civilian market these could be purchased off the shelf from civilian industry. In the Falklands War, the UK could not rapidly produce air-to-air missiles and had to buy Sidewinders, which could be fitted to Harriers, from the US.

Economic effects

At all times, higher military expenditure means other government expenditures are lower; taxes are higher; or the budget deficit is higher. As the economy grows, even with fixed tax rates, tax revenues grow so expenditure can grow in line. Higher budget deficits may mean higher interest rates, which may reduce consumption and investment. In the 1990s the US and UK got a 'peace dividend' as military expenditures were reduced after the Cold War; most of this came through budget surpluses and lower interest rates. If there is unemployment, higher military expenditure boosts demand and can reduce unemployment, as happened with World War II rearmament after the Great Depression of the 1930s. With relatively full employment, using workers for military purposes diverts them from other productive activities. Military Expenditure, by increasing budget deficits and interest rates, may 'crowd-out' investment and may influence technical progress, through Research and Development (R&D), and human capital, through training. The arms trade may have effects on the balance of payments. None of these macroeconomic effects seem particularly large at relatively low levels of military expenditure, below 5 per cent of GDP. There is also a large microeconomic literature on the conversion of military resources to civilian use; through local reconstruction after base closures and conversion of arms factories to commercial products. Michael Brzoska (2007) provides a survey of the experience of conversion after the end of the Cold War.

One would not expect any simple relationship between military expenditure and growth because there are both positive, demand, effects (growing countries can afford higher military expenditure) and negative, supply, effects (military expenditure displaces investment and other factors that increase growth). In the US and UK at the beginning of World War II military expenditure went up and growth increased, while at the end of the Cold War military expenditure went down and growth increased. The net balance will depend on the threat, which influences the demand for military spending, and the growth potential of the economy, which influences the supply response. As a result anything is possible; all four combinations of high and low growth and high and low shares of military spending in GDP are observed in practice. Countries with a high threat, so high military expenditure, but great growth potential, like South Korea and Taiwan in the 1970s and 1980s, show a high share of military and a high growth rate. Countries where a high share of military expenditure displaced investment and other factors hinder growth, show a high share of military expenditure and low growth; the Soviet Union being an example. Countries like post-war Japan and Germany that restricted their military expenditure and could devote it to investment showed low shares and high growth. In most countries of sub-Saharan Africa shares of military expenditure are low, wars are fought with cheap conscripts and low-technology weapons, but growth rates are also low. For developing countries there is a complex interaction between military expenditures, conflict, resources and economic capacity. The economic capacity reflects education and institutions. Thus the outcome will depend on the balance of economic and security factors: there will not be a simple association between military expenditure and growth.

Technological spin-off

The output a society can produce depends on its capital, labour and technology, which will depend on the scientific and engineering skills available to the society. Since there are strong links between the military and society, there will be links between the military and civilian science and engineering.

The military has to recruit from society, though it often has to remedy the deficiencies of its recruits, for instance, in basic literacy or physical fitness, even in societies like the US and UK. Trying to ensure soldiers are literate is something that the army has long done; trying to ensure that they have the advanced engineering skills the military now need is more difficult, when relatively few young people in the US and UK want to study science and engineering. The commercial solution, sub-stituting with engineers from China and India, is less available to the military. The links often go both ways. Global Positioning System, GPS, is a military system that has very wide civil applications. It was also a technology that was crucial to the military in the 1991 Gulf War. Armies have always had difficulty navigating in deserts and Desert Storm could not have been fought in the way it was without GPS. Before that cam-paign most military vehicles did not have GPS, but it could be rapidly fitted using commercial receivers.

The gap between the science, technology and engineering used by the military and by the rest of society plays a central role. During World War II the gap was quite small: civilian factories could be switched to producing tanks and aircraft. After the war the gap widened: military equipment became increasingly specialised and different. Then the gap narrowed again as civilian technology overtook military technology and the military started to buy COTS: commercial off-the-shelf. Even arcane technologies that had once been the sole preserve of the military and the intelligence community, such as cryptography, became dominated by civilian research, because of its commercial importance, particularly in finance. Whereas once the defence industry would have designed and built specialised electronic components and software for the military, increasingly the military rely on standard components from commercial suppliers, though this causes problems with time-scales. The life-cycle of commercial electronics is about 18 months, driven by Moore's law that the computing capacity of integrated circuits doubles every 18 months. The average military procurement time is about seven years, about four generations of electronics. This means when the military system goes into service, the electronics is not merely obsolete but no longer even in production. The gaps between military and commercial technology and time-scales have implications for rapid mobilisation and the provision of urgent operational requirements.

Many military activities became central to wider society: mapping (the name of the UK organisation Ordnance Survey reflects its mili-tary origin), meteorology, air traffic control, Internet and GPS. Often, as their civilian importance grows, they are spun off from the military, like mapping and meteorology. There is a large scientific and engineering component to a range of things that the military do for the wider society: search and rescue, coastguards, protection of oil rigs and aid to the civil power in times of emergency. This aid can include maintaining bio-security during pandemics; providing support during natural disasters like floods; maintaining public order during large-scale disruptions; or, in a previous generation, planning to run the country after a nuclear war. To fulfil these functions the military need the skills to interact with the wider society and have a broad spectrum of technological capabilities. It may be useful to have the military provide these functions, but societies without armed forces like Iceland and Costa Rica provide these services in other ways than the military. The military often leave the armed forces at a comparatively young age and have careers later in civil society and they take their skills with them. There are examples like management education and logistics where commercial firms have learned from the military.

The extent of the spin-off of technology from the military to the rest of society is controversial with strong positions on both sides. Vernon W. Ruttan (2006), an expert on innovation, asks *Is War Necessary for Economic Growth?* He concludes that the answer is yes, though his argument has been widely criticised. It is certainly true that many technologies have military or wartime origins, though many have not. If a large part of national resources and R&D are devoted to the military, as they were during the world wars and Cold War, it is not surprising that many technologies have military origins. However, had those resources been spent on civil R&D without the secrecy restrictions and diversion of scarce scientific and technical skills to the military, there may have been even more innovations.

The military origins of many technologies is not necessarily an argument for support of military R&D. The fact that the US Defence Advanced Research Projects Agency (DARPA) produced the Internet is given as an argument for supporting military research; but the fact that European Centre for Nuclear Research (CERN) produced the World Wide Web is rarely given as a reason to support research into particle physics. If you want to promote technology there are generally better and less expensive ways to do it than relying on the military to spin it off. In any event, it is quite difficult for governments to target innovation effectively. Consider the growth of India as a major software producer. Partly this was the result of an education system that produced very good software engineers. But partly this was because the Indian Government did not treat software as a serious industry. Software benefited from not having the extensive government support and intervention that doomed many other Indian industries, particularly in manufacturing.

Because the military is inter-twined in society, absorbing substantial resources, it does have effects on technology and the economy. It does create employment and those jobs can be politically crucial, particularly if they are in a marginal constituency. But if you want to create employment, there are many more effective ways of doing it than spending on the military; similar is the case with technology. There are strong scientific and engineering links between military and society, but they are complicated, operate in both directions and are difficult to manage. Acquiring the technology the military need and acquiring weapons is difficult enough when the objective is buying the best value military capability. The Government Accountability Office (GAO) and National Audit Office (NAO) regularly document the problems in doing this. If you further complicate the procurement process, by trying to fine-tune the technological spin-offs, there is a danger that the decision makers will be incapacitated by the complexity of their objectives, resulting in even worse procurement decisions.

Economic warfare

There are two aspects to economic warfare. Economic measures can be a complement to military action, used as part of normal warfare; or they can be a substitute for military action, used as sanctions. Economic measures have always been used in war. Retreating armies burn crops and destroy supplies to stop them being used by the enemy. States blockade their enemies to stop supplies; in both world wars, German submarine attacks on shipping almost crippled Britain.

Economic sanctions are usually a substitute for military actions, where the international community disapproves of some policies of the target country but is unwilling to use force. Such sanctions restrict the free movement of trade, capital, technology or people to or from the sanctioned country. They may be widely targeted or focus on particular goods, such as arms, or on particular people, such as the assets or travel of the leadership. There is a large amount of empirical and theoretical work on sanctions, but few clear conclusions. Kaempfer and Lowenberg (2007) provide a survey of the political economy of sanctions. Sanctions may have various objectives. They may be instrumental, intended to change the behaviour of the targeted state: to persuade South Africa to abandon apartheid or to persuade potential proliferators not to acquire nuclear weapon. They may be punitive, punishing apartheid South Africa for its behaviour. They may be expressive, showing the disapproval of the states imposing the sanctions, even if they are ineffective in instrumental or punitive terms; neither changing the target's behaviour nor punishing it. Expressive policies may be adopted because policy makers are under public pressure to do something, however ineffective. The objectives of sanctions are rarely clear, which makes it difficult to judge their success, the extent to which they meet their objectives. Even when countries do change their behaviour in desired ways, South Africa abandons apartheid or Libya abandons its attempt to acquire nuclear weapons, it can be difficult to judge the contribution of sanctions to the policy change.

Analysing the economic operation of sanctions is as complicated as specifying the objectives and outcomes. Sanctions may do more damage to the country imposing them, through lost exports or having to substitute more expensive imports, than to the target. Sanctions may also be a covert form of trade protection: stopping competitive imports from the target country. Sanctions may be more effective on friends, to whom close ties are important, than on enemies. The US financial threats to the UK and France, after their 1956 invasion of Suez, were effective in forcing withdrawal because of the integration of the UK and France into the international system, their desire to maintain fixed exchange rates and the importance of their trade links with the US. Sanctions can strengthen the target regime by increasing domestic cohesion against the hostile powers imposing the sanctions. Sanctions can be evaded at a cost, and the cost of evasion can be much lower than the cost of enforcement. The target state may even benefit from the sanctions through its control of the embargoed item, either at home or abroad. This is particularly the case with high value items: South Africa had little difficulty selling its gold and diamonds. Sanctions may stimulate the development of domestic industries which produce the sanctioned products, such as arms, and may encourage the substitution against sanctioned products, for instance, by replacing conventional with nuclear weapons. Forcing foreign companies to divest their assets in the target country allows those in the target country to acquire productive assets cheaply. The sanctions may hurt the poor or oppressed in the target country more than the ruling elites. In principle smart sanctions target the elite but it can be very difficult to identify the elite and target them effectively. Kaempfer and Lowenberg (2007) point out that in contrast to the economic sanctions on South Africa, which hit blacks harder than whites, the sports sanctions primarily hit whites, the only ones who cared about rugby or cricket.

Empirical evaluation of sanctions is made more difficult because we observe cases where sanctions were imposed and these may not be typical. The threat of sanctions may often be effective in inducing compliance, so we only observe the cases where the threat failed and sanctions were actually imposed. Since these are cases where the target country was willing to incur the sanctions rather than comply, these are hard cases, giving us a more negative view of sanctions than is justified. Alternatively, we may only observe cases where sanctions were imposed because the sanctioning country expected that they would work, giving us a more positive view than is justified.

Markets may impose their own sanctions in response to political actions which they see as threatening to profitability. After the conflict between Russia and Georgia in August 2008, the rouble exchange rate dropped rapidly and the Russian authorities had to intervene to defend it; Russian shares halved in value and the authorities had to close the stock market to restore order; and the inflow of foreign investment more than halved. Markets move in mysterious ways, so it is difficult to know the extent to which this flight of capital was a response to the Georgian war, the credit crunch or the fall in the oil price, since all happened simultaneously.

Another form of economic warfare is to institute an arms race that will impose very heavy economic costs on your antagonist, as they struggle to match your military build-up. Some attribute the collapse of the Soviet Union to economic warfare of this sort by President Reagan, in particular his use of the threat of the Star Wars missile defence system. It is difficult to know if this was a deliberate US strategy and what effect that it had on Soviet decision makers. But if it was a US strategy, it was quite a dangerous one. If the antagonist anticipates that it will be militarily dominated in the future, the incentive is to start the war now, rather than to wait until it is in a weaker position.

A relatively new form of economic warfare, which may be a substitute or complement for military action, is electronic attacks on critical infrastructure. During the Cold War it was planned to use the electromagnetic pulse from nuclear weapons to destroy electricity and communication systems. But it may now be possible for state or non-state actors to disrupt critical infrastructure by hacking into the computers that control electricity, water or transport systems.

The maintenance of economic security, protection against economic warfare, is a natural government objective. Christopher Dent in Collins (2007) discusses economic security in wider terms and brings out the theoretical difficulties in defining it. Economic security is a vague concept, particularly when it is extended beyond protection against economic warfare to protection against any economic change which may endanger a country's livelihood. Economic change is a constant and military–political responses to economic change are rarely effective because of their unintended consequences. Actions designed to increase economic security may well undermine it, inhibiting innovation and other economic processes on which long-term security is dependent. The measures adopted may not only be expensive but also be counter-productive, since adapting to change may be more effective than trying to protect against it. Japan destroyed Switzerland's major industry, mechanical watch-making, by the development of electronic watches in the early 1970s. The Swiss do not seem to have contemplated a military response and managed to adjust, creating a very different type of watch industry.

9
Understanding Military Economics

Neither the study of strategy nor of economics provides clear policy answers. They are primarily ways of thinking: analytical frameworks that identify the crucial trade-offs and illuminate the choices in a way that should help decisions. There are rarely unambiguous right and wrong answers; the trade-offs mean that you have to weigh gains against losses. This is no easy matter. The losses may be apparent and salient, the gains not so obvious, or vice versa. Who gains and who loses matters. A proposed policy may have large net benefits; but if those who lose are politically powerful, it is unlikely to be implemented. One reason strategy and economics can never provide clear policy rules is that they are largely competitive activities. If they did provide a set of rules, and you followed those rules, your economic or strategic competitor, knowing the rules, could predict your actions and thwart them. While there are sensible rules – invest in training and make sure that you have adequate supplies and reserves when you go into economic and military battles – they are rules for avoiding guaranteed failure rather providing guaranteed success. Thus there are no conclusions to this book in the usual sense, no suggestions as to how to stop the killing or save the world, rather there is a discussion of how one can understand military economic issues. The academic term for the focus of this chapter is methodology, the study of the methods one uses to understand a particular subject, though in some disciplines, methodology is used in a narrower sense as the study of the statistical methods used.

There are three dimensions to understanding: description, prediction and prescription. One may be able to understand enough about the operation of a process to describe how it works, but not be able to predict what it will do next, or make prescriptions about how to change it. Efficient market theories are of this sort. If the theory is correct price changes are unpredictable. On the other hand one may have no understanding of the mechanisms involved, but be able to prescribe effectively. For instance, on the basis of empirical observation, aspirin was widely prescribed as an analgesic, long before anyone could describe how it worked.

At the level of description, there are two main annual sources of factual information that are very useful. The SIPRI Yearbook gives figures on military expenditure, the arms trade, arms production and the number of conflicts as well as much other material on armaments and disarmament. The IISS *Military Balance* gives figures on the number in the armed forces and holdings of various weapons as well as figures on military expenditure. For individual factual items Google, or other search engines, and Wikipedia are very useful. Some academics are rather dismissive of Wikipedia because the material is not edited and peer-reviewed. On checking subjects that I knew about, for this book, I found it largely accurate. The Internet is introducing a free-market in information, displacing the traditional regulation of editors, but it brings both liberty and license so a degree of scepticism is required. Disciplines differ on the importance of peer-review. Because publications lags in economics are longer than most other subjects, economists tend to distribute and extensively cite working papers, which have not been refereed; there are a number referenced in this book.

More generally, the literature that is relevant to the subject is very large. The intersection between economics and the military has many pathways that go off in different directions: such as sociology, psychology, law and the environment. I have mainly given references to non-technical literature that is directly relevant to the issues being covered, but the literature is much wider than my references. I have largely treated peace as the absence of conflict, and there is a large prescriptive literature on conflict resolution, devoted to creating that absence of conflict, such as Crocker, Hampson and Aal (2007).

As noted in the Introduction, much of the recent work in defence economics is quite technical using fairly advanced mathematical and statistical tools. But often the main point of the argument can be got from the verbal discussion and the equations can be skipped. The text books by Sandler and Hartley (1995) and Anderton and Carter (2009) are excellent introductions to the technical literature and the two *Handbooks of Defence Economics*, Volume 1, edited by Hartley and Sandler (1995), and Volume 2, edited by Sandler and Hartley (2007), are essential reference works. Many papers on defence economics are published in journals like *Defence and Peace Economics, The Journal of*

Peace Research, Economics of Peace and Security Journal and *The Journal of Conflict Resolution*, though many are technical. Military-related journals like *International Security, Survival* and the *RUSI Journal* often contain less technical articles on the economics of security.

Within the large literature that is relevant to this subject, there are a range of methods or approaches. There are case-studies of particular events, historical or contemporary; there are verbal theories that explain the events; there are statistical analyses of qualitative or quantitative aspects of those events; and there are mathematical models of the processes that generate those events. These four approaches are often presented as substitutes, the proponents of a particular method denouncing the alternatives, often very stridently as academics are prone to do. The approaches are better seen as complements: each has its advantages and disadvantages and an analysis which can draw on all four approaches is likely to be stronger, benefiting from synthesising the different insights each provides. This synthetic approach is becoming more common. For instance, the book by Stephen Biddle (2004), *Military Power: Explaining Victory and Defeat in Modern Battle*, begins with a verbal description of his theory; goes on to consider three historical case-studies chosen to provide crucial evidence for or against the theory; conducts a range of statistical tests using a large sample of battles; and finally uses a formal mathematical model of military capability in combat. The book also has a useful discussion of the relative advantages and disadvantages of the four methods and how they should be applied.

The details of any particular example matter and these details can only be found from case studies, either historical or contemporary. The distinction between historical studies and contemporary case studies lies largely in the nature of the source materials; over time more information tends to become available. Because of secrecy crucial pieces of information may not be in the public domain and contemporary accounts which ignore them will be misleading. For instance, some of the history of World War II was seriously wrong until the details of Ultra, the Allied decryption of Axis codes, were revealed. Primary sources are original documents or accounts of eyewitnesses, secondary sources assemble the primary evidence. This book relies almost entirely on secondary sources; historians tend to emphasise the importance of using primary sources. Documents tend to be given a privileged status as evidence, but many important things are not written down. Such tacit knowledge, undocumented information available to participants, is crucial to the operation of technology and organisations.

Theory, often implicit, provides focus, allowing one to abstract the crucial features, and determine what is important, relevant to the purpose of the particular analysis. The theory can be made more explicit, through definitions of the relevant concepts and an account of how they are related. Making theory explicit makes it easier to evaluate its logic, accord with evidence and possible biases. Some theory is necessary; since it is impossible merely to describe what happened, some selection is inevitable. Including everything is not only impossible, but of no more use than a one-to-one scale map, the same size as reality. But focus can bring biases. If what is regarded as important is what ruling-class white men do, then a lot is ignored. The aspects of the military that interest most men tend to be technology, training and battles. Elements like the role of women and logistics get less attention, but are often crucial. Every fighter pilot has a huge team that gets their aircraft armed and into the air. Military history traditionally focused on battles and operations, but these always happen in a wider context. For example, N.A.M. Rodger (1997, 2004) in his history of the British navy has chapters not only on operations, but also on technology, the ships and weapons; administration and finance; and social history. Each of these has their own evolution and dynamic which impact on the military. Thus although they are less glamorous; administration, finance and social forces need to be analysed in their own right, because they often shape operations.

One generally needs different descriptions for different purposes; what a logistics specialist needs to know about a war is different from what the diplomat needs to know. There are also advantages in the division of labour, since it is difficult to master both differential equations and the details of Soviet archives. Thus various perspectives are important. The need for various perspectives also applies to the range of theories used, hence the fairly eclectic approach in this book.

The verbal theories and the mathematical models are sometimes seen as theoretical, providing explanations; the case studies and statistical analyses as empirical, providing evidence about the facts. While this distinction between the theoretical and the empirical is useful, it cannot be drawn too sharply since they overlap. Theories are heavily influenced by perceptions of the facts and which facts are recorded and thus perceived is heavily influenced by theory, explicit or implicit. The impact of explicit theory on observation is most obvious with quantitative data. The national accounts measures that we have used, like GDP, are based on an explicit theory of the economy. With a different theory one would use a different measure of the output of an economy as the Soviets did, using Net Material Product (NMP). Counts of the number of wars rely heavily on theories of what constitutes a war, for instance that wars involve states and a certain number of people dying. What might usually be called wars might not count because as in Somalia there was no state, or as in the Cod Wars between the UK and Iceland not enough people died. Although it is less obvious, and the theory is less explicit, the same applies to history and case studies, where theory shapes what is regarded as important enough to report and analyse.

At some stage, it becomes difficult to analyse complex chains of interactions in words and it is much easier to do it in equations. Consider two countries in an arms race. One might think that the growth in spending on arms by each country reflects three factors. There is some baseline level; there is a feedback effect in response to the level of arms in the other country; and there is a fatigue effect: as the level of arms gets greater, taking more of national output, it becomes harder to increase arms at the same rate. This would be a verbal theory. Lewis Fry Richardson, the Quaker meteorologist, recognised that this verbal description can be captured by a pair of interacting partial differential equations, very similar to the equations he knew from physics. This allowed him to make more precise statements which depended on the size of the parameters, such as the strength of the feedback and fatigue effects. In particular, it allowed him to examine what combinations of parameters would lead the arms race to explode into exponential growth and what combination would lead it to settle down to some stable equilibrium. This formulation then spurred statisticians to see whether the data on military expenditures or stocks of arms for pairs of countries shed any light on the values of the parameters and whether the arms race was explosive or stable. Having an explicit model makes evaluation easier. Allied casualties in the 1991 Gulf War were lower than most people or models had predicted. With the models, one could find out exactly which assumptions were wrong. Biddle (2004) discusses the reasons for the lower casualty rate.

For those with some mathematics, T.W. Korner's *The Pleasures of Counting* (1996) is an excellent introduction to the application of mathematics. It uses a range or military, peace and other examples where mathematics has been applied including the work of Richardson. Richardson's work on war and peace also had profound implications for mathematics. One of the factors that Richardson identified as influencing the probability of war between two adjacent countries was the length of their border. In collecting the data he noticed that different countries gave different lengths for their common border, the smaller neighbour usually thinking their common border was longer than that of the larger neighbour. He then started to think about how one might measure uneven shapes like borders. Lines are one dimensional, flat surfaces are two dimensional, but squiggly lines like borders have dimensions between one and two. Richardson's work, on non-integer dimensions, was read by Benoit Mandelbrot, who developed fractals. These were introduced in a paper titled How Long Is the Coast of Britain? Fractals rapidly moved from being a mathematical curiosity to the basis for the computer generated images, CGI, of modern movies. CGI, which some see as a crucial technology, was a spin-off not of the military research but of peace research.

While mathematical models certainly help one to follow through complicated chains of interaction with precision, they are only as good as the accuracy of the model as a representation of the phenomena of interest. There are also measurement issues in how you match the variables in the model to available data, particularly when intangible factors are important. The rule 'garbage in, garbage out' applies. There are two responses to the poor quality of much of the data on military issues. Some believe that it is so bad that only the simplest statistical techniques can be applied; some believe that it is so bad that the most advanced statistical techniques are required to separate the signal from the noise. Both have arguments on their side.

Whether one is using historical or statistical evidence there is a fundamental problem of induction. There is no logical basis for drawing general lessons from particular instances. However, many times that you have observed an empirical regularity in the past, there is no guarantee that it will hold in the future. The turkeys, who inferred from observation the general law that every morning the farmer would feed them, were somewhat surprised by what he did the morning before Christmas. In economics this is often summarised by Goodhart's Law that 'any well established econometric relationship will break down as soon as it is used for policy purposes.' Charles Goodhart was Chief Economist at the Bank of England and is a professor at London School of Economics (LSE).

Consider an example of an empirical generalisation, which suggested that globalisation reduced the likelihood of war. Thomas Friedman (1999) noted that no two countries that each had McDonald's had gone to war. However, the fact that the association had held in the past could not be any guarantee that it would hold in the future: Georgia and Russia both had McDonald's when they went to war in 2008. The association between peace and McDonald's was not intended to be a causal relationship; there was no suggestion that eating burgers promoted pacifism, or pacifism promoted a demand for burgers. Rather the argument was that peace and the presence of McDonald's were indicators of a third factor: certain characteristics such as the existence of a sizeable middle class and integration into the world system which were associated with a reduced likelihood of war. Nor was it intended to be a deterministic relationship. It was not suggested that war was impossible if both had McDonald's, merely that the probability of war was lower. A particular counter-example cannot falsify a probabilistic relation, though it can reduce its plausibility.

Inferring causal relationships from the evidence and making predictions is made more difficult because there may be more than one causal relationship between the variables and they operate in opposite directions. A number of such cases have arisen, including the relationship between military expenditure and growth. Trying to separate such relationships is a major task, which in economics is called the identification problem. Consider another example. Suppose an army, fighting guerrillas, decides to put more troops and effort into killing or capturing insurgents. Would one expect more insurgents to be neutralised or fewer? On one hand, a greater proportion of insurgents in the area are likely to be killed or captured. On the other hand, there are likely to be fewer insurgents in the area, since they will melt away in anticipation of the government offensive. It could go either way.

In analysing war and peace there are many dimensions; conflict and the military are linked to society in a large variety of ways. The economic dimension is important because fear and greed are important motivations and power and money are inevitably inter-twined. Understanding this dimension can illuminate many military issues and identify how conflict shapes the economy. However, it cannot be relied on to provide guaranteed predictions or policy solutions; all it can do is illuminate a range of possibilities.

Acknowledgements

Over the years I have learned a lot from lecturing on defence economics, often to audiences who were better informed on many of these issues than I was. I taught defence economics in the UK with Dan Smith at the University of York in 1980, which led to Smith and Smith (1983) and in the US at the University of Colorado 1997–1998. I have also presented some of this material to audiences at the UK Staff College; the Royal College for Defence Studies; the Masters in Defence Administration at what was then called the Royal Military College of Science; to meetings at the Royal United Services Institute; to various other groups of military and MoD Civil Servants at the UK Defence Academy; and to many peace movement groups, campaigning on various topics. Although I teach statistics and econometrics rather than defence economics at Birkbeck, I have greatly benefited from the Birkbeck environment with its part-time students, many of whom had military or peace interests, or who worked at the MoD. In particular, the book has benefited from my many discussions over the years with David Kirkpatrick, who I first met as a student at Birkbeck.

Much of the material in this book draws heavily on more technical research papers, by me and others, which have not been referenced. Some of my research was financed by grants from the UK Economic and Social Research Council, the United Nations, the World Bank and the European Central Bank to whom I am grateful.

Research in economics is a social activity and I am very grateful to my many co-authors on military topics including Jacques Aben, Hong Bai, Terry Barker, Yongmin Chen, Saadet Deger, Paul Dunne, Jacques Fontanel, Maria Garcia-Alonso, George Georgiou, Steve Hall, Keith Hartley, Farouq Hussain, Paul Levine, Tony Humm, Steve Martin, Fotis Mouzakis, Effie Nicolaidou, James Nixon, Sam Perlo-Freeman, Mick Ridge, Somnath Sen, Dan Smith, Martin Sola, Fabio Spagnolo, Ali Tasiran, Bud Udis, Dirk Willenbockel and Sue Willett.

The book was very much improved by those who kindly read and commented on early drafts including Paul Anand, Jurgen Brauer, Vincenso Bove, Malcom Chalmers, Warren Chin, Neil Cooper, Chris Cramer, Neil Davies, Paul Dunne, Maria Garcia-Alonso, Andrew Gibbons, Keith Hartley, Tony Humm, Sandeep Kapur, David Kirkpatrick, Paul Levine, Colin Rowat and Ali Tasiran. The Palgrave Commissioning editor, Taiba Batool, and two anonymous reviewers provided helpful advice. None of these should be held responsible for any errors or opinions in the book, particularly since I did not always follow their advice. Finally my thanks to my wife, Linda Hesselman, who has been advising me on what I have written since my PhD thesis.

Abbreviations

ABM	Anti-Ballistic Missile
AK47	Kalashnikov Assault Rifle
AVF	All Volunteer Forces
BAE	BAE Systems, a British arms-aerospace firm
CADMID	UK description of the weapons life cycle: Concept, Assessment, Development, Manufacture, In-service, Disposal
CAS	Close Air Support
CBO	Congressional Budget Office
CEP	Circular Error Probable
CERN	European Centre for Nuclear Research on the French-Swiss border.
CGI	Computer Generated Images
CIA	Central Intelligence Agency
COCOM	Coordinating Committee for multilateral export controls that restricted trade to the Soviet Union
COEIA	Combined Operational Effectiveness and Investment Appraisal
COTS	Commercial Off-the-Shelf
COW	Correlates of War project
DARPA	US Defence Advanced Research Projects Agency
DEL	Department Expenditure Limit, UK public finance control
DGA	Delegation General Pour Armements, French arms procurement body
DIB	Defence Industrial Base
DoD	US Department of Defence
DRC	Democratic Republic of Congo, formerly Zaire
EADS	European Aeronautics, Defence and Space, arms-aerospace firm
EU	European Union
FDI	Foreign Direct Investment
fMRI	Functional Magnetic Resonance Imaging
GAO	Government Accountability Office (previously called the General Accounting Office), US government auditors
GATT	General Agreement on Tariffs and Trade
GDP	Gross Domestic Product, a measure of a country's output or income
GNP	Cross National Product, another measure of a country's output
GPS	Global Positioning System
IEA	International Energy Agency
IED	Improvised Explosive Device
IISS	International Institute for Strategic Studies, London
IMF	International Monetary Fund
IPR	Intellectual Property Rights
IRA	Irish Republican Army
IT	Information Technology
JDAMS	Joint Direct Attack Munitions
JSF	US Joint Strike Fighter, F35 Lightning II

LIBOR	London Inter-Bank Offered Rate, the interest rate at which banks lend to each other
MIC	Military Industrial Complex
MoD	UK Ministry of Defence
MOTS	Military Off-the-Shelf
MTCR	Missile Technology Control Regime
NAO	National Audit Office, UK government auditors
NATO	North Atlantic Treaty Organisation
NCO	Non-Commissioned Officer
NGO	Non-Governmental Organisation, such as charities like Oxfam
NMP	Net Material Product, Soviet measure of output
OECD	Organisation for Economic Cooperation and Development, rich countries club
OPEC	Organisation of Petroleum Exporting Countries
OSCE	Organisation for Security and Cooperation in Europe
P5	Five Permanent Members of the UN Security Council
PFI	Private Finance Initiative
PPBS	Program, Planning and Budgeting System
PPP	Purchasing Power Parity (also used for Public Private Partnerships in the UK)
PRIO	Oslo International Peace Research Institute
QALY	Quality Adjusted Life Year
RAB	Resource Accounting and Budgeting, UK public finance system
RAND	US think-tank that has done much military research
R&D	Research and Development
RDTE	Research Development Testing and Evaluation
RoE	Rules of Engagement
RUSI	Royal United Services Institute, the oldest military think-tank
SALW	Small Arms and Light Weapons
SIOP	Single Integrated Operating Plan for US nuclear targeting
SIPRI	Stockholm International Peace Research Institute
SSR	Security Sector Reform
UCDP	Upsala Conflict Data Program
UN	United Nations
UOR	Urgent Operational Requirements
WCMD	Wind Corrected Munition Dispenser
WMD	Weapons of Mass Destruction
WTO	World Trade Organisation, also used for the Warsaw Treaty Organisation, called the Warsaw Pact in this book.

References

Ambrose, Stephen, E. (2000) *Nothing Like It in the World*, Simon & Schuster, New York.

Anderton, Charles, H. (2003) Economic Theorizing of Conflict: Historical Contributions, Future Possibilities, *Defence and Peace Economics*, 14(3) 209–222.

Anderton, Charles, H. and John R. Carter (2009) *Principles of Conflict Economics*, Cambridge University Press, Cambridge, UK.

Arnson, C.J. and I.W. Zartman (eds) (2005) *Rethinking the Economics of War: The Intersection of Need, Creed, and Greed*, Woodrow Wilson Centre Press, Washington DC and Johns Hopkins Press, Baltimore.

Arreguin-Toft, Ivan (2005) *How the Weak Win Wars: A Theory of Asymmetric Conflict*, Cambridge University Press, Cambridge, UK.

Asch, Beth, J., James, R. Hosek and John T. Warner (2007) New Economics of Manpower in the Post-Cold War Era, chapter 32 of Sandler and Hartley (eds) (2007).

Axelrod, Robert (1984) *The Evolution of Cooperation*, Basic Books, New York.

—— (1997) *The Complexities of Cooperation: Agent-Based Models of Competition and Collaboration*, Princeton University Press, Princeton, NJ.

Baran, Paul, A. and Paul M. Sweezy (1966) *Monopoly Capital*, Monthly Review Press, New York.

Biddle, Stephen (2004) *Military Power: Explaining Victory and Defeat in Modern Battle*, Princeton University Press, Princeton, NJ.

Bilmes, Linda and Joseph Stiglitz (2008) *The Three Trillion Dollar War*, Penguin, Allen Lane, London.

Blattman, Christopher and Edward Miguel (2009) Civil War, *Journal of Economic Literature*, forthcoming.

Bourke, Joanna (1999) *An Intimate History of Killing*, Granta, London.

Boyer, Yves, Pierre Lellouche and John Roper (1989) *Franco-British Defence Co-Operation: A New Entente Cordiale?* Routledge for the Royal Institute of International Affairs, London and L'Institut Francais des Relations Internationale, Paris.

Brauer, Jurgen (2007) Arms Industries, Arms Trade and Developing Countries, chapter 30 of Sandler and Hartley (eds) (2007).

Brauer, Jurgen and Hubert van Tuyll (2008) *Castles, Battles and Bombs: How Economics Explains Military History*, University of Chicago Press, Chicago.

Brzoska, Michael (2007) Success and Failure in Defence Conversion in the 'Long Decade of Disarmament', chapter 34 of Sandler and Hartley (eds) (2007), pp. 1177–1209.

Cammaert, Patrick (2008) A Peacekeeping Commander's Perspective from Headquarters and the Field, *RUSI Journal*, June, 153(3) 68–71.

Chalmers, Malcolm, Neil Davies, Keith Hartley and C. Wilkinson (2002) The Economic Costs and Benefits of UK Defence Exports, *Fiscal Studies*, 23, 343–367.

Chin, Warren, A. (2004) *British Weapons Acquisition Policy and the Futility of Reform*, Ashgate, Aldershot, UK.

Clark, Gregory, Kevin O'Rourke and Alan M. Taylor (2008) Made in America? The New World, the Old, and the Industrial Revolution, *American Economic Review*, Papers and Proceedings, 98(2) 523–528.

Clarke, Michael (ed.) (1993) *New Perspectives on Security*, Brassey's, London.

Coase, Ronald (1960) The Problem of Social Cost, *Journal of Law and Economics*, 3, 1–44.

Collier, Paul (2007) *The Bottom Billion: Why the Poorest Countries are Failing and What Can be Done About It*, Oxford University Press, Oxford.

Collier, Paul and Anke Hoeffler (1998) On Economic Causes of Civil War, *Oxford Economic Papers*, 50(4) 563–573.

—— (2004) Greed and Grievance in Civil War, *Oxford Economic Papers*, 56(4) 563–595.

Collier, Paul, Anke Hoeffler and Mans Soderbom (2008) Post-Conflict Risks, *Journal of Peace Research*, 45(4) 461–478.

Collins, Alan (ed.) (2007) *Contemporary Security Studies*, Oxford University Press, Oxford.

Cowley, Robert (ed.) (1999) *What If? Military Historians Imagine What Might Have Been*, Putnam, New York.

Craft, Cassady, B. (2000) An Analysis of the Washington Naval Agreements and the Economic Provisions of Arms Control Theory, *Defence and Peace Economics*, 11(2) 127–148.

Cramer, Christopher (2007) *Civil War Is Not a Stupid Thing: Accounting for Violence in Developing Countries*, Hurst and Company, London.

Crocker, Chester, A., Fen Osler Hampson and Pamela Aal (2007) *Leashing the Dogs of War: Conflict Management in a Divided World*, United States Institute of Peace, Washington DC.

Dallaire, Romeo (2003) *Shake Hands with the Devil*, Random House, Canada.

Das, Satyajit (2006) *Traders, Guns and Money: Knowns and Unknowns in the Dazzling World of Derivatives*, FT Prentice Hall, London.

David, Saul (2006) *Victoria's Wars*, Viking, London.

DEG, Defence Engineering Group (2005) *Conquering Complexity: Lessons for Defence Systems Acquisition*, The Stationery Office, London.

Diamond, Jared, M. (1998) *Guns, Germs, and Steel: A Short History of Everybody for the Last 13,000 Years*, Vintage, London.

Dixit, Avinash (2004) *Lawlessness and Economics, Alternative Models of Governance*, Princeton University Press, Princeton, NJ.

Dixit, Avinash and Barry Nalebuff (2008) *The Art of Strategy*, W.W. Norton, New York.

Dixon, Norman, E. (1976) *On the Psychology of Military Incompetence*, Jonathan Cape, London.

Doyle, Michael, W. and Nicholas Sambanis (2006) *Making War and Building Peace: United Nations Peace Operations*, Princeton University Press, Princeton, NJ.

Dunne, Paul and Ron Smith (1990) Military Expenditure and Unemployment in the OECD, *Defence Economics*, 1, 57–73.

—— (2007) The Econometrics of Military Arms Races, in T. Sandler and K. Hartley, *Handbook of Defense Economics 2: Defense in a Globalized World*, Elsevier, North Holland.

Dunne, Paul, Maria Garcia-Alonso, Paul Levine and Ron Smith (2007) Determining the Defence Industrial Base, *Defence and Peace Economics*, 18(3) 199–222.

Ferguson, Niall (2001) *The Cash Nexus, Money and Power in the Modern World 1700–2000*, Basic Books, New York.
—— (2006) Political Risk and the International Bond Market between the 1848 Revolution and the Outbreak of the First World War, *Economic History Review*, 59(1) 70–112.
Findlay, Ronald and Kevin H. O'Rourke (2007) *Power and Plenty: Trade, War and the World Economy in the Second Millennium*, Princeton University Press, Princeton, NJ.
Friedman, Thomas (1999) *The Lexus and the Oliver Tree*, Harper Collins, New York.
Frost, John (1983) *2 Para Falklands*, Buchan and Enright, London.
Galbraith, James, K. (2008) *The Predator State: How Conservatives Abandoned the Free Market and Why Liberals Should Too*, Free Press, New York.
Garcia-Alonso, Maria and Ron Smith (2006) The Economics of Arms Exports Controls, chapter 2 of Daniel H. Joyner. *The Future of Multilateral Nonproliferation Export Controls*, Ashgate, Aldershot, UK, pp. 29–45.
Gat, Azar (2006) *War in Human Civilization*, Oxford University Press, Oxford.
Gigerenzer, Gerd (2002) *Reckoning with Risk: Learning to Live with Uncertainty*, Penguin, London. First published in the USA as *Calculated Risks* by Simon & Schuster, New York.
Goldsmith, Benjamin, E. and Baogang He (2008) Letting Go Without a Fight: Decolonisation, Democracy and War 1900–94. *Journal of Peace Research*, 45(5) 587–611.
Gray, Colin, S. (1992) *Why Arms Control Must Fail*, Cornell University Press, Cornell, NY.
Hartley, Keith (2007) The Arms Industry, Procurement and Industrial Policies, chapter 33 of Sandler and Hartley (eds) (2007).
—— (2008) Collaboration and European Defence Industrial Policy, *Defence and Peace Economics*, 19(4) 303–315.
Hartley, K. and T. Sandler (eds) (1995) *Handbook of Defense Economics, Vol. 1*, North Holland, Amsterdam.
Hastings, Max (2005) *Warriors*, Harper Collins, London.
Hennessy, Peter (2002) *The Secret State*, Penguin, London.
Hirshleifer, J. (2001) *The Dark Side of the Force, Economic Foundations of Conflict Theory*, Cambridge University Press, Cambridge, UK.
Hobsbawm, Eric (2007) *Globalisation, Democracy and Terrorism*, Little Brown, London.
Howard, Michael (1981) *War and the Liberal Conscience*, Oxford University Press, Oxford.
IISS various years *The Military Balance*, annual Routledge for the International Institute of Strategic Studies, London.
Jones, B.F. and B.A. Olken (2007) Hit or Miss? The Effects of Assassinations on Institutions and War, NBER Working Paper 13102.
Kaempfer, William, H. and Anton D. Lowenberg (2007) The Political Economy of Economic Sanctions, chapter 27 of Sandler and Hartley (eds) (2007), pp. 867–911.
Kalashnikov, Mikhail with Elena Joly (2006) *The Gun That Changed the World*, Polity Press, Cambridge, UK.
Keegan, John (1993) *A History of Warfare*, Hutchinson, London.
Kennedy, Gavin (1975) *The Economics of Defence*, Faber and Faber, London.

Kennedy, Paul (1988) *The Rise and Fall of the Great Powers: Economic Change and Military Conflict from 1500 to 2000*, Unwin Hyman, London.
—— (2006) *The Parliament of Man: The United Nations and the Quest for World Government*, Random House, New York.
Keynes, J.M. (1919) *The Economic Consequences of the Peace*, Macmillan, London.
Killicoat, Phillip (2007) Weaponomics, the Global Market for Assault Rifles, World Bank Policy Research paper 4202, April.
Kincaid, Bill (2008) Changing the Dinosaur's Spots: The Battle to Reform UK Defence Acquisition, *RUSI Books*, Royal United Services Institute, London.
Kindleberger, Charles, P. (2000) *Manias, Panics, and Crashes: A History of Financial Crises*, 4th edition, Wiley, New York.
Kirkpatrick, David, L.I. (1996) *Choose Your Weapon, Combined Operational Effectiveness and Investment Appraisal (COEIA) and Its Role in UK Defence Procurement*. Whitehall Papers 36, RUSI, London.
Kolodziej, Edward, A. (1987) *Making and Marketing Arms: The French Experience and Its Implications for the International System*, Princeton University Press, Princeton, NJ.
Korner, T.W. (1996) *The Pleasures of Counting*, Cambridge University Press, Cambridge, UK.
Leeson, Peter, T. (2007) Better Off Stateless: Somalia Before and After Government Collapse, *Journal of Comparative Economics*, 35, 689–710.
Levinson, Marc (2006) *The Box: How the Shipping Container Made the World Smaller and the World Economy Bigger*, Princteon University Press, Princeton, NJ.
Luttwak, Edward, N. (1985) *The Pentagon and the Art of War*, Simon & Schuster, New York.
Lynn, Jonathan and Anthony Jay (1981) *Yes Minister, Vol. 1*, BBC Publications, London.
MacKenzie, Donald (1990) *Inventing Accuracy: A Historical Sociology of Nuclear Missile Guidance*, MIT Press, Cambridge, MA.
Mackinlay, John, Terence McNamee and Greg Mills (eds) (2008) International Peace-Building for the 21st Century: The Tswalu Protocol and Background Papers, Whitehall Report, 2-08, RUSI.
Maddison, Angus (2007) *Contours of the World Economy, 1-2030: Essays in Macro-Economic History*, Oxford University Press, Oxford.
Markevich, Andrei and Mark Harrison (2006) Quality, Experience and Monopoly: The Soviet Market for Weapons Under Stalin, *Economic History Review*, 59(1) 113–142.
May, Timothy (2007) *The Mongol Art of War*, Pen and Sword Books, Barnsley, UK.
Mocan, Naci, H. (2008) Vengeance, NBER Working Paper 14131.
Montalvo, Jose, G. and Marta Reynal-Querol (2008) Discrete Polarisation with an Application to the Determinants of Genocides, *Economic Journal*, 118, 1835–1865.
Myerson, Roger, B. (2008) Perspectives on Mechanism Design in Economic Theory, *The American Economic Review*, 98(3) 586–603.
NAO (1993) Accounting for Inflation in Defence Procurement, December 1993.
—— (2008) Ministry of Defence: Chinook Helicopters, HC 512 Session 2007-2008.
Page, Lewis (2006) *Lions, Donkeys and Dinosaurs: Waste and Blundering in the Armed Forces*, Heineman, London.

Peden, G.C. (2007) *Arms, Economics and British Strategy: From Dreadnoughts to Hydrogen Bombs*, Cambridge University Press, Cambridge, UK.

Porter, Michael (1985) *Competitive Advantage*, Macmillan, London.

Powell, Benjamin, Ryan Ford and Alex Nowrasteh (2008) Somalia After State Collapse: Chaos or Improvement? *Journal of Economic Behaviour and Organisation*, 67, 657–670.

Olson, Mancur (1982) *The Rise and Decline of Nations*, Yale University Press, New Haven, CT.

—— (1993) Dictatorship, Democracy and Development, *American Political Science Review*, 87(3) 567–576.

Richardson, Lewis Fry (1960a) *Statistics of Deadly Quarrels*, Boxwood Press, Pittsburg.

—— (1960b) *Arms and Insecurity*, Boxwood Press, Pittsburg.

Reinhart, C.M. and K.S. Rogoff (2008) This Time Is Different: A Panoramic View of Eight Centuries of Financial Crises, NBER Working Paper 13882.

Rodger, N.A.M. (1997) *The Safeguard of the Sea: A Naval History of Britain 660–1649*, Harper Collins, London.

—— (2004) *The Command of the Ocean: A Naval History of Britain 1649–1815*, Alan Lane, London.

Ruttan, Vernon, W. (2006) *Is War Necessary for Economic Growth: Military Procurement and Technology Development*, Oxford University Press, Oxford.

Sampson, Anthony (1991) *The Arms Bazaar*, revised edition, Coronet, London.

Sandler, Todd (1992) *Collective Action: Theory and Applications*, University of Michigan Press, Ann Arbor.

Sandler, Todd and Keith Hartley (1995) *The Economics of Defense*, Cambridge University Press, Cambridge, UK.

—— (eds) (2007) *Handbook of Defense Economics Vol. 2*, North Holland, Amsterdam.

Sandler, Todd and Keith Hartley (1999) *The Political Economy of NATO*, Cambridge University Press, Cambridge, UK.

Seabright, Paul (2004) *The Company of Strangers: A Natural History of Economic Life*, Princeton University Press, Princeton, NJ.

Schelling, Thomas, C. (2006) An Astonishing Sixty Years: The Legacy of Hiroshima, *American Economic Review*, September, 96(4) 929–937.

Schelling, Thomas, C. and Morton H. Halperin (1962) *Strategy and Arms Control*, Twentieth Century Fund, New York.

SIPRI Yearbook, various years. *Armaments, Disarmament and International Security*, Oxford University Press for the Stockholm International Peace Research Institute.

Skidelsky, Robert (1983) *John Maynard Keynes: Vol. I Hopes Betrayed 1883–1920*, Macmillan, London.

—— (1992) *John Maynard Keynes: Vol. II The Economist as Saviour 1920–1937*, Macmillan, London.

—— (2000) *John Maynard Keynes: Vol. III Fighting for Britain 1937–1946*, Macmillan, London.

Smith, Dan and Ron Smith (1983) *The Economics of Militarism*, Pluto Press, London.

Smith, Ron, P. (1977) Military Expenditure and Capitalism, *Cambridge Journal of Economics*, 1(1) 61–76.

Smith, Ron, P. and Ali Tasiran (2005) The Demand for Arms Imports, *Journal of Peace Research*, 42(2) 167–181.

Smith, General Sir Rupert (2005) *The Utility of Force: The Art of War in the Modern World*, Allen Lane, London.

Taleb, Nassim Nicholas (2004) *Fooled by Randomness: The Hidden Role of Chance in Life and in the Markets*, 2nd edition, Thompson, London.

—— (2007) *The Black Swan: The Impact of the Highly Improbable*, Random House, New York.

Taylor, John, B. (2007) *Global Financial Warriors: The Untold Story of International Finance in the Post 9/11 World*, W.W. Norton, New York.

van Creveld, Martin (1977) *Supplying War*, Cambridge University Press, Cambridge, UK.

Von Hoffman, Nicholas (1992) *Capitalist Fools: Tales of American Business, from Carnegie to Forbes to the Milken Gang*, Doubleday, New York.

Wood, Pia Christina and David S. Sorenson (eds) (2000) *International Military Aerospace Collaboration*, Ashgate, Aldershot, UK.

Index